*The Art of Persuasive Talking*

# The Art

# of Persuasive Talking

*Lynn Surles*

*W. A. Stanbury, Jr.*

*Drawings by Robert Glaišek*

McGRAW-HILL BOOK COMPANY, INC.

*New York  Toronto  London  1960*

THE ART OF PERSUASIVE TALKING

62348

# *Foreword*

Lynn Surles meets lots of people, as individuals and as groups. That's his business. He operates a training service in which he helps people in what he calls "Effective Expression on the Job." He takes his training teams into banks, factories, personnel departments, public-service corporations, insurance companies, lending agencies, business schools, hospitals, institutes, and universities.

Everywhere he goes, he begins with this question: "What do you feel is your greatest need for training in self-expression?" Over the years here are the replies he has heard most often:

"I can't get people interested in my ideas."

"I'd like to be able to talk better when there's no time to prepare."

"I'd like to know how to get people to take action on my ideas."

"There must be a way to keep from arguing all the time."

"How can I develop the techniques of persuasion and conviction?"

"If I try everything and the other person still won't come around, what do I do then? How can I get others to rationalize agreement?"

"I don't know how to prepare to talk."

"I can't generate ideas for a talk in the first place."

"How can I keep people from getting the wrong idea from what I say?"

"Even when I have the facts I run into trouble. I want to know how to convince people."

"I have trouble when I try to wind things up."

"I get jumpy when I have to talk to important people or groups. How can I conquer nervousness?"

"We have a lot of meetings at our plant. How can we stop wasting time?"

"I have trouble with people who want to take over a meeting and run it themselves."

"How can I read a report without putting people to sleep?"

"People say I gab all the time. I need to develop the skill of good listening."

"Can I use some little formulas to help in certain situations, such as giving orders, reprimanding, spiking rumors, and talking on safety?"

These comments and questions reflect the frustrations and feelings of inadequacy that worry most of us when we have to talk to others. They form the framework of this book. The 17 chapters that follow are the distillation of Mr. Surles's wide experience in helping people talk better—communicate more effectively. Each chapter offers practical help to people who have these feelings of frustration and inadequacy.

Dr. Stanbury's work, like Mr. Surles's, is communication. For eight years, as professor of English at colleges in the two Carolinas, he was a communicator with students. With the Navy in World War II he was an instructor in air navigation—a communicator with aviation cadets. Since 1946 he has been an editor with the McGraw-Hill Publishing Company—a communicator, through the written word, with men in a broad cross section of business and industry.

Both authors are convinced that effective talking lies at the root of many a successful career in business, in industry, in the professions, and in public service. It often spells the difference between triumph and failure in dealing with individuals as well as groups in business conferences, in sales meetings, in factory offices, private and general conversations, customer contacts, and community gatherings.

What is the secret of talking effectively?

There's really no mystery about it. Talking is man's oldest and most familiar means of communication. It's his most flexible tool of self-expression. He uses it every waking hour of every day. It's so much a part of everyday living, in fact, that it's easy to overlook simple opportunities to improve it.

Talking situations today don't call for spellbinding eloquence. The best talking, in conversation or in groups, is simple, clear, and straightforward. Those very traits marked the chapel talks of the late Dean Mason DuPre, of Wofford College. He spoke to his boys once a week for many years, and hundreds of men remember to this day the things he said. One of his colleagues explained the Dean's effectiveness this way: "He had something important to say, and he said it simply and clearly, in Anglo-Saxon words and uncluttered, straightforward sentences."

Even in Dean DuPre's day, spellbinding was on the wane. Today it's altogether out of fashion. Rafter-ringing oratory just doesn't fit into the pattern of modern business. This simplifies the task of the man who wants to speak effectively in today's environment. He doesn't need an angel's tongue, or a trumpet voice, or a waving arm. He does need purpose, clarity, and the conviction that what he says is the right thing to say—and that it's worth saying. And he needs to master some simple principles of organization, persuasion, and self-discipline.

These principles—purpose, clarity, conviction, organization, persuasion, and self-discipline—are the substance of this book. The authors treat them not as abstractions, but as real helps in everyday situations in which men talk to each other. Master these helps, and you'll have the key to "The Art of Persuasive Talking."

*Lester R. Bittel*

# *Preface*

Some day you may become a great platform speaker. Indeed, you may discover a power by which you can sway great throngs of people. If that should be your good fortune, don't thank this book. For this book is not about formal public speaking—the formal address, complete with typed manuscript, lectern, glass of water, and breathless audience.

This book is really about informal talking—the kind of talking you do person to person or in a small group. It is written to help you shape your ideas and communicate them clearly and persuasively in the situations that confront you day by day in your business, your plant, your office, in your professional life and your civic enterprises. If this book fulfills its purpose it will add strength, depth, and color to your personality and effectiveness to your communication. It will give you the look and the manner of leadership.

Far oftener than you think, the skill with which you can talk in everyday situations determines whether your ideas meet with action or indifference, whether your convictions triumph or founder, whether your organization flourishes or atrophies, whether your own career advances or falters. This purposeful but informal give-and-take talking is important. It's the reason for this book, which aims at helping you cope successfully with every talking opportunity that comes your way—and thus at helping you become the man you'd like to be.

Many people shared in creating this book. We are deeply grateful to all of them. To name them all would exhaust several pages. But we would be remiss if we did not name the following in acknowledgment of their significant share in what we proudly (if somewhat narrowly) call our book:

The late Professor Lew Sarett, of Northwestern University, much of whose spirit and philosophy has found its way into this book.

James H. McBurney and Kenneth G. Hance, authors of *Discussion in Human Affairs* (Harper & Brothers), and Thomas Gordon, author of *Group-centered Leadership* (Houghton Mifflin Company), who shaped much of the thinking in Chapters 13 and 14 of this book.

S. I. Hayakawa, author of *The Semantic Barrier* (Walter V. Clark Associates), whose studies have thrown new light on the problems of communication.

Permission to use excerpts has been graciously granted by the following publishers:

Harcourt, Brace & Company, for a passage from *Abraham Lincoln: The Prairie Years,* vol. II, by Carl Sandburg.

St. Martin's Press, Inc., for a passage from *Anatomy of a Murder,* by Robert Traver.

*Lynn Surles*
*W. A. Stanbury, Jr.*

# Contents

*I can't get people interested in my ideas.*

# How to Get People
# Interested in Your Ideas

It doesn't matter where you talk—sales meeting, business office, luncheon conference, parent-teacher meeting, or production planning session in your plant—you talk because you have something to say. And you want to talk in such a way that people will listen to you. You want to get them interested in your ideas.

Your first few moments are crucial in achieving this aim. They can make you or break you. They are your best opportunity to show your listeners that you and they have something in common, that this matter is interesting to you and them, and that you have something meaningful to say about it.

1

When you rise to your feet, or ask the chairman to recognize you, or simply draw in your breath to talk across a table or a room, you're promising something to your hearers. They become expectant. They're receptive, willing to listen. But this is a fleeting attitude. It will vanish unless you make the most of it—unless you satisfy the expectancy of your hearers—right at the outset. It's a rare speaker who, having fumbled aimlessly through his first few moments without filling this expectant void, can win his audience later. The initial disappointment will keep on working against him however long he talks and however effectively he frames his thoughts later. His hearers will feel sorry for him, or be annoyed with him —but they won't listen receptively.

Those first few moments are your chance to introduce yourself and your subject, to set the stage for the main body of your remarks and the summing up to follow. They are your opportunity to do three things every persuasive speaker, whether he's talking formally or informally, must do at the start:

1. Make the initial contact with the audience
2. Capture the attention of listeners
3. Tell them what you're going to talk about

## 10 Tips for Making the Initial Contact Effective

Your first move is to make contact with your hearers—to create a bond between yourself and them.

Naturally, you want this contact to be favorable to you and to what you're about to say, whether you're meeting your hearers for the first time or talking to them as long-time associates. You want them to see you as the kind of person who deserves and can command their attention.

Here, then, are 10 tips that will guide you to an effective initial contact:

1. *Be warm and friendly.* This attitude will project itself to your hearers, draw them to you, break down barriers to communication, and, through absence of pretentiousness, disarm those who may be hostile or indifferent to you.

You should aim to be like those unusual people who seem to light up a room when they enter, be it conference room, office, or living room. They're unpretentious and sincere. They have a liking (native or acquired) for other people and an interest in them. They're not like Prime Minister Gladstone, of whom Queen Victoria complained that he addressed her as if she were a public assembly. To be sure, Gladstone was respectful. But he was cold and formal. Lincoln, on the other hand, was a man of different stamp. His fellow circuit riders in Illinois liked to meet him after months of separation. Lincoln would approach them saying, "Now, boys, aren't you glad to see me!" But his whole countenance showed how glad *he* was to see *them*.

Why are warmth and friendliness helpful? Take this real story:

A publisher was dissatisfied with the quality of his printer's work. He asked the printing-plant president and his top assistant to come in and talk things over. When they arrived at the publisher's office he greeted them warmly, thanked them for making the 200-mile trip, told them what he hoped would develop from the meeting, and in every way laid the basis for a friendly, constructive business session. To be sure, differences came to light as the discussion moved on. But the publisher's initial warmth and friendliness had pitched the tone for the meeting on such an agreeable plane that everybody present guarded against saying anything that would bring it down to the level of heated dispute. The publisher won his points—and kept the friendship of his printer. His initial contact won the day for him.

2. *Give your audience your full attention, whether it's just one man or a thousand.* Many a hearer drifts away from the man who fastens his eye on one corner of the room or stares fixedly out the window while he gathers his thoughts. Eye contact with your hearers is important. It signals interest, attention, and purpose. From time to time, of course, you may have to look away while you formulate your ideas. There's nothing wrong with doing that occasionally. But unless you come back quickly to your listeners, you're sure to lose your contact.

3. *Pause a moment before you plunge into what you have to say.*

A brief pause can create expectancy and arrest attention. It tells your listeners, subtly but dramatically, that you have something important to say and that you're willing to wait until they're ready to hear you. It also gives them a moment to settle down in their chairs and prepare to listen to you. This is why, just before the preacher begins his sermon Sunday morning, the organist may play a few bars of quiet music. The pause gives the congregation a little time to ease down in the pews and focus attention on the preacher.

4. *Use contrast to make your first few moments different from those that have just passed.* If other speakers at a meeting or other participants in an informal business conference have been hammering at one theme in much the same way, an entirely different approach can make a successful audience contact for you. A bit of humor can relieve prolonged seriousness. And a suddenly serious approach can be arresting after a long spell of humor.

Former President Hoover once captured the attention of a rather formal audience by using contrast effectively. On this occasion he was one of four people who were to be cited for distinguished public service. He knew he would be the last of the four to be cited. Knowing the other three, he shrewdly guessed that their acceptance remarks would be serious if not solemn. He therefore came prepared to begin his acceptance speech with some amusing parallels on his new gold medal and President Roosevelt's decision in 1933 to take the United States off the gold standard. His humor in the midst of solemnity was refreshing. He made a successful initial contact with his listeners, and they talked about little else as they left for home.

There's a moral here: Humor that follows seriousness is often a welcome relief and an attention getter. For the same reason, you need never dread following a clever humorist in a meeting, a conference, or a conversation, for your change of pace can be an effective contrast.

5. *Look pleasant.* A smile can be disarming if it's sincere and if it's in keeping with your personality. But don't try to smile if you have to work at it—if it cracks your face. A forced smile will tell your hearers at once that you're cloaking insincerity, fear, or un-

certainty. But if you can't smile, at least you can relax the muscles of your face, look agreeable and pleasant, and show that you're well disposed and good humored. A show of antagonism, resentment, or anger (unless under exceptional conditions) can wreck any chance of making your initial contact successful.

To smile at yourself is often a good way to make your first contact. Take the story of an affable purchasing agent, for instance. Though he had had little experience in talking to groups, he was pushed into launching a welfare drive in his community. He faced his audience and took a deep breath. With that, he completely forgot his first sentence. He expelled his deep breath in one great gust and let a broad grin sweep over his face. "How preposterous can I get?" he seemed to be saying to himself. He brought down the house before he had said even a word. His listeners liked him because he was a good-natured person, whatever his lack of merits as a speaker.

6. *Be a showman.* But watch your step. Don't overdo it. Good showmanship in a moderate dose will establish contact with your hearers. But too much showmanship—or poor showmanship—is quickly recognizable as hokum. It will distract your hearers from what you're saying. It may be good showmanship to walk to a blackboard and, without saying a word, draw some lines; or to place visual aids in a chalk trough; or to unveil some charts, exhibits, or other stage props. But it's not good showmanship to bang your fist on your listener's desk, or to let go with a lot of bombast, or to drain a tall glass of water before you begin to talk. You'll be far better off just to be natural.

7. *Be straightforward.* Beware of passing out compliments to your hearers and expressing your pleasure in being asked to talk. No matter how sincere your intentions may be, some people will take this kind of talk as flattery aimed at them or as boastfulness on your part. Either way, you'll lose your listeners fast. It's not the way to win an audience at the outset.

If you really feel you must open your remarks with a compliment to your hearers, do it swiftly, simply, and sincerely. But the fact still remains: The best way to compliment a person or a group at

the beginning of your remarks is to relate what you say to their own
needs and experience. That way, you can establish a bond quickly
and surely.

A simple, straightforward opening, for example? Take this one:
"Your chairman was good enough to ask me if I'd talk about arbitra-
tion for a little while this morning. I'd be glad to share my experiences with you. I hope that what I say today may help you handle
some of the day-to-day labor problems your chairman has told me
about."

8. *Try to sense the mood of your listeners.* Fit the tone of your
remarks to that mood.

Suppose, for instance, you're general sales manager for a food
corporation. On one of your regular swings through your district
sales offices you stop in Atlanta to talk to your salesmen in that area.
Sales are good and competition is on the run. Your salesmen there
generate a lot of enthusiasm in you, and you find it's easy to persuade them to go after a 25 per cent increase in sales. Then you
move on to St. Louis for your next meeting. Sales there have
slumped. Your chief competitor is on the upswing. Your salesmen are
glum and tired. You're tempted to let your brimming enthusiasm,
generated in Atlanta, color your opening remarks to the St. Louis
group. But that would be a mistake. Unless you can sense the
mood of discouragement and frustration among your St. Louis salesmen and pitch your opening to their state of mind, you'll be better
off not to call them together.

What it comes down to is this: Though your general subject matter may be the same time after time as you talk to individuals or
groups, no two audiences are ever the same. The successful talker
is the one who senses these different moods, responds to them at
the outset, and goes along with them until he can transmit his
own mood. Carl Sandburg, for instance, is such a speaker. He once
came to a small Southern town near election time, when feelings
were strong and divisions were sharp. He sensed the tension in his
audience, made some earthy but humorous remarks about politics
in general, and gradually swung his hearers to his own mood of
relaxed tolerance.

9. *Ask for participation.* This is especially helpful when you're dealing with small groups rather than individuals. If you can get the group, or some member of it, to go along with you in some physical participation, you'll have less trouble getting mental participation. The magician often uses this opening gambit. He gets some member of his audience to come to the stage and take part in the act. That person becomes the magician's bond with the group.

Like the magician you, too, can make effective contact through group participation. You can ask people to hold up their hands in answer to a question. You can ask those who are sitting on the back rows to move forward. If it's a warm room, you can tell the men to remove their coats if they wish. You can ask some member of the group to hold your charts or other props for you. If you're one of a series of discussion leaders in a conference, you can ask your hearers to stand up for a seventh-inning stretch before you begin your part of the program. If it's an office meeting, you could suggest a coffee break. If it's a meeting in the plant, you can pass around a sample of the product for your listeners to get the feel of. Or if it's a sales meeting, you can ask one of the men present to unveil your charts and graphs for you.

10. *Refer to what some other member of the group has said.* This can tie you to the group. You can start by summing up what Jones or three or four other members of the group have just said. Then you can relate their views to your own. The group will appreciate your listening to others while you were thinking about what you yourself would say. Also, the group will recognize the fact that you're taking its interests and views into consideration.

Suppose, for instance, you're a member of the local school board. The board is debating the problem of discipline. Two members already have stated their views. Now you feel you should say something. You might begin this way:

"Mr. Hodgins and Mr. Cruikshank have thrown a good deal of light on this question. Mr. Hodgins has given some facts about classroom problems that show we've got to take strong action. And Mr. Cruikshank has told us pretty convincingly about some of our after-school problems. I think they're on the right track. I'd like to suggest we take a look at a third problem area—the parents of our school children. We must find some way to arouse their concern about discipline. We can't do much to improve the situation without their action."

## Six Ways to Catch Attention

After you've made your first contact and created a bond between yourself and your hearers, your next move is to catch their attention and rouse their interest. How can you do this? Here are six suggestions, with examples:

1. *Say something startling.* The unexpected always wakens the mind. It stirs curiosity, focuses attention, gives your hearers something to think about. For instance, a foreman in a machine shop may walk up to a grinder operator who isn't wearing protective goggles. The foreman opens his hand under the operator's nose, revealing half a dozen glass eyes. "Pick your favorite color," the foreman says, "while you can still see." For the rest of his safety talk he'll have an interested listener. His opening was startling.

Or take the real story of a businessman who was a candidate for a top job in financial circles. He was invited to appear before the board of directors for an interview. He knew the men who would interview him, and knew their tendency to talk about background —the best prep schools, then Harvard or Yale, finally a big broker's office, the top luncheon clubs, and Park Avenue apartments. He knew he couldn't match them on those scores. So his first remark after he was introduced at the board meeting was this: "I know why I'm here—to be interviewed for a big job. And I know who you are, all of you. I don't think I'm the man you want, because I was brought up on a farm. I milked cows, and I pitched hay. And I didn't go to college at all. Now if you want to go on from there, let's talk." From that point the interview became a contest to see which director had milked the most cows as a boy and which one had worked hardest in night school. When voting time came, the ballot was unanimously favorable to the candidate. By saying something unexpected, he had captured attention and roused interest right at the beginning.

2. *Work from a narrative.* A real-life story, applicable to the subject you're talking about, is a sure way to catch attention. Suppose, for instance, you're a salesman. Your company has just brought out a new product or has just added a new service clause to its contracts. The move isn't going well, and your general sales manager calls a sales meeting to search for a better approach to customers. You've got an idea that may throw new light on the problem—may even solve it. Your opening might go like this: "Let me tell you how the purchasing agent of Company ABC reacted when I showed him this new service clause." Or like this: "You'll be interested in what happened when I used a new approach on the office manager of a company we've never sold before."

3. *Relate your ideas to the interests of others.* A successful fund raiser in New York had made up his mind to persuade a certain prominent citizen to take the leadership of a campaign. He had been told that this citizen never permitted anything to interfere with his bridge playing. But he set up a date anyhow, and with his opening remarks took dead aim on the man's major interest. "Now, Jay," he said, "I know you're an expert on bridge. So you'll know what I mean when I say this plan to raise money will give our community a grand slam if we can just finesse a few problems. That's where I need your help."

Take the story of a plant supervisor. His best machine operator had just lost a son and now, though back at work, was dispirited and broken. "I think I know how you feel, Ed," the supervisor told him. "I lost a son, too, several years ago. But I've got something that has helped me here in my wallet. It was written by a President who lost two sons. Read it over. I think it will help you, too."

4. *Use humor.* Humor can break tension, deflect anger, relieve tedium, shatter gloom, soften the impact of unpleasant truth, and provide a welcome change of pace on many occasions.

But there are some words of caution about humor. It doesn't fit every occasion. For spotting those occasions it doesn't fit, common sense and good taste must be your guide. There's no hard and fast rule.

What's more, there are some kinds of humor that just don't fit certain occasions or certain groups. You'll want to remember the unlucky man who began his conversation with a group of community leaders by saying, "I see there are no ladies present, so I'll tell you a joke I heard in a bar a few days ago." He was brought up short by a voice from the group: "But there are gentlemen present." The moral: The successful talker senses the attitudes and tastes of his audience and pitches his humor accordingly.

Examples of fitting humor to the occasion? There are many of them. Dr. Ralph W. Sockman, a leading Protestant minister with a rare sense of humor, once was scheduled to speak to a national Protestant group following addresses by two distinguished laymen, one a Republican, the other a Democrat. Dr. Sockman's opening remark was this: "You've just heard one man speak for the Republicans and another for the Democrats. I'm going to speak for the Christians." Then there was the corporation vice president who was to talk at a stockholders' meeting held in a tent on the plant grounds. It was raining, and water had dripped through a hole in the canvas onto his notes. He got to his feet, held up his notes, and said, "This is the first time a talk of mine was all wet before I started out."

The two examples above are humorous quips, not narratives. They grew out of the circumstances of the moment and fitted only those peculiar circumstances. What about narratives, stories, jokes? How do you find those that suit the remarks you prepare for certain occasions? Somebody once asked Colonel Willard Chevalier, a vice president of the McGraw-Hill Publishing Company, how he always found such amusing stories to fit his talks. His reply was this: "You've got it wrong. I don't find stories to illustrate my talks. I find my stories, and then make my talks fit my stories."

5. *Stir up curiosity.* A little suspense will lift your hearers' minds out of lethargy and start them working along the channels you desire. An irate parent rose to her feet at a parent-teacher meeting and held aloft a broken piece of heavy chain. "You wonder why

I've brought this broken chain to our meeting," she said. "Well, it's going to prove a point that comes close to home to every one of us here tonight. A few days ago one of our children fell from a playground swing when this chain broke. This broken chain is only one of the many hazards that threaten our children every day at school. It emphasizes the need for better maintenance of our school property." Having roused curiosity in this way, she carried her audience along as she developed her theme.

6. *State a paradox.* A paradox is puzzling. It challenges the mind to reconcile opposites. Your hearers will be interested in how you develop the paradox and apply it to the points you want to make. Not long ago, for example, an industrial nurse was talking informally with a group of her associates. She began this way: "This is going to be a little talk about salaries. But before I reveal some research I've done, let me tell you that you can take heart, girls. The psychologist at my plant tells me there's plenty of evidence to show a correlation between humble people of great intellectual ability, like us industrial nurses, and lack of money-making ability." Her paradox was ironically humorous, to be sure, but it had real substance —and real meaning for her listeners. It got her off to a good start.

## Telling Where You're Going

"He lost me right at the start."

"What was he trying to get at?"

"Why does he beat around the bush forever?"

"I feel like throwing him out of my office. He talks and talks, and never comes to the point."

How often have you heard those remarks after a conference in the front office? Or after a salesman has made his pitch and left the room? Or after a group has broken up following a meeting? Too often, alas. And not always about the men who hold subordinate positions.

Comments like these point up the need for establishing direction and purpose for what you have to say, and for doing so close to the beginning. Whenever you speak, your purpose must be clear—clear to yourself and to those you are talking to. This is where many a communicator-talker fails. He doesn't bother to clarify his purpose in his own mind. Small wonder his listeners fall by the wayside and, after he has finished, are hazy about his purpose and his ideas and are therefore unconvinced.

The persuasive talker is the one who frames and states his purpose briefly and effectively. He does it while waiting for somebody else to finish, while he's walking down the hall to the vice president's office, while he's waiting in the receptionist's room, while dessert is being served, or while he's waiting for other participants to gather in the conference room. He words his purpose in one short, crystal-clear sentence: "I've got an idea for combining two assembly-line operations and cutting 10 per cent off the cost of our product." Or "I think we're headed wrong in this matter. Our workers will oppose it. Our stockholders will suffer. And we may find ourselves on the street as a result." Or "Let me tell you why this insurance policy is a good buy for you. Its cost is low in comparison with other policies. Its cash value builds up fast. And it provides unusually broad protection." Or "I have two things to say to you. First, this plan will be easy to put into effect because everybody will gain from it—churches, schools, and individuals. Second, this plan will rehabilitate our neighborhood financially, socially, and morally. Now let me develop these points one by one."

If you can begin your talk this way, with a clear purpose and a clear statement of it, nobody will ask later, "What was his point?" And nobody will say, "I don't know what he was driving at. He didn't say."

## Summary

When you begin to talk—wherever you are, whatever the circumstances, and however many listeners you have—your first few moments are crucial. They can make you or break you. Because it's in those first few precious moments that you make your first contact with your hearers. That first contact tells them what kind of person you are, what you're going to talk about, and whether your words and ideas are going to be meaningful and interesting to them.

There are time-tested techniques (discussed in this chapter) for getting off to a good start—for making those first few moments dynamic and attention getting. The net effect of these techniques is to convince your hearers that you're a person they should listen to, that there's a bond—a common interest—between you and them, and that what you expect to say will have purpose and substance. If you can get what you say off to this kind of start, you've won more than half of the battle.

## Exercises

1. Recall a talk you had with some person or group within the last few days about something that was important to you. What was the situation? Who was involved? What was the subject? Remember the first minute of your participation in the event—what you said and how you said it. Try to discover why you failed or succeeded.

2. Now reconstruct that first minute above along the lines suggested in this chapter. That is, use one of the methods for making a sure initial contact, use one of the methods for attracting attention and rousing interest, and then state your purpose clearly and concisely.

*I'd like to be able to talk better when there's no time to prepare.*

# How to Talk Effectively When You Have No Time to Prepare

At one time or another you must have felt the cold clutch of fear that grips most people when they are asked to talk unexpectedly. Your hands get clammy. Your mind goes blank. You can't run for a book. You don't have any notes to fish out of your pocket. You don't even have time to gather your thoughts. And you grope blindly for something significant and rational to say. Somehow you stumble through. Later, after it's all over, you feel you've made a miserable mess of an opportunity to help the group—and improve your own status into the bargain. Later—too late—the logical, helpful things you could have said come to mind.

If that's the way impromptu talking hits you, you're not alone. It hits most people the same way. Yet these impromptu situations come along often—in business, in community service, even in informal conversation. Each such situation is an opportunity and a challenge. Each is also an opportunity for success—or failure.

The roots of failure in impromptu talking are (1) fear and (2) lack of simple approach patterns at your command to fit most everyday impromptu situations. The men and women who stand out as persuasive, effective impromptu talkers are those who have mastered their fears and developed patterns of approach that keep them ready to talk even if they have no notes to guide them, no time to collect their thoughts. That's what this chapter is about—the mastery of fear and the development of approach patterns that will fit most everyday impromptu situations.

## How to Master Your Fears

Why are so many people afraid of impromptu talking? Here's what they often say:

"I might make a lame start. I've agonized through those first few lonely seconds in other meetings, and I don't want to do it again."

"My ideas aren't important. I'd just be wasting the time of the group."

"I don't know enough about the subject. Think I want to get up there and make myself ridiculous? Not me."

"I'd get myself in trouble with the boss (or with the local firebrand). He and I don't see eye to eye on this matter. I don't want to start an argument."

"The people who *are* talking are far abler talkers than I. I just can't measure up to them."

"I haven't settled the question in my own mind. I'd just flounder around and get nowhere. People would laugh at me."

"All those people are watching me. I don't feel comfortable when I'm talking to a group—even a small group."

Fears like these aren't laughable. They're real. If you let them take command of you, they'll be your downfall. But you don't have to give in to them. You can master them. Here are eight ways to bring them to heel:

1. *Face up to your fears squarely.* Bring them out in the open. Learn to live with them, because they'll always be with you. In fact, they may help more than they hinder you. A dinner companion at a fund-raising banquet not long ago asked the after-dinner speaker, an old hand at such affairs, if he still got nervous before he had to speak. "Look at my hands," the speaker said, revealing his damp palms. "Sure, I still get nervous, even after all these years. But I've learned to accept the tensions and live with them. The truth is, a little nervousness sharpens my wits and puts me on guard against letting down."

2. *Build up your self-confidence.* Don't hold back just because you've got misgivings about the significance of your opinions and views. Giving in to these doubts may betray you into passing up an opportunity to make a real contribution to a discussion. Remember, if your boss (or the chairman of the committee, or your business-luncheon host) didn't value your opinion, he wouldn't ask you to state it. You should have at least as much confidence in your views as he has.

3. *Find out how other people feel about impromptu talking.* It's a rare person who isn't a little surprised when you compliment him on some off-the-cuff remarks he made. If you probe a bit, you'll find he had been reluctant to talk, he thought he had stumbled through his comments, and he was sure he hadn't got his point across. Yet you were impressed with what he said and the way he said it. In other words, if you look around you'll find that most people share your misery in impromptu situations. If that discovery doesn't build up your ego, at least it will give you the comfort of knowing you're in the same boat with lots of other people.

4. *Throw off your self-consciousness.* Relax. Be natural. How?

Concentrate on what you're saying—and what you expect to say. If you keep that in mind, you'll forget the color of your necktie, the sound of your voice, and those awkward hands that seem to hang at the end of your arms. So will your listeners. They don't care whether you stand bowlegged or straight, whether your necktie is blue or brown. Why should you?

5. *Stall for time while your ideas take shape.* Again, relax. If it's a somewhat formal situation, get up slowly from your chair. Take your time walking to the front of the room. Pause a moment while your hearers settle down in their chairs. Ask the group leader or chairman a question. Take a minute to review the remarks of the person who has just been talking. Snatch at anything that will give you the few seconds you need—delivery of a telegram to the group leader, the ringing of a telephone, the need to open a window, the need to rearrange some papers—those little opportunities to play for time while your thoughts fall into place. While these delaying tactics are skimming the surface of your mind, keep the wheels turning deep down inside. First thing you know, you'll have your deeper thoughts shaped, framed, and ready to communicate.

How precious just a few seconds of delay can be came clear in a recent discussion between the general sales manager of a corporation and one of his district managers. The sales manager was wrestling with a tough decision that involved short- and long-range implications. He called in the district manager most affected by the situation and, without warning, asked him to outline his views on the question. Just then the phone rang. Twelve or fifteen seconds later the general sales manager put down the phone and said, "Well?" Thereupon his associate outlined a course of thought that put the question in a new light and shaped a constructive decision. "If that phone hadn't rung," the district manager said later, "I couldn't have gathered my thoughts and we might have made an unwise decision."

6. *Pick out a friendly, responsive eye among your hearers and fasten on it.* It may be the eye of an associate with whom you've already talked about the question at issue, or a listener who you now know will agree with you in part if not wholly. It may even be

your wife. It's usually easy to sense the responsive and sympathetic people in a group. Contact with them will give you confidence and ease your fears.

Take the editor who was invited a few years ago to make the commencement address at a junior college for girls in a distant state. He wasn't used to making speeches, certainly not to young girls. Even so, in an unguarded moment, he accepted the invitation. Came the day. He sat in abject fear during the preliminaries. But just as he rose to his feet he spotted an old friend, father of one of the graduates, in the audience. They exchanged a glance of greeting and for the first few minutes of the address he kept his eye on his friend. This contact dissolved his fears and he finished his address, if not in triumph, at least with some equanimity.

Among trial lawyers the technique is a familiar one. For example, take Paul Biegler, hero of Robert Travers's novel *Anatomy of a Murder*. During the first day of the trial Biegler has felt this spark of recognition and sympathy in one of the jurors, a young Finn. That evening, Biegler reflects on how he will conduct the case:

> I thoughtfully lit a cigar and stared out at the lake. Maybe, I thought, I had better pretty well try my case for this intelligent young juror. . . . I remembered that when I was D. A. I had almost unconsciously selected and played to a lone juror during my longer trials. Some small sign usually came along, some tiny tacit recognition that you and the jurors were talking the same language. And that way one seemed to gain—or at least I seemed to gain—a greater sense of immediacy and impact during one's efforts; that way, there seemed to be a tangible goal upon which to concentrate, a discernible target at which to aim whatever arts of conviction and persuasion one possessed.

7. *Say what's on your mind.* Few bosses are men to fear. Many of them are lonely men, plagued with problems. They desperately need help—and welcome it. You can't hurt yourself if you speak honestly from conviction. Your boss is likely to heed your grounds for disagreeing with him, respect your opinion, and admire your courage for stating it. In fact, by speaking openly you may throw an entirely new light on a problem and thus earn the boss's gratitude. But remember this: Though you speak your mind frankly,

you don't have to be blunt or unpleasant. Above all, you must not allow personalities to enter your remarks, whether you're talking to the boss or somebody else.

As for the firebrand or troublemaker who may be listening, don't let him intimidate you. Speak your mind honestly. And if there's disagreement, let *him* fan the fires and stir the trouble. If you're honest and have the right on your side, he can hurt only himself.

8. *Be ready even if not prepared.* And this leads you into the second part of this chapter . . .

## Patterns That Will Solve Most Impromptu Situations

Most occasions for impromptu talking call for one of three things:

• Advocacy, in which, by debate or persuasion, you seek action or agreement.

• Explanation, in which you must make something clear to your hearers.

• Description, in which you must reconstruct an image for those who haven't seen it.

If you can develop a pattern for handling each of these situations, you can ease into impromptu talking with the confidence that what you say will have coherence, unity, and impact.

Here are patterns that will help you in these situations:

1. *Seeking action or agreement.* The pattern is simple: State your point, cite an example, and make clear what you want.

Get used to starting off by saying, "Here's my point." If you've really got a point (and you've got no business talking unless you do have one), you'll have no trouble putting it into words. It will almost shape itself. Stating it will help you avoid the wanderings that are fatal to so many impromptu remarks. It will clarify your purpose for you and your hearers and give you a firm peg to hang your subsequent thoughts on.

Next, swing into an example or illustration. "Let me give you an example," you say, or "Let me illustrate what I have in mind." Your example is the most important part of this pattern. It will probably determine whether you get the action you want or fail to get it. It must be appropriately selected and clearly stated. But

that doesn't mean there's anything difficult about it. On the contrary, the example probably is the easiest part of the pattern to summon up, because it will grow out of the very problem that prompted
you to ask for action in the first place. And it's also the easiest to
follow through with because one thing will lead naturally to another. You won't get lost in a maze of thoughts, stumble around
in uncertainty, or punctuate your delivery with awkward halts.

Finally, wind things up. Draw your conclusion from your illustration, relate it positively and definitely to your opening point—
and then stop. This is no place for leisurely rambling or dull words.
Everything should be clear-cut, crisp, and definite. You should leave
no hearer with any doubt about what you've said.

Take an illustration of this get-action pattern at work in one impromptu situation:

SITUATION: A new worker in a plant has just had a lost-time accident. He hadn't been thoroughly briefed on the hazards of the
job. The safety director wants to strike while the iron is hot. So,
without taking time to prepare a formal meeting, he summons all
plant foremen together. Here's how he uses the get-action pattern:

POINT         There's just one point I'd like to get across to you.
              This is it: Don't assume a new man knows the hazards
              of a job just because you know them.

EXAMPLE       Let me give you an example of what I'm driving
              at. Let's say you're hired to work on a punch press.
              You don't have much experience. You don't know the
              hazards of the job. What's more, the foreman doesn't
              brief you very well on the hazards. In fact, the ma-
              chine doesn't even have a guard during the demon-
              stration setup. Later on, when you're setting up on
              your own, you slip on the pedal. To break your fall
              you grab the first thing in reach—the pivot pin. The
              ram comes down across your thumb. You lose it.

              You'd be bitter toward the company in general and
              toward the foreman in particular, wouldn't you?

ACTION        Well, this case just happened here in our plant. So
              give your new or inexperienced men a good briefing

on all the hazards of their machines. And check up on
them regularly to see that they work safely no matter
how long they stay on the job. It's not always the
new man who gets hurt. Sometimes accidents wait
thirty years to happen.

Take another illustration of the get-action pattern at work in an
impromptu situation:

SITUATION: Homeowners in a cooperative housing development
are meeting to adopt rules and regulations to safeguard their prop-
erties. One of the proposals up for discussion would require periodic
inspection of all homes in the development to eliminate fire and accident hazards. Several homeowners oppose the proposal as an in-
vasion of their privacy. But Bob Upjohn favors it. He gets to his
feet. Here are his impromptu remarks:

POINT            I feel I must speak up on this issue. Here's my
                 point: There's too much at stake—the lives of our
                 children, our investment in our homes, and our own
                 safety—for us to turn down this opportunity for mak-
                 ing this a model neighborhood. To some extent, each
                 of us holds the safety and well-being of his neighbor
                 in the palm of his hand.

EXAMPLE          My experience is very much to the point here.
                 Three weeks ago I inspected my own house and
                 garage. I found a lot of booby traps that might have
                 injured my own children—or yours if they had been
                 playing at my house. Some of these hazards might
                 have kept me from going to work someday.
                     First I went to the garage. I found a wooden box
                 full of paint cans—some of them open—in a spot
                 where the sun could focus. Some brushes were soak-
                 ing in turpentine. I also found a rickety stepladder
                 that my wife sometimes uses.
                     Then I went to the basement. I found my incinera-
                 tor and piping only a foot from a wooden partition.
                 There was a clothesline close by.

In my attic I found an electrical outlet that looked like an octopus. That's where my six-year-old boy plays on rainy days. In a second-floor bedroom I found a broken window-screen latch. That's the room where my two-year-old sleeps and plays. The medicine cabinet in the bathroom contained a large bottle of aspirin and a bottle of Lysol—all within reach of my four-year-old Tarzan. And under the kitchen sink I found a bottle of ammonia—a grand prize for any kid.

ACTION    My little inspection trip made me aware of booby traps right in my own house. And I'm not sure my unpracticed eye caught all of them. I wouldn't say I'd been careless—just indifferent, maybe. But I would say I could be ignorant of many hazards because I'm just not a professional hazard hunter. I've got things pretty well cleaned up now at my home. But I'd like to have a professional trouble shooter come around once in a while and inspect my house. And I believe most of you here would like the same thing. I'm going to vote for the proposal. I hope you will, too.

Now look back at the two illustrations above. The situation was the same in both—no time to prepare. But both speakers were ready; that is, they had at their command a pattern of approach to fit such impromptu situations. Both stated their points clearly at the outset. Both drew appropriate examples from the problem under discussion. The examples came to mind quickly and almost told themselves. Finally they stated, briefly and to the point, the action they wanted.

2. *Explaining something.* Doesn't matter whether it's a policy, a procedure, a theory, or a machine you're asked to explain. There are three patterns for the situation:

• You break it up into pieces, explain each piece, then put the whole thing together again and sum up.

- You take the simple-to-complex approach.
- You try comparison or contrast.

THE PIECE-BY-PIECE PATTERN: Take the case of a man we'll call Hansen. He was an engineer in a large plant. He was called across town to explain a new machine his company had built and installed.

Hansen arrived at his destination and was ushered up to the machine. It stood there in place, seven feet tall, and 40 engineers were gathered around to hear his explanation. Hansen took one look and did an about-face. "I didn't expect an audience," he protested. "I never talk to groups."

But the chief engineer needled him. "Maybe it's about time you did," he said. "Just break the machine up into three units and tell us about each one. What's so tough about that?"

"Well," Hansen said, "it doesn't sound so hard now that you put it that way."

In sequence he took the top, middle, and bottom units. He was pretty nervous as he explained the top unit. By the time he got to the middle unit he had settled down a little. When he finished the bottom unit he knew he had licked his problem. He would never be afraid again of explaining something complex or formidable. He had found an easy way to do it.

Take it another way. Suppose you're a plant superintendent sitting in, by invitation, on a meeting of department heads. The department heads are debating whether to ask for salary increases for foremen. Your company has just published its annual report with a typical assets-and-liabilities balance sheet. One department head says, "Sure, I'd like to see our foremen get raises across the board. But I don't know whether the company can afford to give raises. That annual report is Greek to me."

As plant superintendent, you can't let this opportunity pass. The company report is something you want every department head to understand. Here's the way you go about it:

"Let's forget about assets and liabilities. They're accountants' words. Let's think instead in terms of a right-hand pocket and a left-hand pocket. Into the right-hand pocket we put everything we own. Those are our assets. Into the left-hand pocket we put everything we owe. Those are our liabilities. Accounts receivable, for example, go into our right-hand pocket. They represent money that's due to be paid to us. In effect, that money is ours. We also own our plant and offices. They go into the right-hand pocket. And we've got a lot of nuts and bolts and sheet metal on our shelves. They're worth money, and they belong to us. They're our inventory. They go into the right-hand pocket." And so you go on, breaking the balance sheet down into small pieces and explaining each one in turn. Your puzzled department head begins to see the profit-and-loss statement clearly now, and understands the financial position of the company.

THE SIMPLE-TO-COMPLEX PATTERN: Another way to explain something that's complex is to start with something simple, something that everybody understands, then move on to the combinations and permutations that make simple things seem complex.

Not long ago a mixed group of laymen and musicians took on the task of buying a new pipe organ for their church. The laymen were dismayed when they saw the specifications for the new instrument—60 to 100 stops, several hundred pipes, all sorts of pistons and couplers, and many strange words—German, Italian, and French—to describe the various elements. They felt they couldn't grope their way to the real meaning of the specifications. But a scientist member of the group straightened them out. "Essentially," he said, "we're talking about whistles and reeds. That's all these pipes are, though they've got some formidable names. Some are big, some are small. Depending on the size of organ we want, we can buy few or many. And we can connect them in various ways to get various tonal effects. That's what these specifications do for us. They tell us which reeds and whistles the organ builders think we need, and how they should be connected and combined for greatest tonal flexibility and range."

THE COMPARISON-OR-CONTRAST PATTERN: Like the simple-to-complex pattern (above), this pattern explains something that's hard to understand in terms of something that's easy to understand. Recently, for instance, a manufacturer of military goods played host to 40 or 50 reporters. After lunch a small group of correspondents

and engineers gathered for some informal discussions. Said one of
the reporters: "Frankly, I'm puzzled about all this space business.
Why is it so hard to hit the moon with a missile?"

"I think I can throw a little light on that for you," one of the
engineers said. "Maybe you play golf. If you do, you know how
hard it is to make a hole in one. In fact, if you do make one, luck
plays a pretty strong role. Well, imagine a moon shot as a try for a
hole in one. Except that you're shooting from a truck traveling at
one speed, the green is traveling at a different speed and in a different direction, and there's a 40-mile cross wind blowing. That's
how hard it is to hit the moon with a missile."

For another example, take the case of the plant manager who
has worker problems. Morale is low, rejects are high, and profits
are slipping. He calls his foremen in for a conference and asks them,
each in turn, for their views about what's wrong. Norman, foreman
of the maintenance shop, gets called on first. He doesn't have time
to prepare any notes or to run home for his psychology textbook.
But he has an explanation for low morale in the plant, and he
presents it effectively. He frames his remarks as a comparison—
this way:

"We think people are pretty complicated. And they are, I guess.
We don't always know what makes them tick. But in lots of ways
they're like clocks. You have to wind them up regularly; that is,
you have to encourage them. You have to oil them once in a while;
that is, you have to reward them when they need rewarding. You
have to check them against a radio time signal to see whether
they're keeping good time. Same way, you've got to check up
on your men to see that they're performing their jobs right. Sometimes you have to take your clock to the shop and get it fixed. In
other words, you've got to sit down occasionally with your men,
individually, and find out what's wrong with them—diagnose their
troubles. Set a clock on a sloping mantle and it won't run right.
Deal with your men any other way than on the level, and they
won't work for you. Sure, we've got complex problems here in the
plant. But maybe they're not as complex as we think they are. And
maybe some simple remedies will set things right again."

Both of these men, Foreman Norman and the space engineer, had mastered the art of explanation by comparison. It was a pattern of approach to impromptu situations that made their meaning instantly clear.

3. *Describing something.* Your best help here is to keep space and time in mind. In terms of space you can describe your object or image by moving from north to south, from top to bottom, front to rear, floor to floor, department to department, state to state, plant to plant, office to office. In time you can move from date to date, incident to incident, highlight to highlight, beginning to end, or end to beginning.

Take a description in terms of time, for instance. Suppose you're an insurance salesman. You're attending a sales conference. The sales manager asks you to describe your chief competitor's most recent move. You take the time approach: "Let's start right at the beginning," you say. "A year ago, in April, I called on a prospect in the Gray Building. He gave me the first inkling that X Insurance Company was about to bring out a new policy. X's salesman had just called on him. It was July before I got the first solid information about the features in X's new policy. In October, making a call in the Horton Building, I ran across the first man in my territory to buy this new policy. Up to now, I've counted a dozen more."

Suppose, on the other hand, you're a plant engineer. At a staff meeting the vice president for operations springs the news that your company plans to build a new plant. Then and there you decide that right now is the time to get some of your ideas across. You've just visited a new plant on the other side of town, where you've seen some pretty good things. You decide to draw on your descriptive powers. You rise to your feet, the vice president recognizes you, and you launch into your comments, describing what you saw as follows:

"Last week I visited Company A's new plant across town. It's well planned and laid out. I saw some things there that I'd like to see built into our new plant. Take the entrance. It's inviting and colorful, the kind of entrance the company and its workers can be proud of. Just behind the reception area are the personnel offices, with medical offices adjoining. Going farther inside, I found locker rooms right next to the production floor and foremen's offices arranged as islands in the middle of the production floor. At the rear of the plant, receiving and shipping are right next to each other, served by one long dock, so that raw materials come in, travel through a U-shaped process line, and return as finished goods to the shipping dock. The whole plant adds up to efficiency and good working conditions. I'll be glad to go into more details at the right time, but this brief guided tour will give you some general ideas that I think we can explore profitably for ourselves."

## Summary

Don't worry about your fear of impromptu talking.

In the first place, you can conquer your fear by facing up to it squarely, building up your confidence, comparing your fears with the fears of others, thrusting your self-consciousness aside, playing for time to gather your thoughts, seeking a sympathetic eye among your hearers, saying what's on your mind, and mastering three patterns of approach.

With three patterns at your command you can be master of almost any impromptu occasion. With them you can:

1. Win agreement and get action. You'll use the point-example-clincher approach.

2. Explain something—a policy, a procedure, a theory, a machine. You'll use the piece-by-piece pattern, the simple-to-complex pattern, or the comparison-or-contrast pattern.

3. Describe something—a house, a scene, an action, a process. You'll call on the time pattern or the space pattern.

## Exercises

Following are six typical impromptu situations in which you might find yourself. They lend themselves to development by the three patterns discussed in this chapter. Don't read the situations. Instead, hand this book to your wife. Ask her to read Situation 1 to you and give you fifteen to thirty seconds to plan your approach. Then talk for two minutes on Situation 1. After you have finished, ask her to criticize what you said and the way you said it. When you have finished Situation 1, go on to Situation 2. Now hand the book over to your wife—right now, before you read any further.

## Win Agreement

SITUATION 1: You're a salesman for a paper products company. Major markets are in the Eastern states. Your territory is upper New York State. Other territories, each with its own salesman, are New England, metropolitan New York, New Jersey, Pennsylvania, and the Washington-Baltimore area. Your general manager calls a sales conference. In that conference the subject of territorial boundaries comes up. The general manager asks you how you would like the lines redrawn for your territory. You have a plan. Now is your time to put it across.

SITUATION 2: You are superintendent of a plant that manufactures toys. The president, the vice president (operations), and the sales manager ask you to meet with them. You find that retail stores have complained about delivery of faulty toys. The president asks you to comment. This gives you an opportunity to ask for a new electronic inspection device you have read about.

## Explain Something

SITUATION 3: You go to the bank to arrange a personal loan for paying taxes. The bank officer asks you to explain how you budget your income and expenses.

SITUATION 4: You're entertaining a visitor from India on his first trip to the United States. He asks your advice in planning a nationwide tour. You explain our transportation system to him.

## Describe Something

SITUATION 5: You're a member of the local school board. The board is meeting to plan a new school. You have just returned from a visit to a nearby city where you saw a newly completed school. You liked its layout. Describe it.

SITUATION 6: You're a claims adjustor for a casualty insurance company. Your company is planning to launch a program of safety education. You think that's a good thing. When the boss asks you why, you describe an accident that could have been avoided.

*I'd like to know how to get people to take action on my ideas.*

# How to Get the Action You Want from People

A talk can be graced with nearly all the attributes of good communication—purpose, conciseness, and clarity, and a beginning, a middle, and an end—and still be ineffective. It can be perfect—except that nothing happens when it's finished. Yet the aim of most talking is to get action. And unless action follows, you can't call a talk successful.

The key to getting action is motivation. Motivation is what this chapter is about—your own motivations, which can attract or repel

31

your hearers; and the motivations of others, to which the skillful talker tunes his remarks. This chapter will tell you what people respond to in a speaker. It will also tell you the basic human motivations that you must appeal to if you want action to follow your speech.

## How to Be a Persuasive Speaker

Some speakers have a quality that draws people to them. In some measure they were born with that quality. But in a larger measure this ability to draw others is the fruit of studied self-development of their own character and personality. From this conscious self-development come the attributes and motivations of a speaker that command attention, respect, and a willingness among his hearers to follow.

What are these attributes to which people respond? They are sincerity, integrity, conviction, empathy, and respect for others. None of them is enough. All of them must work together.

Take them one by one:

*Be sincere.* Sincerity always shines through. The sincere man talks from his heart, says what he thinks, meets issues head on, avoids trickery and double talk. That's not to say he is blunt and rude. On the contrary, he is tactful—not because he wishes to save his own skin by evasion but because he earnestly strives to spare the feelings of those who may disagree with him.

Tact and sincerity are not contradictory. Take the case of the young editor whose senior asked for his comments on an editorial that took a strong position on industrial labor unions. Suppose the young editor, after reading the article, took it into his senior's office with these words: "I think you're all wrong. If I were doing it I'd go at it in an entirely different way." To be sure, that would be sincere talking. But it wouldn't be persuasive talking. The young editor would be equally sincere—and at the same time tactful—if he put his case this way: "Your experience in this field is much wider than mine. But in all honesty I can't share the position you take. If you'll give me a few minutes I'd like to tell you why."

Like sincerity, insincerity sticks out all over a talker. It's easy for his hearers to spot. Not long ago, in a large city, a group of tenants in a large apartment building met to discuss their landlord's proposal to raise their rent. Whether the landlord was entitled to an increase is not the question here. Maybe he was entitled to it, maybe he wasn't. But in secret he made the mistake of offering to redecorate the apartment of one tenant if that tenant would speak in favor of the increase at the meeting. At the proper time, that tenant rose to his feet, extolled the virtues of the landlord, and launched a plea for the rent increase, saying it was nothing more than fair. But the audience sensed his insincerity quickly, became restless and inattentive, and at last made it impossible for him to continue.

*Build integrity.* This is a compound virtue. It's made up of honesty, morality, fairness, and dedication to duty and right causes. It colors a man's reputation in his business and among his neighbors. It imprints itself on his face. It's implicit in his very mannerisms and gestures. It's what the late Ernie Pyle described when he wrote his classic dispatch about the death of Captain Henry Waskow, of Belton, Texas, in World War II. Pyle told how one soldier after another looked into the dead man's face and said, "I'm sorry, Old Man," "I sure am sorry, sir," and how another knelt down and straightened the points of the captain's collar, rearranged the torn uniform around the wound, then got up and walked away down the road in the moonlight, all alone. Pyle told why the captain's men were devoted to him, why they wanted to do what he wanted them to do. "He always looked after us," said one soldier. "He'd go to bat for us," another said. "I've never known him to do anything unfair," said a third.

What does the story of Captain Waskow have to do with your talking? Just this: Captain Waskow's integrity spoke for him. In the same way, your own integrity can speak for you—shine through what you say and make people do what you want them to do because, knowing you, they trust you.

*Show conviction.* The successful talker must believe that what he's saying is the right thing to say, that what he's asking his hearers to do is the right thing to do. Take the story of the saleswoman in a large department store. Her job was to sell household cleaning equipment. Her department stocked five different brands of rug cleaners. All five looked much alike on the shelf. She had tried them all in her own home. One stood head and shoulders above the others. She was convinced it was the best. Yet her instructions from the manager were to offer all five brands impartially to customers. Even so, at the end of the first month customers had bought 200 units of the rug cleaner she preferred. Sales of the other rug cleaners in the same period ran in the order of 10 to 25. The point is, she just couldn't keep her conviction from showing through in her talks with customers. Her conviction shaped her words, and her words swayed her customers to her way of thinking. Same way, your conviction will swing listeners to your side.

*Practice empathy.* What's empathy? It's the projection of yourself into another person's situation, thus sharing his experiences, seeing his point of view, and understanding his feelings. In a sense it's oblivion of self, for the time being, and absorption in others. Its root is interest in other people. Its fruit is the ability to talk in terms of the everyday experiences and emotions of other people and thus bind them to you. One woman put it aptly when she described the effect of Dr. Ralph W. Sockman's sermons at Christ Church, Methodist, in New York City. She said, "When I hear him preach I feel he's been following me around all week, so he knows what I've been doing, what I've been thinking, and what he ought to say to me."

*Respect others.* You wouldn't invite guests to your home for dinner and serve them leftovers. You wouldn't talk to a grown person as you would to a four-year-old. And you wouldn't knowingly deliver a molehill to people who deserve a mountain. Persuasive communicators and effective talkers take time to prepare their remarks. They seek out significant things to say. They clothe the substance of their talk in well-chosen words. If they have nothing to say, they don't get to their feet. They respect people too much to try to fool or mislead them, to let them down, or to send them away empty-handed.

## How to Appeal to Basic Human Drives

There are five basic motivations that account for most human actions:

1. Self-preservation and security
2. Self-improvement and self-fulfillment
3. Love for others
4. Curiosity
5. The need for purpose

The effective communicator—the man who gets the action he wants from his hearers—is the one who casts his comments in terms of these basic human drives. They are the push buttons that make the lights flash.

The most gifted talkers seem to touch the right buttons instinctively. For less gifted mortals (most of us, that is), this appeal to basic drives takes a little thought. But it's not a difficult strategy to master, and anybody can learn the rudiments and put them to work. There's nothing underhanded or sly about this appeal. It's simply a way of creating a climate in which the ideas you plant will thrive and blossom into action. The strategy is reprehensible only when it serves an unworthy or sordid end, as was true of Hitler—and as has been true of some rabble-rousers of smaller stature in our own country. Even these regrettable episodes in history prove the power of appeal to the basic human drives—a power that is far stronger when turned to good ends.

When you seek action from a person or a group, how can you frame your remarks in terms of these basic motivations? Here are a few examples:

1. *Self-preservation and security.* Take John Wilson. He's superintendent of a warehouse. He wants his company to buy 800 feet of steel guardrail to go around the edge of an elevated storage area. The treasurer has turned him down: "It's not in your appropriation," he says. At the next regular weekly meeting of executives in the general manager's office, Wilson puts his case this way:

"In the last year our business has grown so much that we've had to store some of our packaging materials on a mezzanine above the packing area. That mezzanine overhangs part of the aisle. I'm afraid somebody's going to get hurt. In fact, just a couple of days ago after our treasurer passed through the packing area with some visitors, I discovered one of the cartons was hanging over the edge of the mezzanine. It wouldn't have taken much to tip it over. I expect to keep my eye on that storage area and correct anything I see that's unsafe. But I'd feel much better if I could know that in the meantime we've placed a purchase order for a guardrail."

Needless to say, Wilson got his guardrail.

Or take the case of a certain small manufacturing company. At a regular quarterly meeting a major stockholder pushes hard for doubling the dividend rate. He argues that earnings have increased and that markets look strong. But the treasurer demurs. He states his position this way:

"I'm as proud as anybody of our improved earnings. But I don't think we ought to pass out all of our increase in higher dividends. We're in the midst of a fast-developing technology. We need more money for research into new products and new applications. And we need to hold something in reserve to buy new machines and modernize our processes. Let me remind you of the sad case of one of our neighbor companies. It passed out all its increased earnings in dividends and held back nothing for research and modernization. When the time came for change, it had no money to support change. It simply had to go out of business. I'd regret it—and I'm sure all of us would—if the same thing happened to us. I hope we'll vote to hold our dividend where it is. If we do, I believe the time will come when we'll be in position to do more than double it."

Both men in these two examples wanted action. One made a plea for something special outside his appropriation. The other asked for action to protect his company's future. Both took the right approach to get the action they wanted. They appealed to their hearers' desire for self-preservation and security.

2. *Self-improvement and self-fulfillment.* All of us seek satisfaction for our yearnings, our ambitions, our desire to grow in stature

and in the esteem of other people. And few of us can resist an appeal for action if it promises something for our advancement.

Suppose, for example, you're a district sales manager for an insurance company. You have a promising young salesman on your hands. Thus far he's had pretty good luck—but you know it's mostly luck. You want him to get ready for a really tough problem that you expect to throw his way—working out a pension plan for a small enterprise with about 200 employees. How can you impress him with his need for a night course at a nearby college? You can order him to enroll. But that wouldn't really do him much good. He needs motivating. Here's one way you could approach him:

"Les, you've made a pretty good showing up to now. And I think you've got the energy and drive to keep up the good work. But I'm sure you don't want to level off where you are. There are too many opportunities in the insurance field. Life insurance is just one of them. The newest and most promising area right now is the pension field. Not many of our agents have gone into it yet. So for those who get in on the ground floor and who master the principles of pension administration and investment, the future is bright from the standpoint of promotion in our company as well as earnings. There's a new night course beginning next week at the college uptown. It will give you a good start on pension plans. I hope you'll give it some serious thought. I think you'll be glad in the long run if you sign up for it now."

Or maybe you're cashier of a bank. You've got a bright young assistant named Frank—knows accounting, knows banking, and studies hard to learn even more. But he's shy, and doesn't make friends easily. In fact, you are one of the few people who have broken through his shyness and know his real worth. You want him to move ahead in banking, maybe take over your position when you retire. Can you get him to throw off his shyness and widen his acquaintances? You might try this approach in one of your conversations with him:

"Frank, you're my good right arm in this bank. Don't know what I'd do without you. And you've got abilities that can send you right to the top. But you've got one obstacle. Your shyness hides your abilities from all except just a few people, like me. What's more, success in banking is like success in lots of other businesses—to a big degree it hinges on relations with other people. I want you to succeed in all the ambitions you've told me about. But you're going to have to break out of that shell you've built around yourself. I want to help you. And the best way I can help you is to let some of my friends know that you'll accept their social invitations in the future. You've been turning them down, you know, saying you had to work or study. May I tell them they can count on you next time they invite you to Rotary, or the country club, or a dinner party? They'll see what a fine fellow you are. And you'll find there's no good reason why you should shy away from them."

3. *Love for others.* You can make a strong appeal to your hearers through their love for people—their wives, their children, their parents, their close friends.

Take Jim Fisher, for instance. He's drafting-room supervisor for a construction company. Recently a rash of home accidents has left him shorthanded in the drafting room. That's why he's worried about Paul Henley, one of his draftsmen. Paul's hobby is woodworking. His home workshop is well equipped—planer, band saw, lathe, and power drill. But like all other home workshops, it's somewhat hazardous. Fisher decides he'd better talk with Paul.

"Paul," he says, "I think every man ought to have a hobby—fishing or baseball or collecting something. Gets a man's mind off his work at night so he can come to work next day fresh and rested. But I do hope you'll be careful with that band saw in your workshop. If you lost a couple of fingers we'd be in a bad spot here in the drafting room. And that twelve-year-old boy of yours would be in a bad spot, too. I doubt that he could find anybody else to finish that boat you're building for him. Tell you what I want you to do. I want you to set up a guard on that band saw. That way, I can be sure you'll keep coming to work regularly, and your boy can be sure you'll finish his boat. With a boat like that one, he'll grow up to be a real bass fisherman—not just an amateur like me."

4. *Curiosity.* All of us have some of it. We want to know how things work, what's behind the curtain, why people act as they do,

where the magician hides his rabbits, when predictions will come to pass. We like to explore the unknown—or have it revealed to us.

You can use this desire for knowledge to good effect when you ask people to do something. Say you're superintendent of operations for the local bus system in your town. You find you've got to double your night schedules because a new manufacturing plant has just opened up and it's running around the clock. It's doing secret work for the government. You'll have to get some of your drivers to switch to the night shifts. You expect some reluctance. Maybe you could put it to them this way in a group meeting:

"We've got a new situation here in town. This new plant is going onto a three-shift schedule next week. Its employees will need transportation to and from the plant. I don't know what they're making. But they're doing top secret work, and every one of them has to be screened by the FBI. Nobody can get inside the gate without a pass. But buses have got to get in. And that means bus drivers. Now I doubt that any of you has ever been through an FBI investigation. And I don't know how many of you could pass the screening. But I think some of you might like to know how the FBI runs a check on a man. And I believe some of you might like to get inside the plant fence and see a little of what's going on. Will those of you who are interested give me your names before you leave this meeting?"

5. *The need for purpose.* Most of us need something we can give ourselves to, wrap ourselves up in, tie ourselves to. We need a cause or a mission, something that gives direction and purpose to our energy and skills, that takes us out of ourselves and challenges the best that's in us—something that calls on our combative instinct, for the very words *purpose* and *cause* suggest struggle against opposition and conquest over obstacles.

There's a shining example of this kind of motivation in a talk given not long ago at the meeting of a personnel managers' association. The speaker was seeking to persuade his hearers to play a more positive role in business and industry. He described the personnel manager's job—and his sense of mission. Here's the way he brought his talk to an end:

"And so I think the attitude the personnel manager should strive to establish in his own mind and in the minds of others is this:

"He is a 'sensitive spot' between two giant forces—management and labor. He tries his best to gain insight into the problems of both—with an alert mind and a big heart. . . . He rarely has a vote in high-level policy meetings and he seldom holds large blocks of stock in his company. But management weighs his words carefully at the conference table.

"He sometimes takes on the teaching role, not in an atmosphere of the college campus and ivy-covered towers—but in an atmosphere in which he can carry out one of the vital purposes of education, to light up dark places. . . .

"In an atmosphere of results, profits, efficiency, speed, quantity, quotas, overtime, and getting, he gives. He approaches all people with one idea uppermost in his mind: 'How can I help you?' "

That's fine speaking about a noble cause. But your cause needn't be glorious or globe girdling. It can be simple and close at home. The important thing is that it be purposeful, that it be something your hearers can do for others, and that it motivate your hearers to give their best.

Suppose you're general manager of a manufacturing plant that makes a new kind of paper carton. Until recently, no other paper-carton maker has tried to duplicate it. Now, though, you've got a strong competitor. You decide that the only way you can stay ahead of your competitor is to rely on superior quality in your cartons. You resolve to raise quality standards in your plant. You call your plant department heads together—production, maintenance, electrical, warehousing, shipping, purchasing, and personnel. You tell them the situation and your decision. Here, in brief, is what you say:

"We had things all our way a long time. Our customers came to us, and what we sold them was good enough to keep them coming. But things are different now. We've got a strong competitor. In general specifications his cartons are just like ours. He's out to get part of our business—and he'll probably do just that.

"But there's one way we can stay well ahead of him. We can see to it that every carton that leaves our plant is flawless. That way, we can beat him on quality.

"What do we have to do to achieve that kind of quality? All of us here must muster our skills, our experience, and our dedicated best. We must be vigilant against imperfection. In our production department, shearing machines must cut precisely so joints and mating edges will be perfect. Our employees must keep working surfaces spotless—not a drop of oil anywhere. Our electricians must see that there are no line losses in bringing power to our machines, so they'll cut, fold, and shape exactly. In warehousing and shipping we must handle finished goods with tender care—no jamming, no dropping, no crude stacking. Our personnel department must set up a rigorous training course that will boost the skills of our experienced employees and give new employees a good start. More than all that, we've all got to work together, generating methods, improvements, and new ideas that will help us turn out still better cartons.

"I can't promise you any material reward for all this—no big salary increases, no better office space, no stock options, no higher pensions. All I can promise you is the satisfaction that comes from doing a better job, the pride you'll have in a product of peerless quality, and the well-earned esteem of our loyal customers. I'm asking you to do something that calls for our best—and deserves it. Will you go along with me?"

## Do's and Don't's in Motivating People

Here are some helpful hints about using these basic drives to spur your hearers to action:

1. *Use stories, examples, comparisons, and descriptions.* These devices get attention—and hold it. They create suspense, conflict, and climax. If they're from your own experience, good. If they're from the experience of your hearers, so much the better. Such devices make your material come alive. They make your remarks realistic and persuasive.

2. *Look for illustrations and narratives that your listeners have experienced.* These things will bring your remarks close home to

them. One man was asked to talk to a small group of businessmen in a town where the main business was serving vacationers. He used an hour before dinner to stroll through the town and observe the problems and challenges of its businessmen—the specific day-by-day events that affected their motivations. He saw traffic tied up, sidewalks littered with paper cups, women wearing shorts who shouldn't wear shorts, fine old homes shouldered aside by hot-dog stands. He listened to harassed clerks and impatient customers, talked with weary travelers and old settlers. Later, in his speech, he drew on what he had seen and heard on the streets and in the shops. In other words, he wrapped up some objective, far-from-home points in material that was familiar to the people who heard him. His method gave meaning to his talk and made a lasting impression on his hearers.

3. *Aim at frequency, timeliness, and intensity when you choose experiences to relate your remarks to your hearers.* The more frequently your listeners have experienced what you're talking about, the more recently they've experienced it, and the more intensely they've experienced it, the more it will penetrate their minds and stimulate a response.

4. *Keep in mind that appeals to basic drives are mostly non-logical.* These drives are associated with fear, love, hate, and pride. These feelings, in turn, are associated with the five senses—sight, sound, smell, taste, and touch. So frame your thoughts, choose your examples and illustrations, and select your words in terms of such feelings.

5. *Don't overlook the appeal of logic.* Knowledgeable use of statistics, for instance, can put you in psychological command of an audience, and carefully reasoned material can win the respect of your listeners. Even so, clothe your statistics in some close-to-home significance and make your reasoning palatable by relating it to your listeners' experience. This way, logic can take on an emotional as well as an intellectual appeal.

6. *Don't overwork the self-fulfillment drive.* It can easily veer over into flattery. You really can't win an audience by flattery.

People see it quickly for what it is. They resent it, and turn their resentment against you. They see you as an opportunist who is exploiting them.

7. *Don't scatter your shots.* In other words, to make one point you should appeal primarily to just one motivation. Other motivations will slip in by implication, because they're all interwoven and overlapped (self-preservation and self-improvement, for instance) and some may conflict with others (self-preservation and love, for example). Those that slip in by implication will be subordinate to the main motivation. Though they'll sometimes strengthen the main drive, you'll be better off to pick one drive only and concentrate on it—and let the implied drives take care of themselves. An appeal to more than one drive at once can easily confound your hearers and defeat your purpose.

## Summary

The principal aim of talking in business, in industry, and in many civic and social relationships is to get people to do what you want them to do. If the action you want follows your talk, then your talk is successful.

Getting the action you want depends on your own attitudes and personality and on the effectiveness with which you appeal to the basic drives that motivate your listeners.

As for yourself, you must show by words and manner that you are sincere, that you have integrity, that you are convinced that what you want done is the right thing to do, that you understand other people and can put yourself in their place, and (by putting substance into your remarks and not wasting their time with trifles and nonsense) that you respect your hearers.

As for your hearers, they are normal human beings. Accordingly, they act in compliance with certain basic human drives: desire for self-preservation and security, the wish for self-improvement and self-fulfillment, love for others, curiosity, and the need for purpose and direction. The successful communicator knows these basic motivations and couches his talk in terms that will stimulate them. As his talking skills develop, he learns more about how (and how not) to bend these motivations to his own purposes.

## Exercises

1. Talk this one over with your wife or the man you share an office with or the friend you have lunch with:

You tried not long ago to get action from a person or a group of people. Reconstruct the whole situation. Was it at your office? In your plant? At the bank? On the street corner? At your church? What did you want your hearers to do? Did you get the action you wanted? If you didn't, how could you have motivated your hearers to act your way? Did some shortcoming in your own attitude or personality keep you from getting what you wanted? If you did get what you wanted, could you have stirred more enthusiasm and perhaps won unanimity by an appeal to basic drives?

2. Take any one (or several) of the topics below. First decide what you would like done about that topic. Then construct a one-minute talk in which you ask for action. As you prepare your talk keep clear in your mind just what it is you want done—your purpose. Construct your talk so that you appeal to one—only one—of the basic drives discussed in this chapter. Try it out on a friend, or on your teen-ager. Here are your topics to choose from:

There are many hazards on the job.

Paychecks get lost pretty easily.

Some people drink when they're depressed.

You'll often find petty jealousies in an office (or plant).

Some people conclude that if they're not fitted for a particular job they're a failure.

There's a night school right here in town.

It's hard to work with Charlie.

A good many people have joined the new bowling league.

Most buildings these days are called "fireproof" but none of them are 100 per cent fireproof.

Many people who are handicapped turn out good work.

*There must be a way to keep from arguing all the time.*

# How to Turn Disagreement
# to Agreement

Could you win another chance for a foreman who persists in showing up drunk? A man who keeps on trying the patience and forbearance of his workers, his fellow foremen, and his plant supervisors? One plant superintendent did.

Here's what he said to win the day:

"For the past half hour we've been saying we ought to dismiss Jim Curtis.

"I agree with you. What he's done these past few months is enough to warrant firing him out of hand. I know he's got a trigger

temper. And I know he's come to work intoxicated a few times.
But I didn't know, until I heard it a few minutes ago, that Jim
had been in a fist fight right here in the plant. I agree with you that
a fellow who shows such a poor example, a fellow who doesn't work
cooperatively, ought to be removed from any position that carries
responsibility.

"Yet I'm going to ask for another chance for Jim Curtis.

"I can't forget he's been with us fifteen years. In the past he's
been a good man, in and out of the plant. During the war he earned
one of the highest decorations the Army can confer. Only three
years ago he developed an idea that netted our company at least
$20,000.

"I believe we owe Jim Curtis something. And I believe that now
is the time to repay him. Let me take the responsibility of trying
to straighten him out. I think it can be done."

When the superintendent sat down, there just wasn't any more
argument. He carried his point hands down. Could you do as well?

You could if you mastered the techniques of winning agreement
from disagreement. Our friend the superintendent used a simple
pattern effectively. He took the conciliatory approach—admitted
that his hearers had a great deal on their side of the argument. But
having put them in a receptive frame of mind by agreeing with
them, he then switched artfully to a new point of view and capi-
talized on the frame of mind he had created.

This is just one of the argumentative situations that arise a
dozen times a day. Your department, for instance, tangles with the
purchasing department and you have to soothe ruffled tempers. Or a
representative from the auditing department storms into your office,
argument written all over his face. Or you have to talk the sales
manager into a move you know he will oppose. Or you have to take
part in a heated debate on policy in the vice president's office. Or
you have to ask a hostile group to do something it has already made
up its mind not to do.

The conciliatory approach, used so successfully by the superintendent above, is only one of several techniques that will help
you win support for your views and bring agreement out of dis-

agreement. Others are the common-ground approach, the circuitous gambit, the blunt assault, the cards-on-the-table strategy, the subtle suggestion method, and the technique of simply listening. The successful talker keeps all of these techniques at his command and calls on them as befits the occasion. They are vital to every person who wants to succeed in business, in industry, in community enterprises, in social contacts.

## People You Must Win to Your Side

Who are the people and groups you are most likely to have to win to your side? Here they are:

1. *Hostile groups and individuals.* You can feel the hostility bristling all over them. They're often angry about something. They've already made up their minds—and feel strongly about their decision. They resent anything that might force them through the agony of decision making again. Or they're people who know you've come to take something away from them, or to tell they can't do what they've decided to do, or to tell they must do something they don't want to do. You'll meet them, for example, when you face a union shop committee after you've had to fire an employee. Or when your church or synagogue gets embroiled in a dispute over moving to a new location. Or when you have to tell your salesmen that you've got to make an economy move—cut their entertainment allowance.

2. *People with grievances or complaints.* If you're in industry, they may be your employees. If you're a landlord, they may be your tenants. If you're a politician, they may be your constituents. If you're a rabbi, priest, or minister, they may be your parishioners. Whatever they are, they feel they've been mistreated. They expect you to listen to them and to correct whatever, in their opinion, you're doing wrong. They can be pretty indignant—and pretty blind to your side of the question.

3. *Doubters.* These people are skeptical of everything you say. For some reason, your own fault or their prejudices, they just don't trust you. They doubt your facts, your illustrations, your con-

clusions. They show their attitude by restlessness, inattention, whispering among themselves, the expressions on their faces, even by open questioning. Sometimes they're harder to deal with than those who openly oppose you. They're like the chronic doubter, a citizen of Dayton, who heard about the first flight of the Wright brothers at Kitty Hawk, N.C. "I don't believe it," he said. "I don't think man will ever fly. And if anybody ever does, it won't be anybody from Dayton."

4. *Chronic "aginners."* There's usually one of these in every group. Whatever comes up, he's against it. He's against modernizing the office because it costs money or moves him away from his favorite view. He's against buying a new boring mill for the machine shop because the old one still works pretty well. He's against modern classroom methods because he remembers (or likes to think he remembers) the hickory stick and the old-fashioned speller. He's against a new proposal because he doesn't like the person who offered it. In short, he's the guardian of the *status quo.* Most of all, he likes to hear himself talk.

5. *The defeatist crowd.* They're the ones who think your idea just won't get anywhere—won't do any good—even if they do go along with you. So they don't go along with you. "What's the use, anyhow?" they ask. "All that work for nothing."

6. *Divided groups.* They're deadlocked, and neither side will give an inch. They look on any easing of their position as appeasement or surrender of principle. And whatever anybody suggests in an effort to bring them to common ground brings down wrath from both sides.

These various people—and groups of people—can thwart your best intentions when you're talking. But don't let them get you down. You're not the first speaker to come up against them. And you won't be the last. Less skillful speakers than you have carried the day in spite of them. So can you if you go at them the right way.

Your success hinges on talking to your hearers in such a way that you lead them to a willing surrender of their position and an acceptance of your views. There's much to be said for the old adage: "A man convinced against his will is of the same opinion still. And a woman convinced against her will is not convinced, nor is she still." In other words, there's little lasting value in the support you win by main strength of logic and statistics. What you want, like every effective talker, is willing support. To win it you need an even, unruffled disposition and respect for opinions that differ from your own. You need to see the views of your opponents against the background of their likes and dislikes, their fears and doubts, their education and conditioning, their religion, and their personal and business problems. And you need to know the rudiments of the art of persuasion. That's what the remainder of this chapter is about.

## Six Ways to Swing People to Your View

### 1. The Conciliatory Approach

This is the method used so successfully by the superintendent at the beginning of this chapter.

You start out by taking the other side's argument or position—or part of it—as your own. You agree. You tell the other side where it is right, though you may hint at some reservations of your own. You repeat its points and sum them up. In fact, if you can, you state the opposing position even better than the people who uphold it. The important thing is this: to show that you do more than tolerate opposing views—you respect them.

What have you done thus far? By repeating or summing up the other side's points you have won acceptance for yourself as a person. Your hearers have opened their minds to you. They're saying to themselves: "That fellow's all right. He's a sound thinker." Now that they have accepted you as a person, you seek to transfer this acceptance to your stand on the question at issue. Here's where you first begin to suggest your own view.

The way you make this transition from the opposing view to your own is important. You must do it tactfully and skillfully, without jolting your hearers and without making them feel that you've betrayed their acceptance of you. Also you've got to give them a way to move over to your side without losing face. Your opponents put a pretty solid value on their own views, and it may be hard for

them to give in to you without some loss of pride. In fact, you can
win many an argument by reason and evidence, but unless you give
your hearers a way to come to your side without embarrrassment,
you'll only convince them against their will. That's not the kind of
conviction you want. You want willing conviction. And your transition is a key step in winning it.

Here are some handy patterns that will get you started on the
transition from the opposing view to your own:

"There's just one little angle I'd like you to think about."

"This may be farfetched, but I'd like to throw it in here."

"Lots of intelligent people agree with you. So do I, except in this
one aspect."

"What you say is thought provoking. Let's see how it would work
out in our situation."

"A man in Texas went along with the same idea. Here's his story."

"Here's a good example of what we've been discussing."

"It's just like a policy we had in the Navy."

"Here are some interesting facts in connection with this matter."

"Let me describe this new plan to you."

"It's like the story of the two drunks who went into a funeral
parlor."

You can make this transition from the other side's view to your
own in various ways, somewhat as follows:

• *Tell a story.* People will follow a story with little or no resistance as you tell it. It needn't be elaborate. Indeed, the simpler
the better. But it should be interesting and in point and it should
have suspense and climax, so that your hearers will turn their attention to the story and away from the fact that it's being used as a
bridge between their views and yours.

Take the editor who publishes a strong editorial on a new city
tax program. His editorial provokes a storm of abuse, much of it
personal, from a councilman. The editor's associates, loyal and
angry, recall an administrative scandal that involved the councilman some years ago. They dig up the facts, take them into the

editor's office, and urge him to hit back at the councilman. But the editor wants to stick to the tax issue. Here's how he conciliates his associates and wins them to his view:

"I couldn't agree with you more. The councilman's attack on me was reprehensible. And in attacking me he attacked all of us. He's a pretty low type of politician. And I agree with you—he doesn't have a moral or a scruple to his name. He ought to be run out of town. And if we refreshed people's memories about his connection with that scandal, in the heat of this dispute they really might run him out of town.

"All this takes me back to the time when I was a kid on the farm. I got home from school one day with a black eye and a bloody nose. I'd had a fight with a boy who called me a dirty name. My father asked what had happened, and I told him. I remember right now what he said: 'Can't say I blame you much, son. It's pretty hard not to do just what you did. But I don't think you helped yourself much. When you've lived as long as I have you'll know you can't win a smelling contest with a skunk.'

"That's why I'm not going to use this old scandal you've dredged up. And I hope you won't talk about it among your friends. Our newspaper's reputation for decency and honor stands up pretty well. All of us share that reputation. The best thing for us to do is to fight this tax issue on its merits. We're going to fight issues—not men. That's what we're going to do—all of us. With the newspaper skills we've got among our staff, we'll come out well ahead."

Now look back at how our editor won a willing surrender from his associates. He recited their views and showed his agreement. He gave almost no early warning of a shift. He made a smooth transition to his own position by telling a story that was directly related to the situation. Then he stated his own position and, reminding his associates of their high purpose and their skills, gave them a way to change their views without embarrassment to themselves.

• *Describe something.* The closer to the experience of your hearers it is, the more effectively it will swing them from their position to yours.

Say you're the superintendent of manufacturing in a plant that makes small metal parts. You've got a twenty-five-year-old stamping machine that turns out one part every three seconds. You want a new machine, one that will turn out parts ten times as fast. But this has been a slow year for your company and you know you'll meet opposition if you ask for anything that costs money. In fact, the general manager was downright nasty the other day, when you asked for just a small appropriation. But you decide to go ahead anyhow. Here's how you might approach him:

"You and I have been around this plant a long time, Phil, and I don't remember a worse year since the Depression. That's why I should have known better than to ask you to buy that new gear for the stamping machine last week. We patched up the old one, the way you suggested, and now it will work all right for a while. Saved a little money, just as you said we would. I keep trying to remember that we're all in this thing together, trying to keep our costs down.

"That reminds me of something I saw last night. I took my grandson to the fair—followed your advice and let him play that ball game, the one that pitches out balls for you to hit. Did you take a look at that pitching machine, Phil? I did. It's a simple mechanical setup. Works on compressed air. Nothing in it to go wrong. Takes just one man to run it—and he takes in the money, too. You can speed it up to throw out twice as many balls per minute as it did last night.

"And that brings me back to the plant. We've got to cut costs, as you say. But we saved only $25 by repairing that gear. What we need is something that will save big money. I saw something yesterday in a catalog that will do just that for us. It's a new stamping machine. In some ways it's like the pitching machine I saw at the fair. Our old machine takes two men—one to feed steel strip in, the other to take off the stampings. This new machine takes only one man. He just refills the magazine periodically on the feed side and takes filled boxes off at the finish side. There's a compressed-air ejection device that throws finished parts off the die and down a chute to a box. And it's fast. We'll get 200 stampings a minute with the new machine. With only one man to run it, our labor cost per finished stamping will be only one-twentieth of what it is now.

And, with air ejection, we'll have no more mashed fingers and no more accident claims. I figure the new machine will pay for itself in six months, and what we make on it from then on will be clear profit."

• *Reveal the facts gently.* You don't have to charge headlong into an argument. If you do, chances are you'll only harden the resistance of your opponent, because belligerence begets belligerence. Unfolding the facts gradually, in a friendly way, will ease your opponent into the truth and give him a chance to adjust himself with the least embarrassment possible.

To see how this gentle revelation of facts works to the advantage of everybody, put yourself in the unhappy position of Stewart in the story that follows:

Stewart was a guest at a party. Not realizing that the owner of the local hardware store was also a guest, Stewart told of a recent visit to that store and complained bitterly about the service he got —or didn't get. All other conversations halted while Stewart pursued his grievance. The store owner, too, kept silent, even though his wife fixed a look on him that seemed to ask, "When are you going to punch that guy in the nose?"

As Stewart talked himself out, the store owner moved tactfully into the conversation—almost as if he were drifting into it. He agreed that sometimes the service left much to be desired. "But here are some interesting facts in connection with this matter," he said. He gradually unfolded fact after fact—the lunch-hour rush, the summer-resident trade, a magazine advertisement for a new do-it-yourself kit that everybody seemed to want at once, the wave of grippe that kept two clerks at home for a week. This way, he justified occasional below-standard service. He also intimated that service in his store was pretty good compared to service in some other stores in town. At last he let it drop that he owned the store in question. He said also that he would do his best to improve the service there.

See how the store owner dulled the edge of Stewart's embarrassment by his gentle approach. He revealed the facts gradually. He made it as easy as possible under the circumstances for Stewart to accept them gracefully and to inch backwards from his position. He artfully turned the conversation to constructive channels in which Stewart could share, thus saving face for Stewart. He avoided spoiling the party—and avoided punching Stewart in the nose, however strong the temptation was. And he swung Stewart over to his point of view.

Could you have talked to Stewart as effectively as the store owner did? Next time you're in Stewart's fix, hope for a man like the store owner to rescue you. And when you're in the store owner's position, remember how he did it.

• *Use comparisons and analogies.* Comparing one situation with another is often so fascinating in itself that your opponents don't realize you're making a transition to a different point of view.

Suppose, for instance, a recent direct-mail campaign your company launched has fallen flat on its face. Now your boss won't touch direct mail with a 12-foot pole. But you're convinced that just one little change in technique would spell success, and you want to try direct mail again. So you go into the boss's office.

"That last campaign cost us a lot of money," you say to the boss, "and we haven't got a fraction of our money back from it. Maybe, as you say, direct mail gives us a shotgun approach that's just not right for our product.

"It brings to mind what a cake-mix manufacturer found out. It may be a little farfetched. But I'd like to bring it in right here. For a while, you know, he made a mix that required nothing except a little milk and some stirring. It made a perfect cake. But housewives didn't buy much of it. He put his motivation researchers to work on the problem and they came up with the answer. Housewives who used the mix developed a secret feeling of guilt—felt the mix left them too little to do. They didn't feel creative when they used it. The motivation-research men suggested that the eggs be left out of the mix and that the directions instruct the housewife to beat up two eggs and add them to it. That solved the problem. Housewifery once more became a skill, and sales of the mix climbed almost straight up. The trouble was, the original mix didn't take that one little human element into account.

"Now I can't believe there's anything basically wrong with direct mail for our product. I think the failure of our first campaign can be charged up to just one small human element we overlooked. People don't like to buy a pig in a poke. They want to see what they're buying—touch it, watch it work. I believe that if we tell people we'll send them our product on a ten-day free trial basis, a direct-mail campaign will work wonders for us."

• *Bring humor in.* But bring it in only if you're skillful at it. (Your wife will tell you truthfully if you're not a humorist.) And bring it in only if it's the right kind of humor. A situation that calls for conciliation is no place for sarcastic or ironic humor. What's needed is jovial, indulgent humor that brings smiles and laughter. The man who is gifted with this kind of humor is worth his weight in gold. He provokes people to laughter, and while their guard is down he brings them over to his side. Such a man was Alben Barkley, President Truman's beloved "Veep." So was Lincoln. So is "Red" Motley, publisher of *Parade.* When such men persuade you, they have fun—and so do you.

• *Illustrate with examples.* Best, of course, are those examples from your own experience or from the experience of your opponents. In bypassing the principal bone of contention and talking about something that's different but related, you divert your hearers' attention from the main issue while you prepare their minds to accept your solution.

Say you're in charge of quality control in a small plant. The union has negotiated a new contract with a sizable wage increase. Your president tells you you've got to transfer one man from your quality-control payroll to the assembly line, where he'll replace a man who quit. You feel you can't spare him. Here's the way you might put your case:

"Basically, I think your idea is sound. With this new wage contract, I know we've got to cut corners wherever we can. It's not an uncommon problem these days.

"Back in Illinois, you know, before I joined this company, we had much the same problem. It's a good example of what we're talking about here. We took an oiler off our maintenance crew and put him in our shipping department. This way, we cut our maintenance payroll and filled a need in shipping. What happened? Things went along all right for a few days. Then a machine broke down because somebody hadn't got around to oiling a bearing. And in a couple of weeks we began to get returns—goods broken because they hadn't been properly packed. Somebody figured that one payroll change cost over $10,000 all told.

"I think we're talking about the same sort of thing here. If I lose that man in quality control I figure we'll lose at least $100 a day in waste, in rejects, and in goods returned because they're faulty."

### 2. The Common-ground Approach

This is not unlike the conciliatory approach, in which you seem to take the opposite side's view, then make a smooth, disarming transition to your own view. But there's a difference. In the common-ground approach you have to search for a common denominator between you and your hearers—something you both can agree on, something you both can say "Yes" to. Your attitude of mind, not necessarily spoken, is this: "Let's talk over our points of agreement." This approach gives the other side a chance to accept you as a person before you move into the sensitive areas.

This approach is especially useful in business circles, where disagreements may be sharp, tensions high, and tempers short. Many a high-keyed businessman works well under a controlled head of steam but becomes difficult when pressure gets too high. The common-ground approach is most likely to succeed with such men. It gives them temporary respite from stress and brings them back to a base where calm judgment is possible again.

Beware, though. This common-ground approach, like the conciliatory approach, must be sincere. If it's less than sincere it becomes only a tool for exploiting others—and a quickly recognizable (and therefore ineffective) tool at that. Its success hinges on your ability to project yourself into your opponent's state of mind and see his problems. To do this, you must call on your own intellectual, emotional, and spiritual experience.

If sincerity is the basis for your common-ground approach, there's nothing underhanded about it. It's simply another manifestation of tact and understanding in human relations. Who wants a dispute or quarrel anyway? In those unhappy situations in which you see trouble approaching, emotions building up, personalities edging into controversy, common ground is your safest and, in fact, most effective way of forestalling disagreement. It may be your only way of turning mounting emotions aside and bringing sweet reason into play.

When you're using the common-ground approach, try to keep all differences, even minor ones, out of the picture until you have made your transition. Your transition can be gradual. It can move slowly and subtly from areas of disagreement to those of agreement. You can probe now and then to see if your opponents are softening up —are seeing their way to move to your side. If you have miscalculated, if they still show signs of hostility or disagreement, you can drift back to common ground. You can even try gracefully to break off the talking and wait for another day. Sure, it's often hard to break off just when you have warmed to your subject. But in many instances that may be just the right time to break off—when you're getting warmed up emotionally. You'll be much smarter if you keep yourself under close observation and, when you sense your feelings rising, back off and wait for another day.

Example? Well, not long ago a certain banker went to Chicago on business. He went to his hotel, where he had stayed several times before, and showed his reservation confirmation to the room clerk. "Sorry, sir," the clerk said, "we're filled up. No rooms for anybody."

Never one to take defeat easily, the banker walked over to the desk of a harassed assistant manager and there awaited his turn to talk. At last it came. Here's how the conversation went:

"There's nothing I can do for you, sir," the assistant manager said. "Not a room in the house."

"I sympathize with you," the banker said. "You've got a really tough problem. You know, I have to deal with disappointed people sometimes in my business. Something goes wrong and a customer

complains. People can be pretty nasty in those situations, and I've
had many a bawling out, like the ones you're taking today.

"In a small sense, you know, you and I are in the same business
—a service business. Know what I mean?"

"That's right, sir," said the hotel man. "If you only know what
I have to go through on a day like this!"

"That's why I feel free to talk to you this way," the banker said.
"Now I know you're in a tough spot. The clerk says your rooms
are all filled. But I wish you'd do me a favor. Go over and check the
board yourself and see if you can't find me a room somewhere, somehow. I'll wait right here."

The banker didn't get the best room in the house, to be sure. But
he did get a place to sleep—a room the hotel was holding in reserve
for just such an emergency. He found common ground with the
hotel man—similarity in the problems they both had to deal with.
He probed to see if he was making progress—"Know what I mean?"
Finding he had made headway, he swung to his point—his need
for a room—and won agreement.

Take it another way. Maybe you're office manager in the downtown office of a large corporation. Your clerks and typists belong to
a union. Their shop steward, Beth Ramsay, long an employee of
your company, comes in with a complaint. Seems some of the girls
think you haven't been assigning overtime equitably. Beth is pretty
wrought up about it, says the girls are talking about a slowdown.

"Now, Beth," you say, "this reminds me of the time when you first
came here to work. I think it was right after the war. I was in
charge of files then, and you started with me. Do you remember
the ruckus we had that year?"

"Sure I do," Beth says. "Some of us really hit the roof."

"That's right. You know that was about overtime, too. The girls'
wages were pretty good, and a dollar went a lot further those days.
They didn't want overtime, and they got mad when I insisted that
a few of them stay a couple of hours one afternoon and help us
over a hump. Even sent a committee in to argue with me. I think
you were on that committee, Beth."

"I think I was, now that I remember."

"Well, things have changed a lot since then, Beth. The girls used to fuss because they got overtime work. Now they fuss if they don't get it. Let me suggest this to you, Beth: Get your girls together and review the overtime clause in the wage contract, then look at the overtime record. I think you'll find that everybody has been offered a fair share of overtime work and that those who have had the least overtime are the ones who passed up overtime offers because they had a date or didn't want to work for some other reason."

Now analyze the conversation with Beth. The common ground was old friendship and bygone days in the plant. The probe for acceptance: "Remember the ruckus we had that year?" Finally, with the probe indicating acceptance thus far, a persuasive statement of position. The result: agreement from disagreement.

### 3. *The Circuitous Gambit*

When you use this approach your hearers don't know where you're going. You seem to ramble. You move from one apparently unrelated point to another. But each point is unusual or interesting in its own way, and so your hearers go along with you, though they're riding blind. Gradually, though, all the points fall into place, you establish the over-all pattern, and your purpose becomes plain. Like the conciliatory and common-ground approaches, this one gives your hearers a chance to accept you as a person before you lead them into the controversial area.

If you work at this gambit skillfully, your listeners won't feel let down or tricked as your pattern unfolds. The key to success is a friendly, good-natured attitude, perhaps even humor if you're skilled in handling it. This attitude will disarm the opposition and give them no reason to feel they've been taken in. Again, though, as in other situations in which humor can be helpful, no sarcasm, no irony.

How do you use this circuitous gambit?

Suppose you're a division head. A young engineer in your division makes a mistake that costs your firm thousands of dollars. He knows it, too, and he's hurt and angry about it. You've got to dress him down, but you want to do it constructively and helpfully. So you start in by telling him stories about your own experiences as a young engineer—how you once raced ahead on an excavation project without thinking to have pumps standing by, and how a sudden cloudburst damaged two costly electric motors and a compressor; how you once overlooked scheduling delivery of some critical steel structurals, and thus held up construction for a week; how you misplaced a decimal that cost your company a contract. You also tell him what you learned by those mistakes—to think ahead, to work with care, to guard against unforeseen bad luck.

Gradually, incident by incident and lesson by lesson, you move closer to the young man's blunder. At last, when you bring it into the open, there's little need to dwell on it. You've made your point without laboring it and almost without personalizing it. And the young engineer doubtless will say to his friends on the job, "Ever talk to the old man? He sure knows his stuff."

### 4. The Blunt Assault

"I'm going to be blunt with you. I'm opposed to your proposal in every way. I'll do everything I can to defeat it. Here's why I'm going to fight it—and you."

Many a man has made a frontal assault like this one and has won his point—without provoking rebuttal. It's a difficult strategy to bring off successfully and it fits few situations. But at the right time and in the hands of the right person, it can turn disagreement to agreement.

Words like those above take courage. But that's not enough. When you take that stand you must be absolutely honest. One false sign, one innuendo that reveals melodrama or hokum, and you're through. What's more, you can't quit midway of your attack, or backtrack. When you throw punches like that one, you're in for keeps.

When can you use that blunt assault effectively? Only when there's a proper issue for righteous indignation. A proposal that will clearly wreck your company, for instance. Or a conspiracy to thwart or ruin somebody. Or a plot to deceive innocent people who don't realize what's going on. First be sure you're right. Then go ahead.

### 5. *The Cards-on-the-table Strategy*

In situations that aren't desperate enough to call for the blunt assault, the cards-on-the-table (or plain-talk-and-fair-play) method will stand you in good stead, especially if you use it at just the right time.

What's the right time? It comes when people are tired of speakers who screen their purposes, who dodge and turn, who resort to double talk and evasion. It also comes when people are tired of debate that drags on and on. In these situations plain talk is refreshing and —more important—persuasive. It puts you in the position of being straightforward and honest, in contrast to your opponents, who seem shifty and sly. It can be a strong weapon for winning harmony out of dissent.

Getting into the cards-on-the-table approach is simplest of all. You need just a few key lead-ins—and the facts that will support your position. Here are some typical lead-ins:

"I know you oppose me. But I want you to know exactly where I stand."

"I'll put my cards on the table. All I ask is that you hold your minds open to me for a few minutes."

"I'm going to be perfectly honest with you. I don't agree with you and I want you to know why."

"I want us to get down to some plain talk about this matter."

"I think it's about time we cleared the dust out of our eyes and looked straight at the facts."

### 6. *The Leading-question Approach*

The proudest triumph of your career as a persuasive talker will come when you get your opponent to state your case for you.

That takes some doing. But it can be done, through thoughtfully worded questions that will lead your opponent to state your view and through provoking his habitual responses and then turning them to your own ends. That way, you lead him to tell you what you wish him to believe and he, believing he thought of it in the first place, accepts your idea as his own. There's really no trickery involved. In fact, it's often done openly and accepted cheerfully. When you do it, you're simply being thoughtful enough to let the other person do the talking.

Indeed, this is about the only way you can handle some people. There are people, you know, to whom you just don't *tell* things. They've got chronically fixed ideas, or they're overbearing, or suspicious, or uneducated, or sensitive, or bigoted. You know them as "difficult" people. The only way to persuade them at all is to answer their unreasoned arguments with subtly leading questions and to steer them with quiet statements of your own that relate to their interests. They're not the kind you'll win with a blitzkrieg. You've got to get at them gradually, turn them slowly and gently to your way of thinking.

Few people are as passionately fixed in their ideas as the old man whom the late Professor Irving Lee liked to describe. The old man had three great and abiding hates—liquor, religion, and Democrats. One morning the town hall burned to the ground. All afternoon that day the old man sat brooding in his kitchen, bringing his fist down on the table and declaiming: "I tell you, when they find out who burned down the town hall—and they will find out—it will be a rum-drinking, hymn-singing Democrat."

But you do come across a man sometimes who takes a position only slightly less inflexible than that of the old man above. Can you make this kind of man relax his views? Can you steer him subtly, so he'll swing himself your way, even state your position for you?

Suppose you're an official of a labor union and you have to settle an issue with an employer who is convinced the union intends to ruin him. What kinds of questions of comments could you frame that would bring him to state your views? There's no pat formula, of course, because you'll have to fit the questions and comments you interject to the drift of the employer's arguments. What's more, this strategy takes a good deal of subtlety and tact. The following, therefore, are only suggestions. But they are typical examples of leading questions, and they point out that there's a wrong way and a right way to ask much the same question:

| *The Wrong Question* | *The Right Question* |
|---|---|
| 1. How has inflation affected your scale of living, Mr. Haworth? | 1. Have you talked with your wife lately about how much it costs to run the house these days? |
| 2. What do you think lies at the root of this dispute? | 2. Joe Quick is one of your old-timers around the shop. Have you talked with him about this question? |
| 3. Your dislike of unions goes back a long way, doesn't it? | 3. I'm interested, Mr. Haworth. How did you get started in your business? |
| 4. How long do you think you can hold out if the union strikes? | 4. Remember that long strike we had right after the war? |
| 5. Do you really think young Joe Whipple is an upstart? Do you really think he's a trouble maker? | 5. Have you seen those figures on the number of college-trained men on your payroll now? |
| 6. What rights do you think a man has in your plant these days? | 6. Do you remember when you first hired Clem McGill? Nearly fifteen years ago, wasn't it? |
| 7. What makes you think men won't work as hard now as they used to? | 7. I saw you talking to Henry Fort out in the shop a few days ago. Did he tell you about that new automatic punch press he's working on? |
| 8. Don't you think that if the company can increase officers' salaries, it can afford a wage increase, too? | 8. What do you think about the new production record in the stamping department last month? Pretty good, isn't it? |

## 7. The Quiet-listening Technique

There are times when silence is your strongest ally. It gives your opponent a chance to blow off steam and get back to normal pressure levels. It gives him a chance to satisfy his need of self-expression. And it gives him a chance—sometimes his first chance—to hear his own views and recognize their weaknesses. In fact, it's not unusual to hear a man spout off for a long while—and finally wind up by saying, "You know, the more I think about this the more I think you may be right." When that happens, agreement comes easily and naturally. Even if your opponent doesn't openly admit you're right, if you let him talk long enough he's likely to waver at some point and thus give you a chance to move in.

In his long career as dean of men at Duke University the late William H. Wannamaker used the silent-listening technique time and time again to win agreement from indignant students and student delegations. Complaints about food, about parking regulations, professors, about regulations for dances and restrictions on week-end absences—whatever it was, it didn't matter. He sat quietly and listened attentively. More often than not the students boiled off their indignation, or wavered enough to give him an opening for persuasion, or simply talked themselves out of their position. It's a technique that will work equally well, if the circumstances are right, with college boys, union committees, stockholders, parishioners, customers, civic and church committees, and almost any other group or individual.

## Summary

One of the most difficult problems in business, in industry, in committee work, in civic projects, and in social conversation is to win agreement out of disagreement. Yet it's a familiar problem, because you'll stumble across differences of opinion, clashing personalities, and conflicting aims wherever you go. You'll find hostile groups and individuals, people with grievances or complaints, doubters, chronic "aginners," defeatists, and groups divided within themselves.

Bringing harmony out of dispute is a richly satisfying experience. And there are tested ways of doing it—ways that can win success if you adapt them to the kind of opposition you face, the context of the dispute, and the circumstances under which you meet your opponents.

Your keys to success are a cool head, calm thinking, a controlled temper, patience, refusal to show annoyance or irritation, sincerity, respect for the honest views of those who differ with you, and conviction that your own view is the right view. With these keys to success in your possession, and with command of this chapter's seven basic techniques for winning agreement from disagreement, you can face almost any difference-of-opinion situation with confidence.

## Exercises

1. Recall a recent experience in which you had to face hostility in a group or individual. Make a pencil outline of the position your opponents took, noting the points they made and the facts they cited. Make notes also on their personalities, their likes and dislikes, their experiences, and the reasons why, in your opinion, they held the opinions they stated. When you have completed your outline and notes, draft a plan by which you can win them over to your side, using one of the seven techniques described in this chapter.

2. Ask your wife or friend to take a position opposing your views on an imaginary issue. See how successfully you can use, in turn, each of the seven techniques described in this chapter for bringing agreement out of disagreement. If you have trouble imagining situations and issues, select one from the following list of controversial subjects:

Let's change this fifteen-year-old method.
We need to expand our department.
Negroes should be allowed to work on this job.
The mistake isn't as bad as it seems.
Charlie shouldn't be fired.
You should take another job at lower pay.
Production is just as important as sales.
Those jobs on the night shift are good jobs.
We should pay day rates instead of piecework rates.

I need an assistant.

There's some good in both political parties.

We should reelect our present mayor.

Let's buy a new pipe organ for our church.

We should pay our schoolteachers higher salaries.

Our state should impose a sales tax.

Our minister (or priest, or rabbi) deserves our support.

It's time we gave our employees a raise.

Seniority shouldn't protect a worker against penalties for careless workmanship.

We jurymen shouldn't convict this man.

How can I develop the techniques of persuasion
and conviction?

**5**

# How to Use the Power
# of Suggestion

Doesn't matter whether you're talking to just one person, a small
group, or a big crowd—whether you're talking formally or informally
—whether you're arguing, explaining, describing, or narrating.
Whenever you talk, you're really making two talks at once. One
of them, expressed in the words you use, hits your listener in the
center of his attention. The other talk, of which your hearer is less
aware, plays on the margins of his attention and carries him beyond
the words he hears.

This second talk, the one that stirs marginal thinking, is what you leave unsaid. You convey it by suggestion only. You plant impressions on the fringes of attention—in those areas that the psychologists call subliminal, where reactions take place covertly or intuitively. Yet this second talk, wordless though it be, can be more important to your success than the very words you speak. It can suggest many things—and much about you. This chapter will tell you what suggestion will do for you, how to develop your skill in using suggestion, and how to avoid suggesting the wrong thing.

## What Suggestion Will Do for You

In general terms, suggestion can (and does) reveal what you are and what you intend. And, without your seeming to impose your views on them, it can lead your hearers to form the very opinions you want them to form. Specifically, here are some of the things suggestion will do for you:

• *Impress your personality on your hearers.* The image of what you are is inherent in what you say and how you say it. Emerson put it aptly when he said, "What you are shouts so loud I can't hear what you say." Your unspoken words tell your listeners whether you're honest or shifty, sincere or superficial, strong or weak, dependable or evasive, stable or nervous, deep or shallow. They tell whether you're eager to share your thoughts, whether you're earnestly concerned about others, whether you're using stratagems and tricks or talking from the heart.

Every effective talker wants to impress his hearers favorably. While he's talking and after he has finished, he wants thoughts like these to run through their fringe consciousness:

"This man is friendly and pleasant. He's natural and sincere, not affected or pretentious. He knows and respects his job, and he expects me to respect it. He's emotionally stable and has a sense of proportion. He believes in himself—and in me. His sense of values is sound. He doesn't judge me by the length of my car, or the elegance of my house, or the size of my bank account. He's trying to help me."

Suppose, for instance, you're foreman of an assembly line. The assembly job is light work that requires nimble fingers, so you employ women. Parts and subassemblies converge on moving belts. Many of the parts are sharp-cornered. From overhead, compressed air lines and electric power lines drop down at every work station to serve lightweight power tools. Fork trucks often run up and down the aisle behind the girls. In short, there are several hazards associated with the work. It's part of your job to keep accidents at a minimum. So you call the girls together.

You could go after them this way:

"Listen, you girls. The superintendent bawled me out when Lola got her hair caught in a power drill day before yesterday. He's sick and tired of these accidents—and so am I. The rules say you girls have got to wear hair nets on the job. I don't want to catch any of you without them from now on."

You wouldn't get much acceptance that way—for yourself or your idea. The girls would see your main objective: to avoid another bawling out by the superintendent.

But you might try it another way and win the cooperation of the girls. Like this:

"I stopped in yesterday to see Lola. She lives with her mother, you know, and all they have to get along on is Lola's check. She'll be laid up at home for another week or so. Got some pretty ugly scalp wounds. Lola's accident was needless. It brings me to say this: The rule about wearing hair nets on the job is a sound one. It's there to protect you. I hope I won't have to remind you of this again."

This way, you've got something direct to say, and you say it directly. But your approach and your manner say even more—and say it eloquently. They tell the girls that you're sincerely interested in them as people, that you earnestly want them to avoid injury, and that you'll stand behind every effort to make the job safe for them.

• *Convey a meaning.* When you'd rather not be blunt or specific, you can often make your point tactfully and effectively by suggestion. You say what you want to say indirectly, leaving it to your hearers to draw conclusions. Indirection opens up a different frame-

work of imagery and experience for expressing your thoughts and
purposes. It gives you an opportunity to use stories and parables
and thus make abstractions concrete and sentiments real. With indirection you can avoid being blunt or candid in sensitive or ex-
plosive situations, and you can ease yourself out of awkward and
unpleasant situations.

Lincoln was a master of suggestion and indirection. Shortly before
the Lincoln-Douglas debates, for instance, he had a talk with Judge
Beckwith, an old friend from Vermillion County, Ill. The judge expressed some doubt that Lincoln would come off very well in the
debates.

Lincoln sat down on the steps of a hotel, asked the judge to have a seat,
and then drawled, "You have seen two men about to fight?" "Yes, many
times." "Well, one of them brags about what he means to do. He jumps
high into the air, cracking his heels together, smites his fists, and wastes
his breath trying to scare somebody. The other man says not a word. His
arms are at his side, his fists doubled up, his head is drawn to the shoulder, and his teeth are set firm together. He is saving his wind for the
fight, and as sure as it comes off he will win it, or die a-trying."

With that, Lincoln bade the judge goodbye and left him to draw
his conclusion. Lincoln had stated his determination to win, and
he had done it more impressively and dramatically than by saying
simply, "I expect to fight and win."

In our own time there are many situations in which suggestion
can be equally successful. Suppose, for instance, you're an office
manager. You've got a seventeen-year-old boy working as a mes-
senger. He's a bright youngster, quick to learn, ambitious, prompt,
energetic. Maybe a little too energetic, in fact, for an orderly office.
He darts here and there, slams doors behind himself, always looks
busy even when he's idle for a few minutes. You figure you'd better
have a talk with him, but you want to handle him gently because
he's a sensitive boy. So, in a slack period one day, you walk over
to his mail table. Here's what you might say to him:

"Billy, you see the old man sitting over there in the corner? Ever
wonder why we call him 'Slammer'? He's been here thirty years,
and he's still just a clerk. They tell me he used to bounce around

here at high speed, always on the move. He'd dart in and out of the office with his hands full of papers, bang things down on desks, shove chairs out of his way, and slam doors every time he went in and out. That's why everybody called him 'Slammer.' But he doesn't move around now the way he used to. And I don't think you'd call him a great success in business. Trouble was, he never got much done. He was too busy to work or think, and he never got things organized."

Take it an even simpler way. Say you've got a prize girl as your assistant. You get along fine with her, and you wouldn't risk offending her or losing her. Her one failing: Three or four mornings a week she comes in late—anywhere from 9:10 to 9:20. How do you handle her? Try suggestion. Catch her one of those mornings when she's on time and say to her: "Peggy, I'm glad you came in early this morning. Things pile up, you know, and we've got a lot to do. Can we get started right away?"

• *Keep your hearers alert.* Suggestion gives the marginal consciousness of your hearers something to work on—something that's allied to subject and purpose—something that creates concrete images and thus makes the thought processes vivid.

The Twenty-third Psalm is a classic example of the use of concrete imagery to stir the fringes of the mind and keep it moving in the desired direction. The same is true of many of the parables of Jesus. They suggest abstractions in terms of sensory experiences and visual objects—"still waters," "green pastures," or "the sower and the seed," for instance.

Few of us can do as well as the Scriptures in using suggestion to hold hearers. But even the inexperienced among us will find it a helpful tool that often spells the difference between ineffective and effective talking.

A young woman was graduated not long ago from a school of fashion design. She took a job with a large department store and, being a bright girl, rose rapidly within her first year—so rapidly, in fact, that the head of the school invited her to talk to the next year's graduating class. "What will I say to them?" she kept asking herself. Then she remembered. Many of the things she had been

asked to do as a student of design seemed a pointless waste of time
when she was in school—a paper she had had to write on different
kinds of carrying handles for bags, pocketbooks, or purses—a visit
she had been required to make to an art gallery. It was only later,
when she began work in the department store, that she found these
projects taking on significance in her everyday problems.

So she built her talk around those apparently wasteful projects
at school. But she did it only by suggestion. She told simple stories
of her day-to-day experiences on the job—how a few remarks about
the handle on a bag had swayed a customer toward a better buy
and how an eighteenth-century portrait she had seen in an art gallery had given her a new idea for draping a fine fabric for display
on a mannequin.

Her talk wasn't schoolteacherish. Never once did she say, "The
things you're fussing about today won't look so foolish a year from
now." Yet every girl who heard her got the drift—imagined herself
in the same role—saw for the first time how purpose breathed in
every assignment at school.

• *Endow your business or institution with a personality.* Perhaps
the most dramatic way to show how suggestion works here is to approach it negatively, because negative suggestion often is the root
of failure in a business or enterprise.

For instance, the hardware store operator who grumbles over having to make a refund for faulty goods inspires little confidence in
his business. The bank teller who doesn't respond to pleasantries can
leave a trail of quietly terminated accounts behind him. The nurse
who's cold and heedless of complaints can turn patients away from a
clinic in droves. The clergyman who is too preoccupied with office
details to listen sympathetically to a story of trouble can reduce his
church's hold on the community to a slender thread. The chairman
of the board who runs a stockholders' meeting ruthlessly gives the
impression that his corporation is just like him—that it's ruthless
and runs roughshod over customers and competition alike. The
jeweler who talks only in terms of price and tries to thrust his goods
on his customers will repel customers rather than attract them.
And the senator with the slick gestures and the grand manner can

become the victim of the "defect of perfection" when the TV cameras move in close and thus can lose the campaign for his party.

If the power of suggestion can work against the group or institution you represent, it can also work favorably in personal contacts and in less informal situations, such as a talk before a small group. If your bearing is dignified yet friendly, if your interest in people genuinely shines through your words, if you talk knowledgeably yet simply, if you are well groomed and courteous, you will automatically create a favorable impression for your business, your organization, or your constituents. Grover Whalen, for instance, long an official greeter for New York City, by his dignity, friendliness, and courtesy imparted his own character and personality to the city and at the same time endowed his perfume business with prestige and stature. The wry candor of Robert Frost gave warmth to the Library of Congress during his term as consultant on poetry. And the selfless drive of Frank Pace, president of General Dynamics Corporation and tireless worker and speaker in behalf of good causes, suggests the vigor and public-spirited attitude of his company and the other interests he is associated with.

• *Obscure your overt faults as a speaker.* Here's where earnestness, conviction, and character play a strong hand in effective talking. Granted, it's desirable to talk grammatically, to have a pleasing voice, to gesture aptly. But even if you don't have these qualities and skills, the things you can otherwise suggest about yourself and your cause can add impact to what you say—enough impact, in fact, to cancel out your obvious imperfections as a speaker.

There's the foreign-born girl, for instance, whose sentences are badly jumbled and whose accent is an obstacle to understanding, but who holds her hearers spellbound with her conviction, born of experience, that communism is evil. There's the ex-cancer patient who makes $12,000 a year as a salesman—he's had to learn to talk by swallowing air and releasing it through his esophagus because his larynx has been removed. There's the unlettered man of simple faith whose sense of right and wrong is a guide for his fellow churchmen, though his gestures are clumsy and his grammar leaves much to be desired. There's the inarticulate businessman whose words stumble one over another but who rises to the presidency of a rich corporation because his judgment is always sound, his facts are accurate, and his energy is limitless.

## Six Do's for Developing Your Skill in Suggestion

Here are tried and tested ways for becoming a better user of suggestion.

1. *Cultivate a cheerful, pleasant attitude.* That doesn't mean you should try to be funny. Few people can. Nor does it mean you should be a pushover, giving in with a vapid smile when opposition develops. It simply means that if your own attitude is optimistic, if your brow is clear of furrows and frowns, if you relax the muscles of your face, you'll create a climate about you that will make dispute difficult—a climate that will encourage your hearers to reflect your own good will and thus go along with your views. In short, what you suggest about yourself will strengthen what you say about your subject.

2. *Cultivate your interest in other people.* Try to understand and respond to their needs and desires. Seek opportunities to talk with people about their hopes and fears, their beliefs and doubts, their careers and hobbies, their families and friends, their experiences and opinions. Sensitivity and understanding come from wide acquaintanceship, close observation, and attentive listening. If you develop these qualities of sensitivity and understanding, your thoughts will automatically clothe themselves in terms of the experiences and needs of your listeners, and what you say therefore will suggest far more to them than the naked words you use. While you talk and listen, people will be saying to themselves, "This fellow really understands me. He knows what's worrying me. He sees things the way I see them. He's not asking me to *do* something for him. He's really trying to *be* something to me."

3. *Be simple and concrete.* High-flying language will only suggest that you're pompous, that you're putting on an act, that what you're saying is contrived and artificial, that you're interested mostly in covering yourself with glory. What's more, big words that come

from Latin and Greek tend to express abstractions. Simple language and short words, on the other hand, build a bond of sympathetic understanding between speaker and listener. The shorter words of our language are mostly concrete. They evoke images in the mind's eye—images of objects, actions, experiences. To be sure, they won't evoke the same image in every listener's mind, because each listener will react in his own way. But whatever the image may be, it will flicker on the borders of conscious thought and thus make vivid and real the ideas your words suggest.

So don't worry if you can't command a multisyllabic vocabulary. Your hearers, in fact, might back away from those long words. Granted, it's good to study your dictionary. It's a fascinating book. But store away in your mind the strong, simple words that come from Anglo-Saxon roots. By and large, they are the colorful words, the picture-making words, those that are rich in association and meaningful in terms of other people's experiences. Think again of the vivid images in the Twenty-third Psalm. Reread Lincoln's Gettysburg Address and see how simple it is. And remember Winston Churchill's rugged, stirring words: "We shall not flag or fail. We shall fight in France. We shall fight on the seas and oceans. . . . We shall fight on the beaches. We shall fight on the landing fields. We shall fight in the fields and in the streets. . . . We shall never surrender." Hardly a Latin word anywhere. Yet Churchill's words evoked a heroic response seldom matched in history.

4. *Study your subject.* You must have the facts at hand and know what you're talking about if you expect to suggest authority and conviction. If you hesitate because you lack information, or if you waver because you haven't made up your mind between two conflicting sets of data, or if you're trapped while pretending to know what you don't really know, you're lost. In this situation the only thing you suggest to your hearers is that you (and the organization you speak for) are unsure, shallow, and weak and that you don't respect your hearers enough to prepare for them.

On the other hand, you can suggest the best about yourself and those you represent by careful preparation of what you say. Just a few years ago a rising young journalist, an expert in general business, was made editor of a specialized technical magazine serving an industry he knew little or nothing about. Shortly afterward, he was asked to address a large conference of leaders in that industry. By concentrated study of this new field and its problems he equipped himself to make a stirring and brilliant address—so brilliant that the foremost technician in the audience rose voluntarily to his feet to praise the young speaker for the depth of his perception and the clarity with which he had probed the industry's problems. As one listener put it, "This young editor, who didn't know a kilowatt from a kiddycar a year ago, put the experts to shame."

So bone up before you speak up. Go to your account books, study the record, spend a while at the library, get hold of a reference book, seek out an expert and talk with him, go to the place in question and see for yourself. In short, find out whatever you must know to talk with conviction and authority. Thus prepared, you'll have your listeners saying to themselves, "This man knows his subject. We trust him. Knowing what he knows, he can't be wrong."

If you don't have time to bone up before you talk, at least pause a moment while you plumb your experience for significant materials and examples.

5. *Explore new fields of knowledge.* This way, you'll acquire broader understanding, sharper perceptions, wider experience. And while you're acquiring these things, the talking you do will automatically take on richer meaning for your hearers and stir more meaningful images in their fringe thoughts. You'll become a more interesting, stimulating person and, what's more, you'll increase your store of examples for illustrating or explaining what you say.

The late George Smith, art director of *Factory* magazine, was such a person. He knew the arts of presentation and illustration. He knew far more, too. George had a restless mind. And he never let go of any subject until he had mastered it—fishing, marine navigation, genealogy, punched-card data-processing equipment, and chess, to mention only a few. The result? His conversation was refreshing, his language was rich in allusions, and what he said always suggested the best about himself.

How do you get into new fields of knowledge? George Smith, like many people, was driven into them by natural curiosity. Others, like the young editor above, drive themselves into them by strength of will and ambition to succeed.

Doesn't matter which way you break into a new area of knowledge, there are lots of opportunities everywhere—books in your home or in the public library, training or study courses offered by your company, city- or state-sponsored adult education programs, night classes at the local high school or college, private study groups (like those voluntary adult groups in some towns that study "The 100 Best Books"), correspondence courses and extension courses (in history, art, and other subjects) offered by many state university systems, educational TV lectures (many of which, to be sure, come along at a chilling hour of the morning), friendships cultivated with experts in various fields, well-informed public speakers, forums on public affairs, and a host of other opportunities. The wider your knowledge and experience, the more interesting person you will be —and the more effective you will become at expressing ideas.

6. *Keep yourself well groomed.* Nobody seriously argues that clothes alone make the man. In fact, there are rare people (like Dr. Samuel Johnson, whom Boswell immortalized) whose gifts of charm and intellect make us forget their rumpled, untidy looks. But it takes more charm, more intelligence, more wit than most of us can muster to offset the negative suggestions created by dingy fingernails, unshined shoes, gravy spots on a necktie, twenty-four-hour whiskers, baggy trousers, unkempt hair, badly mixed colors, flashy jewelry, and the like.

That's not to say you must spend big money on clothes to put yourself across to your hearers. All it means is this: One key to creating favorable marginal thinking about your person (and therefore what you represent) is personal cleanliness, general tidiness, and quiet good taste. These virtues are within reach of all of us, whether we spend $20 a month for clothing, or $500.

## Six Rules for Avoiding Trouble with Suggestion

If you control it skillfully, suggestion will work in your favor. But it can also work against you if you talk when you should stay quiet, if you say the wrong thing when you do talk, or even if you stay quiet when you have good reason to speak up. That's why these six rules are good ones to follow:

1. *Don't talk unless you have something to say that's helpful and meaningful to your hearers.* People are quick to catch the fact if you ramble aimlessly, if you're unsure of your facts and your purpose. They're even quicker to catch on if you're talking simply to hear yourself talk, to bring yourself before the public eye, to bask in the attention of the crowd.

Talking when you have nothing to say is a sure way to create negative suggestions in the minds of those who hear you. The effect can be fatal, now and in the future as well. For the time may come when you really do have something to say—when it's important that you summon up all your resources and hit your listeners' attentions directly and indirectly. If you have formerly given people negative suggestions about yourself, those suggestions will still flicker through your hearers' minds and crowd out the favorable suggestions you're now trying to create.

2. *Don't argue or debate unless you've got convictions.* If you do, you'll be a sitting duck for any opponent who does have convictions. In comparison with him, you'll look weak, uncertain, confused. And that's not the way you want people to think of you.

3. *Don't speak in anger.* Indignation, yes—if the situation warrants it. But not anger. Anger can betray you into extreme positions, provoke you to say things you'll regret, reveal an ugly prejudice or a side of your personality that you've outgrown or schooled yourself to subdue. Anger can even paralyze your reason, erase facts from your mind, and thus alienate people from a cause that you would have won them over to if you had waited for your anger to subside. Anger suggests the worst about you—that you're undisciplined, careless of the feelings of others, irrational, stubborn, narrow, and unforgiving. It hurts you, it hurts any group you may be representing, and it hurts any cause you may be advocating. So calm down before you speak up.

4. *Don't bring personalities into argument.* Not unless you can say something pleasant about them. To let an attack on an issue slide over into an attack on a person reveals your own prejudices

and animosities. What's more, it breeds prejudices (or stirs them up) among those who hear you. Both ways, it's bad strategy. In the first place, you show yourself in an unfavorable light, just as you do in anger. In the second place, prejudice being negative by definition, you create a negative attitude of mind among your listeners. Though you may win a few followers among those whose prejudices you can shape or guide, you'll alienate those whom you attack and those who sympathize with your victims.

5. *Don't fawn or flatter.* Keep your compliments dignified and sincere (though they need not be devoid of humor if it's light, good-natured humor). Most people can detect the difference between genuine compliments, which they welcome, and toadying, which they resent. You don't have to manufacture nice things to say to people. If you really feel kindly toward them, good things to say will come to you naturally and tastefully.

Also, don't pander to the vulgar tastes of a few. If you cross the borderline of good taste to please a handful of people, you're more than likely to lose the discriminating persons whose respect and support you value highly.

In short, avoid anything that will give your hearers the impression that you are insincere, self-seeking, weak, self-abasing, or vulgar.

6. *Don't let your little shortcomings keep you from speaking up.* If your grammar isn't simon pure, don't worry. Real purists are rare in business, in industry, in sales, in politics, and in civic or community work. The hazard in imperfect grammar is not the imperfection itself, but the sense of inadequacy or uncertainty that it creates in a speaker, and hence the suggestion of inadequacy or uncertainty that he leaves with his listeners. So if you've got something to say, go ahead and say it. If you talk with sincerity and conviction, faulty grammar won't stand in the way of a favorable impression.

Of course, if you are guilty of flagrant misuse of basic grammar rules, you should accept the challenge and do something about it— as you would accept any other challenge to improve yourself. Just walk into a library or bookstore and ask for a practical, everyday book on grammar. Then have the fun of wrestling with it in your spare time. Lincoln did. He found grammar an "easy science" and was glad he spent the time and effort.

The same is true of voice and diction. Time was when speech textbooks for people in business and industry had long chapters on these subjects. Not now, though. Today the emphasis is on the desire to communicate. If you've really got the desire to share what's in your mind and heart, voice and diction will take care of themselves. You never fail to understand a man who makes an impassioned speech about something he really believes in. You never pay attention to the voice or diction of your wife when she gets excited about something you did or failed to do. Instead, you focus your attention on what she's saying. When your seven-year-old gets immersed in telling you about an adventure at school, you don't notice the pitch of his voice or the excited slurring of his words. You listen to his words, not his voice. So did the millions of people who heard Wendell Willkie in his historic campaign for the Presidency. Though his voice always rasped and often was made worse with hoarseness, his conviction and enthusiasm made people oblivious of these imperfections.

The impassioned speaker, your wife, and your seven-year-old are all alike. Their desire to communicate is so strong that it overshadows the imperfection of voice, diction, and grammar. Their manner conveys sincerity, purpose, and conviction. This is more important in effective communication than all the formalities of grammar, diction, and gesture.

## Summary

Every communicator, consciously or unconsciously, delivers two talks when he speaks. One is made up of the words he uses. The other consists of the overtones and impressions he creates by what he says and the way he says it. This second talk, which finds its strength in the power of suggestion, hits his listeners on the fringes of their attention. It can affect them more profoundly than the words he actually says. It can impress his personality on his audience, convey a hidden meaning, keep his hearers alert, endow a business or institution with personality, and obscure the little imperfections that often give a talker a feeling of inadequacy.

The effective communicator knows this power of suggestion—and what it can tell his listeners about himself and his subject. That's why he conscientiously cultivates his personality—seeks to mold it so it becomes consistently cheerful, pleasant, sincere, and earnest. That's why he develops his interest in other people. It's also why he holds fast to simplicity, masters the subjects he knows he will have to talk about, and continuously explores new fields of knowledge.

At the same time, he guards against talking without purpose or substance. He never argues unless he has convictions, never (or seldom) speaks in anger, never drags personalities into a debate on issues, never fawns or flatters, never lapses into vulgarity.

With his personality thus always under discipline, he can count on this power of suggestion to work in his favor whenever he opens his mouth to talk.

## Exercises

1. Remember the last time you had to be firm with a group or exhort people to do something. Reconstruct your phrasing in such a way as to improve the impression you made on the group. Stand before a mirror and watch your facial expression as you talk. Is it friendly and relaxed?

2. Assume you're going to talk for one minute, using the point-example-action technique described in Chapter 2. Decide what your point will be and what you want done about it. Then construct an example that will suggest clearly what your point is and what action you want taken, without stating them explicitly. Now recite your example to your wife (or some other convenient listener) and see if she can tell what point you're making and what you want done. If you're short of points, try one of the following:

We should do something about a faulty condition in the plant or office.

We ought to start a company recreational program.

You should join our club (or organization or committee).
Excessive drinking is harmful to the drinker and others as well.
This sales campaign must be made more dynamic.
There's a better way to do something (office paper work, machine
    operation, traffic control).
One small flaw can spoil an entire campaign.
That's not the way to be a leader.

## 6

*If I try everything and the other person still won't come around, what do I do then? How can I get others to rationalize agreement?*

# How to Rationalize with People

Did you ever know a good woman who married a no-good man, thinking she would reform him? A youngster who dropped out of school and joined the Navy, saying he wanted to see the world? A driver who passed a giant trailer truck on a curve because, he said, it blocked his vision? A company president who plunged into extravagant new-plant construction because "research" warranted quick expansion? Yet that good woman ruined her life—and did her shiftless husband no real good. The youngster missed his chance at a college education. The driver piled into an approaching car. And the president buried his company in bankruptcy.

How valid were the reasons these people gave for what they did? Not really valid at all. The woman simply wanted marriage and security. The young man wanted to escape studies in which he was less than brilliant. The reckless driver just wanted to satisfy his ego. And the company president wanted to be known as a bold, enterprising businessman. All four people were rationalizing their actions.

There's nothing unusual about these four. In fact, rationalization is a familiar friend to most people—a bolster-upper of ego, a refuge from failure, balm for disappointment, a defense for unwise or impetuous action. You see it in the teen-age boy who blames the umpire for a lost ball game. In the foreman who blames his wife because he's late at the plant day after day. In the salesman who blames unfairness of a competitor for a sag in his sales. In the priest who does no parish visiting because panhandlers dropping in at the church take too much of his time.

Rationalization is a method of thinking that follows the formal patterns of logic but lacks the substance of logic. It's unsound because it's wishful. Its root is wish, and the pattern of logic is shaped to fit the wish. With most people it's habitual in some degree.

Can you, as a speaker or talker, bend this habit of rationalization to your own aims and thus bring your listeners to your way of thinking? Yes, to some extent you can. All great persuaders—St. Paul, Benjamin Franklin, Lincoln—used it. The remainder of this chapter will tell you how you can use rationalization in your favor and why, on the other hand, you should use it sparingly.

## How to Get People to Rationalize in Your Favor

From time to time everybody is that boy who blames the umpire for the loss of the ball game. People alibi, procrastinate, and dream up reasons for doing (or not doing) this or that. There's always a battle between their feelings and what the facts spell out, between their fixed attitudes and their objective judgments. People wrestle with conscience and rationalize conscience into retreat. In seeking answers to adult problems, they play the childhood game of "Let's pretend."

When the occasion calls for it, the effective communicator directs his appeal to this habit of mind among his hearers. He approaches them from the standpoint of what they wish to believe or do. He gives them reasons for doing what they want to do—if it's what he wants them to do. Or he uses their own reasons, spoken or unspoken, for persuading them to do what he wants them to do. Thus he gradually brings them to his view or persuades them to take the action he wants them to take.

Four steps will help you be persuasive—show you how to fall in with (and capitalize on) the tendency of your hearers to rationalize their position. Here are those four steps:

1. Probe for what your listeners really want. (This may be quite different from what they say they want.)

2. Fit your remarks to their desires.

3. Start your comments with what is familiar and acceptable.

4. Reconcile their wish with your own purpose.

Now take five typical people you're likely to meet in business, industry, or elsewhere and see how, by following along with their rationalization, you can lead them to accept your view.

• *The aggressive shop steward.* Lately there has been an upsurge in the number of grievances this man has thrust at you. Right now he's demanding a hearing on a discharge case he wouldn't have fought six months ago—a steam fitter who attacked a helper with a pipe wrench.

The shop steward argues that the steam fitter was fired unjustly. He contends that the man was working under trying conditions (cramped work space, high temperature, and a helper who was new on the job) for which management alone was responsible. He admits the steam fitter deserved a rebuke—but not an out-of-hand discharge.

You cast about for reasons why the shop steward recently has become more aggressive. How does he rationalize his position on this discharge case? What's his hidden wish?

You know there's a split in the union. You suspect this split threatens the shop steward's status. You conclude that his real wish is to create issues to which his union members will rally unanimously, and thus strengthen his own prestige. This strong wish, you believe, is father to his rationalization that the steam fitter was fired unjustly. With this as your clue, here's how you might approach the shop steward:

"You know, Mike, you're coming in to see me oftener than you used to. I take it this means the split in the union is closing up now and that your members are solidly behind you, because if they weren't supporting you, you wouldn't be coming in. This is a good thing for employees and the company, because management can't always see the employees' point of view unless they have somebody to speak for them straightforwardly and honestly. It must make you proud to think how many people depend on you to represent them fairly. And I must admit that I, too, rely on you to give me straight facts.

"Now let's come to this steam fitter. I'm glad you brought this case up. Steam fitters do get some tough assignments. And this particular job had to be done fast because the breakdown was holding up the whole line. We just couldn't afford to shut down long enough for the whole system to cool off. But we're going to put in a new hatch so there'll be more room to work in next time there's a breakdown. The new hatch will let more air in, too. I don't think you'll have any more complaints on this point. If you hadn't brought this case up we wouldn't be making this improvement. Every steam fitter in the shop can thank you for it.

"I admit it's too bad we had to fire Joe. That was a tough job he had to do. But a man who lets the necessary discomforts of an emergency job get the best of his temper and takes out his anger on a fellow worker just isn't the kind of man the company can depend on in a pinch. And he's not the kind of man you and the union can depend on, either, because he'll always let his temper and his selfish impulses guide his conduct. That's why the company and the union agreed long ago on a rule against fighting in the plant. It's a rule we can't trifle with, or the company and the union both will suffer. I think Joe was fired for good reason, and I believe you'll agree the discharge ought to stick."

• *The unhappy salesman.* Will Jenks, one of your salesmen,

comes into your office and asks you to redraw some territorial boundaries. He contends that some formerly good customers in the farthest reaches of his territory have tapered off in their buying because he can't call on them often enough. And when he does get there, he says, it's usually at the end of a long spell of travel, when he's tired and ineffective. He says it will be easier for a salesman in an adjacent territory to call on them oftener. All that's needed, he points out, is to swap a small piece of his territory for a small piece of the other salesman's area.

From your conversation with Will you get a clue about what he really wants. He's a proud young man, and the sagging sales in that distant town have wounded his pride. He wants that wound healed. He wants to be thought of as a successful salesman.

Can you get at Will this way?

"I've been studying this problem, too, Will. It *is* a long trip out there, and there's a good deal in what you say about the reason for the dropoff in sales. A fellow does get pretty tired toward the end of the week. Everything considered, though, you've handled these accounts out there better than anybody else we could have sent. The people you call on tell me they're always glad to see you because you give them more than just a sales pitch. You really help them with some of their problems. And they've really got problems. That's the kind of salesman we like to represent our company.

"Now let me tell you how I feel about this thing. You've invested a lot of yourself in those accounts. It would take a new salesman over a year to make himself as well known to them as you are. The potential is there, and we can do a good business with them if we work this thing out right. In fact, I've got a couple of new ideas I believe you could use successfully on them. Let's go over them now. If they work out as I believe they will, I think you'll change your mind about this shift of territory."

• *The late-arriving file clerk.* She comes in at 9:15 or 9:20 morning after morning. Every time, she has a plausible excuse—the alarm clock ran down, the bus pulled away just as she ran up, she turned her coffee cup over and had to change her dress, her kid sister was sick, or she just plain overslept.

The truth of the matter, you discover, is that she wants to feel she "belongs" to the organization. As things are, she doesn't feel needed—doesn't feel that what she's doing is important enough to earn recognition. In fact, the rebuke she gets for being late is her only indication that her job is a job that needs doing. And that's the real reason why she persists in being late. It's her way of calling your attention to herself.

Can you handle this one with effective talking? You might try something like this next time she comes in late and makes her usual explanation:

"I know how these things are, Lois. There are some mornings when everything goes wrong at my house, too—the kids tie up the bathroom, the water runs cold, or the coffee won't perk, or the bus driver doesn't see me. I guess the same things happen to all of us. And that's why all of us are late one time or another.

"But I realized just a few minutes ago how important it is for you to be here at nine every morning. That's just another way of saying how much we need you here in the office. First thing this morning the general manager came in looking for the correspondence on that Homer Fields order. Said he had to have it by 9:30 for a big meeting. We had everybody around here looking for it, and it took us ten minutes to find it. Turned out the boss needed it to close a $10,000 contract. You could have put your finger on that correspondence in less than a minute—spared the general manager and all the rest of us that much anxiety. Shows you how important it is to have somebody here, like you, who knows our files and can spot things right away."

• *The diehard opponent.* This is Vice President Lucas (or Department Head Lucas, or Head Nurse Lucas, or anybody in the upper echelon). Say he fights your proposal to create a new division. He argues that it will dilute management responsibility, that it will be a risky investment, that it's not needed anyhow. "What's wrong with the way we're set up now?" he asks.

This man doesn't really oppose creation of the new division. He's just afraid his own division (and he with it) will lose stature in the change. He's proud of what he has done for the organization and he wants to hold onto his prestige.

Can you rationalize with him—and bring him over to your side?

You might get at him this way:

"There's no person in this room who hasn't made a significant contribution to our organization—those who were in it at its founding and those who were brought in from the outside as it grew. We've all shared in its growth.

"There was a time, most of us remember, when everybody pitched in and did everything that had to be done, without any clear divisional lines. As we grew I guess we all sort of gravitated to the work we liked best because we did it best. That, I suppose, is how we finally developed our divisional organization.

"When old Mr. Smithson retired we looked everywhere for the best man we could find to take over his work. We found Mr. Lucas. Under his leadership that division has grown by leaps and bounds. It has taken on new responsibilities every year. And it has paid off handsomely because Mr. Lucas always calculates his risks carefully. Now, thanks to him, it has grown so big and so diverse that it's unfair to ask any one man, even Mr. Lucas, to run it alone. We need him to work on those problems that call for his unique skills and his undivided attention.

"That's why I'm proposing this new division. It will relieve Mr. Lucas of a burden that grew on him without his inviting it—a burden that he assumed simply because nobody else was willing to bother with it in its early stages of development. Now it's grown far beyond anything any of us expected. I think it's time now for this activity to stand on its own feet as a separate division. Setting it up that way will relieve Mr. Lucas of a great deal of petty detail and will spare him many a sleepless night."

• *The hesitant buyer.* Sometimes your listener's rationalization, unlike that of any of the four people above, is already running in your favor. That is, he really wants to do what you want him to do. But he also has doubts about whether he should. If this is your problem, it's fairly easy. You believe in your product. You know (without rationalization) that he needs your product and has the money to buy it. So you just play down your own anxiety and give him an occasional nudge in your direction. He may well solve your problem for you.

For example, take the story of the young assistant professor who walked into a music store in Syracuse. It was three weeks before Christmas. He had decided to give his wife, an accomplished musician, a piano for Christmas. So far, so good. But he was still wavering in an area of decision: Should he give her a piano that was strictly within his narrow means as an assistant professor? Or should he do what he really wanted to do? That is, veer over, just a little, into extravagance and thus give her an instrument better suited to her talent and more demonstrative of his affection for her?

Could you, as a piano salesman, nudge this young professor into doing what he really wants to do? Yes. And you could do it without being a sinner, too. Listen:

PROFESSOR: I'd like to give my wife a piano for Christmas if I can find one that's not too expensive. Do you have any second-hand, reconditioned uprights?

SALESMAN: Sure. A basement full of them. Come this way.

PROFESSOR (now in the basement): You've really got a lot of them. Probably sell them to YMCAs and churches and the like, don't you?

SALESMAN: That's right. People paint them up and they look fairly good.

PROFESSOR: These do look a bit beat up.

SALESMAN: I guess you're right, at that. But they sound pretty good. Try one.

PROFESSOR: Yes, this one sounds all right.... And so does this one. ... But I don't know. My wife is a fine pianist. She deserves a good piano. But we live in the university apartments and we don't have much room. What about a new spinet? Do you have any in the store?

SALESMAN: Up on the fourth floor. Let's take the elevator here.

PROFESSOR (now on the fourth floor): These are beautiful.... This one has a fine tone. I'm sure she'd like it.

SALESMAN: If she's a good pianist, she certainly would. It's a lot better than a reconditioned one. And you want her to have the best you can buy.

PROFESSOR: That's right. You know, now that I think of it, my father wants to give us a new refrigerator for Christmas. That would cost about $300 or more. Maybe I could talk him into using that money as a down payment on this spinet. We could make do with the old refrigerator for a while. My wife is different from most. Music is important to her. This would make her very happy. And it would be a real Christmas present. Can I finance it some way?

SALESMAN: Any way you like. Let's go to the office and see about it.

The young professor bought the spinet and asked for delivery just before Christmas. His wife was ecstatic. And he got more joy from her happiness than from anything else he had ever done. He knew he had rationalized himself into doing what he wanted to do. But, with a little help from the salesman, he had rationalized consciously and had cheerfully accepted the consequences—a lean purse for some time to come.

Now look back at four of these people—the shop steward, the salesman, the file clerk, and Vice President Lucas. All of them were rationalizing their situations. That is, they unconsciously manufactured reasons to explain away their plight, their actions, or their views. Yet none of their reasons was the real reason.

Look also at the ways in which these four people might be handled. The talker sensed—or probed for—what his listeners really wanted. He found the real reasons for their conduct. He framed his remarks around their unspoken wishes. He started on familiar and agreeable ground and at last reconciled their wishes with his own. His method was persuasive because it bolstered ego, expressed sympathy and understanding, showed respect for his hearers and their views, and avoided argument.

The fifth person, the young professor in search of a piano, is a somewhat different story. So is the technique of handling him—of turning his rationalization in your direction. In fact, persuading him to buy the new spinet did not involve steering his hidden wish in

another direction, but simply bringing it to the surface and giving
it free scope.

## Four Caution Flags about Rationalizing

You can talk effectively and persuasively to people who rationalize, as the examples above show. But you must pick your occasion
carefully and appeal to rationalization sparingly, because this
thought pattern can be treacherous.

Why treacherous? Four reasons:

1. *An argument based on a listener's rationalization is sometimes
easy to rebut and hard to defend.* This stands to reason because such
argument is often contrived, and the moves by which you advance
from one step to another may not be altogether sound.

What's more, since you start out on common, familiar ground,
it's easy for your listener to interrupt when you state one of his
reasons, snatch the conversational ball from you, and run off with
it in his own direction. Suppose, for example, the shop steward
above had interrupted your opening remarks by saying, "And that's
exactly why I'm here in your office—to state the employees' view
straightforwardly and honestly. Here's what I have to say to you."
With this interruption, he could go on with his own line of reasoning. Even if you didn't lose the battle then and there, you'd have
a long, hard job getting the conversation back on the line you had
laid out.

So, before you go ahead, be sure your path is straight. In most
instances (except when your listener, like the young professor, is
already rationalizing in your favor) you should try to maintain command of the conversation. That is, talk confidently and steadily until
you reach the logical conclusion of your remarks.

2. *You run the risk of mistaking a man's real reasons for rationalization.* Your assumption that he's rationalizing is your own guess.
That guess may be shrewd and right. Or it may be dead wrong.
If it's wrong, you'll be in double danger: You'll base your argument
on an unsound premise and thus will make little or no sense to
your listener. Or you'll antagonize him by attributing motives to

him that he doesn't have. There's no better way than the latter to make a man angry.

Suppose, for instance, you should be wrong about Vice President Lucas up above. Suppose he's really concerned about just what he said he was concerned about—dilution of responsibility, the risk of investment in a new division, and the possibility of creating a new division that's not really needed. Suppose, not realizing how earnestly he feels about these matters, you assume that he wants nothing except to preserve his little kingdom in the organization. And suppose you base your remarks on the false assumption and therefore make no recognition of his real views. Lucas will give you a real fight.

So, before you go ahead, be sure you've sized up your listener right.

3. *Your argument can collapse of its own intricacy.* It takes some pretty subtle maneuvering and some involved thought sequences to analyze somebody else's unspoken reasons, show your concurrence, move across neutral ground, and finally come convincingly to your own side of the discussion. And there's always the danger that you'll lose your point in the concessions you make at the outset. The late-arriving file clerk, for example, might remember only your agreement that there are many reasons for being late and forget your point that she's needed in the organization.

So, before you go ahead, lay out your argument step by step so neither you nor your listener will stumble over it or misconstrue it.

4. *Your persuasion can end in disappointment or resentment on the part of the persuaded person if the action that follows doesn't turn out as expected or promised.* Take that salesman who asked you to redraw some territorial lines. You've talked him out of his view, you've made him feel he's a better salesman than his record really shows him to be, and you've promised him some help of your own. But suppose sales in that far-off city keep on sagging, in spite of all you and he together can do. He'd be perfectly justified in taking an "I told you so" attitude. And next time he came in with a proposal you wanted to talk him out of, you'd have a hard time

talking him out of it. Chances are, in fact, he'd start looking for another company to work with—maybe even a competing company.

## Summary

Rationalization is a thought process that's familiar to all of us. People use it to justify or explain away their views, their shortcomings, their mistakes, their unwise or impetuous actions. It presents a surface reason, often untrue or only half-true, that conceals a real and valid reason for what people do or think.

The effective talker learns to recognize rationalization in others and to bend it in the direction he wants his listener to move in. He does this in four steps:

1. He probes for what his listener really wants—the deep-seated reason that's hidden beneath the surface reason.

2. He adapts his remarks to this concealed, unspoken reason.

3. He lays his groundwork on what is familiar and acceptable to his listener.

4. He reconciles his listener's hidden wish with his own purpose.

Even so, though you follow these four rules, there are hazards in persuading people who rationalize. That's why the effective speaker chooses his occasions cautiously and uses rationalization sparingly. The hazards are these:

1. Such persuasion is often easy to rebut and hard to defend.

2. There's a danger of assuming that a man is rationalizing when he really means what he says. Such a mistake is fatal to persuasion and offensive to the person whose motives you misinterpret.

3. The argument based on rationalization can collapse of its own intricacy.

4. Unless the listener's wish is satisfied, now or later, successful persuasion that overcomes rationalization can lead to disappointment, even resentment, in the person who gives up his views.

There are, therefore, five cardinal rules to follow in talking effectively to a person who rationalizes:

1. Be sure your own thinking is sound.

2. Keep command of the conversation.

3. Be sure you size up your listener (and his deep-seated motives) correctly.

4. See your way clear to the end of your statement before you start out, and thus avoid stumbling over the intricacies of your reasoning.

5. Be sure you can satisfy the hidden wishes of your listener. This way, you'll avoid creating false hopes and laying the foundation for disappointment or resentment later.

## Exercises

1. Recall the most recent decision you made—for example, buying a new car, selecting a gift for your wife, mapping a vacation, firing an employee, investing some money, launching a new product, changing your job. What reasons did you give for deciding the way you did? Were there other reasons—reasons you didn't state, maybe didn't even admit to yourself? Be honest, now.

2. Assume it was somebody else who was on the point of making the same decision that you made above—and for the same hidden reasons. Make a two-minute impromptu talk (to your wife, your luncheon group, or your fellow students) that would aim at those hidden reasons and then persuade the other person to make a different decision.

3. Get someone (your wife, a friend, or a fellow student) to play the roles of the following people. For your part, try to fathom the hidden reasons of these people and rationalize them into taking the action you want them to take.

*The wealthy donor.* A wealthy member of the church or synagogue wants to give a big sum of money to double the size and tonal range of the present pipe organ. But exterior repairs to stonework, windows, and roof are needed far more than a larger organ. This wealthy donor is a self-made man, close to fifty years old. He moved into your community and joined your congregation only two or three years ago. His wife died some six months ago, leaving two children—a twelve-year-old boy and a ten-year-old girl. His stated reason for making the gift: to memorialize his wife.

YOUR PURPOSE: To secure the big gift for the repairs that are so badly needed, rather than for the additions to the organ.

*The valuable employee who is resigning.* This man has been with your company only a short while. He lives with his wife and three school-age children in a huge new housing development, still only partly completed, on the outskirts of town, some 12 miles from the office. At the outset he showed a great deal of promise. He worked hard and made a substantial contribution to the organization. You know he has good potential. But lately his performance has slumped. He comes into your office and offers his resignation, saying he feels the company just isn't the right place for him—doesn't recognize his talents, doesn't offer a bright future for him.

YOUR PURPOSE: To rationalize him into withdrawing his resignation, with the conviction that you can shape him into a valuable employee.

*I don't know how to prepare to talk.*

# How to Prepare a Successful Talk

If you know in advance that you'll have to make a talk sometime in the future, count yourself lucky—whether that future is one hour or six months from now, and whether your audience will be one man or five men, a small group or a big crowd.

Why lucky? Because, if you're put on notice, you'll have time to prepare what you'll say. That means time to think about your subject and time to think about the people you'll be talking to.

That's not to say that you can't talk effectively without preparation. Fact is, impromptu talking can be effective, as Chapter 2 tells you. But impromptu talking is different. Your speaking time is nearly always quite short. You have to think right there on your

97

feet. And though you may be ready in the sense that you can fall
back on certain patterns or formulas, you really have no time for
preparation—no time for research or reflection, no time for organizing or arranging your ideas. You have to plunge ahead, depending
mostly on your wits or your shining conviction to pull you through.

If, on the other hand, you have time to prepare your talk, you can
muster a wealth of thoughts, array them in coherent marching order,
clothe them in the right words, and thus talk logically, interestingly,
and convincingly. That's what this chapter is about—the ways in
which preparation can help you make a better talk, and the steps
you can follow to construct an effective talk.

## How Preparation Can Help You Make a Better Talk

Preparation will do seven things for your talk—and for your
listeners, too. It will:

• *Make your purpose and your central idea clear to you and your
listeners.* If you can state your purpose in one crystal-clear sentence,
and keep that one sentence clear in your mind, you'll follow a
straight course from beginning to end, and your hearers will know
exactly what you're talking about. When your talk is over they
won't ask, as they drift back to their desks or their homes: "What
was he really driving at?" "Do you think he knew what he was talking about? I didn't." "Why did he waste our time that way?"
"Doesn't he know the difference between woolgathering and straight
talk?"

• *Enrich what you say with concrete ideas and lively illustrations.*
Nothing dulls the edge of a talk and lulls people to sleep quite as
successfully as abstractions do. With time to prepare what you will
say, you can screen out these abstractions, frame your ideas in
terms of everyday experience, and call up from memory the events,
the stories, and the images that give body and meaning to ideas.
Also you can talk with people, watch them at what they do, listen
to them as they talk. And you can read books and magazines. This
is how effective talkers pick up illustrations (narratives, events,
parables, situations, jokes, and so on) to give life to their talks. So

next time you have a speaking assignment, keep your subject actively in mind everywhere you go and in everything you do. You'll be surprised at how many useful, colorful things you stumble across that will make your abstract ideas vivid and meaningful.

• *Get the meaningful, significant words and phrases.* Keep in mind that the best language is simple, direct, and concrete. But most of us need an iron discipline to achieve this kind of language. Why? Because we're tempted, when we have time to prepare a talk, to seek polish and refinement through bigger words and longer sentences. The truth is, the greater art is simplicity, and the polishing you do should be aimed at that end.

For example, suppose that instead of offering the British people "blood, toil, sweat and tears" Winston Churchill had tried to stir them with a promise of "sacrificial dedication and burdensome expenditure of energy, excretion of sudorific moisture and lachrymose lamentations." Maybe the Royal Air Force still would have won the Battle of Britain. But it would have been an uninspired and uninspiring victory. If Sir Winston didn't spend midnight hours polishing the speech in which he uttered those immortal words, it was only because he had already spent a lifetime learning the discipline of simple speech.

You may not be able to match Sir Winston's skill in stating abstractions in stirring, concrete imagery. But you'll improve your language, at least in some measure, if you use part of your preparation time to replace your heavy-sounding polysyllabic words with simple, clear words that suggest images to the minds of your listeners.

• *Weed out what's unneeded, unrelated, and inconsistent.* It was a wise speaker who said, "Give me a couple of minutes to gather my thoughts and I'll make you a two-hour speech. But if you want a twenty-minute speech, you'll have to give me a week's notice." He was saying, in other words, that it takes a little while to gather thoughts, but much more time to select the thoughts that will have the most telling effect. It also takes time to select the words, the sentences, and the illustrations that will state a purpose and develop a subject with utmost force and clarity.

Selection will help you take your talk straight down the line to its conclusion. The successful talker is ruthless in discarding material. He cuts out everything that's irrelevant, everything that's superfluous, everything that's not in line with his purpose and his subject. He eliminates every expression or statement that would distract or annoy his hearers. He also protects himself against any embarrassing slip of the tongue that would destroy all hope of achieving the purpose of his speech. For example, preparation would have spared Senator Everett Dirksen the embarrassment of an unhappy turn of speech not long ago. In the heat of floor debate over Clare Boothe Luce's nomination as ambassador to Brazil he asked the Senate to forgive the intemperate things Mrs. Luce had said in a political campaign some years back. But he put his plea in these words: "Why thrash old hay or beat an old bag of bones?" The galleries roared. So did many a senator.

• *Arrange your ideas in logical order.* When you have to talk without time to prepare, your first words usually state the first point that comes to mind. After that, you continue with other points as they come to you. That is not always the best sequence, because the first thought that occurs to you may be the most effective, most dramatic, or the strongest point, and the points that occur to you later may be less persuasive. The result is that you'll fire your heavy ammunition first, then trail off into less forceful thoughts. Even if you can stall for a few minutes while you gather your ideas (as suggested in Chapter 2) there is still precious little time for a considered arrangement of ideas into a convincing structure.

On the other hand, if you have time to prepare your remarks—and if you take advantage of that time to work thoughtfully at what you will say—you can write down all the points that occur to you, study them, and evaluate them in terms of the best possible sequence. You can spot your strong and weak points and structure your talk for an interesting start and a strong conclusion.

• *Foresee objections and prepare to answer them.* With time to study your subject you can cast yourself in the role of your listener and thus weigh your talk as he would weigh it. Are your facts right? Have you got all the facts at your command? Are there other data that contradict your information? Can your facts be interpreted another way? Have you overlooked a point of view that your listener might reasonably hold? Have you got facts or reasons that can counter his prejudices or give vision to his blind spots? Are there weak links in your logic? Have you omitted background information that he needs for complete understanding of your subject? For complete understanding of your views?

If you expect your listener to oppose you, you can weave your counterarguments into your talk and thus blunt the edge of his opposition. If you think he may not know the background, you can set the stage so he'll understand the facts or the situation. If you find gaps in your logic, you can fill them—or, if you can't fill them, at least you can bridge them over so they won't be too obvious.

• *Help you tailor your talk and its tone to your listeners.* Suppose you're invited to make a talk before a group of people a week from now. Among the first questions you should ask the person who invites you are these: "What does this group represent? What does it stand for? What bond holds the members of the group together? Why is the group meeting now? What is its problem? What experiences do its members share? Is there a split in the group? Is it a group of men? Women? Is it a mixed group? Old? Young? Wealthy? Is it political? Business? Social? What do I have in common with this group? Why have I been asked to talk to these people? How can I help them?"

Or suppose it's a private conversation you must prepare for. You know you'll have to discuss a given subject. You should ask yourself much the same kinds of questions: "How does this person feel about the subject? What is his background of education, experience, social contact? What environment does he live in now? What environment was he reared in? What experiences do he and I have in common? What are his interests? What approach will have the strongest appeal to him? What position is he known to have taken on this subject? What kind of personality does he have? Is he quick-tempered? Sensitive? Argumentative? Easygoing? Good-humored? Impatient? Talkative? How can I help him?"

With answers to these questions in hand you can develop your subject knowledgeably, select your material for greatest impact on the people you will talk to, and thus shape your talk to evoke a favorable response among your listeners.

## Five Steps for Preparing a Successful Talk

A few gifted speakers can command an orderly flow of ideas and words that fall easily and quickly into a logical, persuasive progression. Most of us, though, are less gifted. We need time for preparation. What's more, we need tools and a favorable environment for work.

Different people take different ways of preparing their talks. They have their favorite tools and their favorite settings. Some work better with paper and pencil; others, with a typewriter; still others, with a dictating machine. Some people prefer full-size sheets of paper and others work better with 3- by 5-in. index cards. As for working environment, some of us prefer a quiet room; others, a long walk alone; still others, an office or room that's active, or noisy with accustomed sounds. Some can best prepare a talk by talking with other people, picking their brains, and trying out ideas on them. Others are most productive when they mull over a subject in solitude.

Whatever may be the method or tools or environment you find best for yourself, you'll probably follow a pretty generally accepted pattern in preparing your talk. As speaker-to-be, you'll move forward from the original concept and end up with your finished product— your talk. You'll start with a subject. You'll reflect on this subject, develop your central idea or purpose, evolve ideas that are related to it (see Chapter 8), evaluate these ideas, and set them up in logical sequence. You'll clothe them in appropriate words. Finally you'll fix them—sorted, arranged, and stated—in your mind, on note cards, or in full manuscript.

Roughly, you'll do all this in five steps, as follows:

Step 1. *Word your purpose.* Think over your subject in terms of the people you expect to listen to you. Look for what you can contribute to them. Adapt your subject to their background—to their pattern of thought and conduct. Then, in one clear sentence, state your purpose.

Suppose, for example, you're a civil engineer. The chairman of the program committee for your local civic club has set up a series of programs in which two members per meeting will tell about their professions or businesses. He asks you to talk about engineering for twenty minutes at one of these meetings. A broad subject for such a short time. Even so, you say you'll do it.

In your audience will be 25 men of different interests and backgrounds—doctor, lawyer, hardware merchant, building-material supplier, stationer, cotton-mill manager, insurance agent, mayor, preacher, banker, writer, newspaperman, high school superintendent, stockbroker, farmer, wholesale grocer, college professor, clothier, and others. So your first question as you sit down to prepare your talk is this: "In the time that I have, what can I say about civil engineering that will be helpful and interesting to a group of nonengineers? To what purpose can I best use my time?"

The tie that binds this civic club together is dedication to a better business community—and therefore a better town to live and work in. The aim of the civil engineer in this kind of community, you tell yourself, is to lift the standards of construction in housing, in manufacturing plants, in city streets, and in public services such as water supply and sewage disposal.

Putting all this together, you decide that the purpose of your talk will be this:

To convince your hearers that the civil engineer plays a creative role in community life—in your town.

Step 2. *Gather your ideas.* Some people call this "tabulating the topics." List your thoughts as they come to you. At this point, order or sequence doesn't matter much. The idea is to spill everything down on the page in front of you. Here's where you let your own background come into play. Your list of thoughts will be made up of the things you have felt and observed, the things you have lived through, the things you have read and seen.

It doesn't matter how you get these thoughts. Just get them the way that's best for you. Maybe you like to turn your desk lamp on, rest your head on your hand, and scribble on a pad. That's all right. Maybe you like to get up at five in the morning and walk across the fields or take a turn around a few city blocks, stopping now and then to jot down a few ideas. That's all right, too. Or maybe you work best when the radio is going. If that's true, turn it on. You may even prefer the rattle and sway of a commuter train. Fine—get out your pad and pencil, or your portable typewriter, or your dictating machine, or whatever you work best with. But whatever method you use to get your ideas down, and wherever you work, you'll need two things that every thoughtful speaker needs: time and contemplation.

To see how this works, keep on imagining yourself the civil engineer who will make a talk to his civic club. Here are some of the ideas that might come to you at random if you took time to contemplate your subject and your purpose:

Civil engineers go through a tough course of training. Compare with doctors, lawyers.

They know structural materials—concrete, steel, wood, plastics, new materials. Information useful in building schools, manufacturing plants, office buildings, dams.

They apply principles of physics to construction problems—bridges, buildings, schools—cantilevers, trusses, stresses, load-bearing surfaces, etc. Principles of safety, economy, efficiency.

They build things that are useful—raise standards of living—manufacturing plants, schools, city streets, highways, public buildings, skyscrapers, railroads, water systems, electric power plants.

They spend a lot of time outdoors. Good health. Fresh outlook.

They are practical men who put theory to work, make useful applications of laboratory findings. Relation to college professors.

They are cost conscious—know the least expensive ways to get best results. Similar to plant managers, merchants.

They master mathematics, estimate costs, work within budgets. Compare with city officials, school superintendents, cotton-mill managers.

They work to high standards of efficiency, safety, economy. Effect on community life.

They're in a highly competitive business—must bid against others for contracts. Must watch dollars. Often deal in big sums of money. Compare with merchants, with bankers.

They work with precision. Cost (in dollars) of a misplaced decimal point. Cost (in lives) of a miscalculation of stresses in building a school. Risks involved permit no relaxation of standards. Compare with doctor. Dealing with human lives—school children, auto drivers, traffic, etc.

They move from place to place—wherever jobs take them. Break provincial barriers, bring in new ideas. Compare Herbert Hoover.

They maintain high moral standards. Often deal with public funds. Conscience a strong element. Refer to preacher, mayor, taxpayers.

They keep local business active. Deal with local suppliers—hardware, building materials, gas and oil, pencils and paper for paper work, insurance, bank loans, cars and trucks, local electrical and plumbing contractors. Side effects in higher sales for grocers, clothiers, filling-station operators, farmers, etc., because of construction crews brought in. Also employ local labor and provide more jobs for community.

Now look back over these rough notes. If you're worried because they look like random jottings, stop worrying. Random jottings are just what you started out to get at this stage. They're your second step in preparing your talk. (Your first step was to state your purpose, you remember.) Your task now is to whip them into organized form—arrange them so they'll serve your central purpose and so they'll be logical, interesting, and persuasive. Now go on to Step 3.

Step 3. *Select and arrange your ideas.* The random ideas above are just that—random ideas. They need order. They need pointing up and weeding out. They need a consistent and pleasing point of view.

Arranging your random ideas and selecting the best of them, then, is your next job. If you follow the pattern by which most talks are constructed you'll settle on a three-part arrangement: Introduction, Body, and Conclusion. You'll shape that three-part arrangement to effect the purpose you stated earlier: to convince your hearers that the civil engineer plays a creative role in your town.

As you study your random jottings you'll see that they fall into three major groups:

*a.* What a civil engineer does

*b.* How he does his work

*c.* How his work affects the community

These three groups of ideas will become the Body of your talk.

Now that you have a fairly good idea of what you will say and the order in which you will say it, you can give a little thought to your Introduction. You'll want it to state your purpose, clearly and simply, so your hearers will know exactly what you're talking about. And you'll want it to be lively, to command attention, to establish a bond between yourself and your hearers. A little humor, in fact, might get you off to a good start.

Humor brings to mind a cartoon you saw not long ago. In the cartoon two men, dressed in the plumed hats and flowing cloaks of the late Middle Ages, stood talking confidentially in front of the Tower of Pisa. The tower, just being finished, stood straight up. One of the two men was obviously the engineer on the job—he held a blueprint in his hands. According to the caption beneath the cartoon, here's what he was saying to his crony: "I skimped a little on the foundations but nobody will ever know the difference." You decide the cartoon, which is about engineers and construction work, will give you the start you want. You note it for possible use in your Introduction.

Now get to work in detail on those random ideas. First, blue-pencil the weak ideas, those that express an unpleasant point of view, those that won't appeal to your hearers, those that aren't closely related to your main idea, those that don't give strong support to your purpose. If you're ruthless (and you must be, because you've got only twelve minutes for your talk), you'll blue-pencil the following:

Civil engineers go through a tough course of training. (Not closely related to the engineer's role in community life. Little appeal to audience.)

They spend a lot of time outdoors. Good health. Fresh outlook. (Doesn't give strong support to main purpose.)

They master mathematics. (Sounds conceited.)

They move from place to place, wherever jobs take them. Break provincial barriers, bring in new ideas. (Pretty weak idea. Can't be proved.)

YOUR NEXT MOVE: Set up a sequence among the remaining ideas. You'll probably want to hold the strongest and most attractive ones for use as you near the end of your talk. And you'll want to sustain balance and proportion throughout the Body.

In terms of the people who will hear you—this cross section of community leaders who are members of your civic club—your strongest idea is that the civil engineer helps keep the wheels of local business turning. That, you decide, is the one you'll use just before your Conclusion. You'll arrange the remaining ideas in your random notes in a sequence that seems logical and convincing.

Your Conclusion? It will summarize the high spots of your talk and restate your purpose.

Step 4. *Outline your talk.* You're making good headway now. You've settled on your Introduction, you know the substance and the main ideas of the Body of your talk, and you know what your Conclusion will say. Now draw up a full outline of your talk.

Some speakers use key-phrase outlines. Others prefer complete-sentence outlines. Still others like to write things out in full, word for word. It doesn't matter much which method you use, as long as it's the clearest and most helpful to you. If people in business and industry do use one method more than another, it's probably a combination of the complete-sentence and key-phrase outline, with complete sentences expressing major thoughts and key phrases leading into secondary or supporting thoughts.

If you're still going along as the engineer-turned-speaker, here's how the outline of your talk might look in its final version (of course, you'll have to flesh it out with examples and illustrations):

   I. Introduction.
      A. Story of the cartoon about the Leaning Tower of Pisa.
      B. Statement of purpose.
      C. Quick review of main points to be made.
  II. Body.
      A. What a civil engineer does.
         1. He builds useful structures.
            *a.* Manufacturing plants.
            *b.* Public buildings.

        *c.* Schools.

        *d.* Highways.

        *e.* Streets.

        *f.* Dams and bridges.

        *g.* Water and sewage systems.

        *h.* Skyscrapers.

    2. His work differs from that of other engineers.

        *a.* Electrical engineers

        *b.* Mining engineers.

        *c.* Chemical engineers.

        *d.* Aeronautical engineers.

    3. He deals with three principal elements.

        *a.* Men.

        *b.* Materials.

        *c.* Money.

B. How a civil engineer does his work.

    1. He uses his professional training (compare with doctors and lawyers).

    2. He puts new theories to the test and applies historic principles and laboratory findings to practical everyday problems (refer to college professors and doctors).

        *a.* Longer-lasting concrete for highways and streets.

        *b.* Stronger but lighter metals for building construction.

        *c.* Better fireproofing materials for safety (refer to school principal).

        *d.* Use of the laws of mechanics in construction.

        *e.* Use of mathematics in computing stresses, surface loadings, etc.

    3. He keeps abreast of the latest and best developments in his field (refer to doctor, merchants, manufacturers).

        *a.* New earth-moving machinery.

        *b.* New building materials.

        *c.* New designs.

        *d.* New methods of material handling.

    4. He holds fast to high ethical principles (refer to preacher, mayor, taxpayer).

        *a.* Best use of public money.

        *b.* Best value for dollars spent.

        *c.* Best good for the most people.

5. He works in an environment of facts and figures.
    *a.* Engineering a competitive business (refer to merchants, insurance salesmen).
    *b.* Objectivity required (refer to banker, newspaperman, stockbroker).
    *c.* Precision required (refer to stockbroker, banker, doctor, college professor, cotton-mill manager).
  *C.* How the civil engineer's work affects the community.
    1. Public safety (fire laws, building codes, traffic controls).
    2. Public welfare (water supply, transportation, schools).
    3. Manufacturing efficiency (plant design, plant location, availability of power, water, transportation).
    4. Civic economy (local purchases of goods and services; new jobs).
III. Conclusion.
  *A.* The civil engineer touches everybody's life in the community.
  *B.* He plays a creative role in civic life.

Step 5. *Familiarize yourself with what you will say.* Put your outline in your lap, put your feet up on your desk, and talk through your ideas quietly, referring as often as you need to your outline. Don't write it out. If you do, you'll think more about words than ideas. Your best bet is to get your words and phrases flowing orally, put the key sequences of ideas at your command, and thus avoid the hazards of memorizing word for word.

The hazards of memorizing? Yes, there are hazards. People who memorize their talks word for word are relying on a pretty frail instrument for their performance. If memory fails, what then? Embarrassment—and lost listeners. You'll be far better off to keep your thought processes going while you talk than to trust all to a fallible memory. Memorizing makes you inflexible. A good talker needs flexibility to deal with the unexpected.

So, without trying to memorize, go over your talk as often as you need to fix it firmly in mind. Try to find a practice audience—your wife, your teen-age son or daughter, your secretary, or anybody who will listen attentively—and go through your speech in full. With that accomplished, you'll be all set for the big day—confident and eager to talk.

## *What to Do When You're Prepared to Talk*

On the day of your talk it's better not to do very much except look over your outline quietly. Save your energy for what happens when you meet the group. If you've prepared yourself well, everything will go all right. You'll "feel" the group—its desires, its needs, its mood. You'll sense intuitively what you should stress or what you should eliminate. And if you should overlook saying something you had planned to say, don't worry—you're probably just as well off for not having said it.

Should you get notes ready to take with you? Should you take your outline along? There's no rule to go by. Do what makes you feel most comfortable—what gives you most assurance. Many people do use their outlines, or some notes. But the best speakers glance at such helps only occasionally. They use them mostly for moral support—to banish the fear that they might forget what comes next. With that assurance, they can give their talk everything they've got.

## *Summary*

It's a lucky man who knows in advance that he'll have to face a talking situation. He's lucky because he has time to get ready.

This advance notice, be it five minutes or five weeks, means time —time to think through a subject, frame the purpose of his talk, gather his material, organize it, analyze his hearers, settle on an approach, clothe his thoughts in meaningful language, and enrich his comments with illustrations and examples.

If you want to make a good talk, don't do anything until you've stated your purpose in talking—why you're talking and what you hope to achieve—because your purpose will shape every step in your preparation. It will be the yardstick by which you'll measure how deep to go with your subject, how far to go in your search for material, which material you'll use and which material you'll discard, and how much of your talk will be humorous or serious, folksy or impersonal, conciliatory or firm, formal or informal.

If your purpose is clear to you while you're preparing your talk, it will shine through when the time comes to make your talk. That means you will communicate in unmistakable terms to your listeners, leaving in their minds no shadow of a doubt about your intent in asking for their attention and taking up their time.

*Exercise*

Choose one of the following subjects:

Why I chose my business (or profession) for a career
How ethics guide me in my business (or profession)
Why fraudulent advertising must go
How advertising helps a community
How selling measures a man
How to prepare for retirement
How ignorance breeds fear
What makes a great salesman
What makes a great statesman
Why human relations is important in business
How failure can lead to success
What makes a persuasive man

Go through all five steps of preparing a five-minute talk on your chosen subject. That is, (1) word your purpose, (2) collect your ideas and materials, (3) select and arrange your ideas and materials, ruling out those that are weak or irrelevant, (4) make an outline, and (5) familiarize yourself with what you will say.

This may take you a whole day (or the equivalent of a day in your spare hours). When you're all set, ask your wife, your classmates, or your friends to listen to your talk. When you've finished, ask them to criticize it from the standpoint of the clarity of your purpose, the quality of your ideas and materials, the arrangement of your talk so the important ideas stand out, and the effectiveness with which you delivered your talk.

*I can't generate ideas for a talk in the first place.*

*8*

# How to Get Ideas to Talk About

Do you sit through meetings with your associates and never utter a word? Never feel an idea flicker across your mind? Do you stare out of your office window waiting for ideas to come and finally give up in frustrated disgust at yourself? Do you walk away from business discussions feeling you've added nothing of your own to them?

If you often—even sometimes—feel this way, take heart. You're not alone. Lots of people have the same trouble. What's more to the point, many of them have conquered this feeling. So can you. This chapter will show you how. It's designed to help you in Step 2 of preparing your talk—the step in which you summon up ideas and

113

mull them over (Chapter 7). It's a crucial step. Failure to carry
it through can bring trouble—deep trouble and disappointment.

Why trouble and disappointment? Because failure to produce
ideas when they're needed can mean failure to win a coveted job
or promotion. It can mean collapse of a favorite project—the one
you've given such tender care to. It can mean that a growing
business, for which you're responsible, can falter and fail simply
because you don't generate ideas to cope with changing needs. It
can mean loss of a crucial sale. It can mean that the glib but misguided man will carry his point on company policy while you, who
might save your company from a disastrous mistake, sit silent because you can't produce ideas to counter his.

## The Key to Idea Output: Your Habits of Mind

Listen to this true story:

One night a young man we'll call Tom sat with a friend, an older
man. Tom said:

"I'm not happy at all. I don't know what's the matter. I just can't
get excited about anything. If somebody wanted to push me off a
cliff, I'd hardly put up a fight. I'm not happy in my work. I don't
even like the product I sell, though I suppose it's the same with
lots of men. I couldn't get the job I wanted with a computing-
machine company because I wasn't a college graduate, though other
men without degrees have done so. Why can't I be happy? What
makes *you* happy, old friend?"

"I don't know," said the older man. "I never thought about it."

"But you *are* happy," Tom went on. "Why?"

The older man tilted back in his chair and squinted at the ceiling.
After a while he said, "Well, I suppose I'm happy when I'm dreaming up something."

"What do you mean by that?" asked Tom.

"Oh, when I'm planning something, some way to improve my
business. Or when I'm working on an idea—a different way to go
about doing something. Things like that."

Tom thought it over. Then he said, "O.K. That's it. I have to try something, right away. So I'll try that. I'll go around dreaming up things."

And that's what Tom did. He began by trying to dream up a way to land the job he'd thought he couldn't get because he wasn't a college graduate. In two months he had his job. After the company trained him he began dreaming up original ways to promote sales. Today Tom isn't selling more machines than anybody else in his company. But he's selling a lot of them. And he's happy. He has ideas—lots of them. And he talks about them enthusiastically. As a side effect, his ability to express himself has improved noticeably. What's more, his creative enthusiasm puts other people in a creative mood—stimulates open minds and experimental attitudes, breeds enthusiasm, sharpens senses, builds up self-confidence. It's a cycle that makes everybody happier and more creative.

Tom's secret is just this: He has acquired a creative, inquiring habit of mind. The wheels never stop turning. Everything he sees, does, and hears gives the wheels another spin.

## 10 Tips for Creating Your Own Ideas

What Tom has done, you can do, too. In fact, you might even outstrip him. How? Simple. Here are 10 tips to guide you.

1. *Open your mind.* A training director at a large plant was often asked why he didn't attend meetings of his state training directors' association. His answer was always the same: "Why should I go to those meetings and listen to a lot of guff? They never say anything, anyhow. I've got enough to do without that." Few people were surprised when our friend lost his job. Those in his company who knew him said, "He always talked about the same old things. Other companies were passing us by in the methods and know-how of training."

Trouble with the training director was this: He got the idea his fellow directors weren't saying anything because he didn't listen with an open, imaginative mind. He grew shallower and shallower, and at last thinned out to nothing.

Many of us are like that training director. Our minds are closed to the voices and actions of other people in our field, and we spend so much time defending our well-worn, established ideas that we have little or no time left to explore new frontiers.

The open mind is fertile ground. Seeds fall into it from all directions, sprout, and grow to full stature. The successful idea producer is the one who welcomes the fresh thinking of others. He breaks up the neatly arranged files that have accumulated—and petrified—in his mind. He knocks down the prison-house walls of his own background, experience, and purpose and opens up his mind to the background, experience, and purpose of others. Later he can give critical examination to what he gets from others. Right now, though, he does the important thing—he gets all he can from them.

2. *Look at familiar things with curiosity and wonder.* Walt Whitman did. To him a simple leaf of grass was many things: "the flag of my disposition," "the handkerchief of the Lord," "a scented gift and remembrancer," "a child," "a uniform hieroglyphic," "the beautiful uncut hair of graves," "the journeywork of the stars." To him, a mouse was "miracle enough to stagger sextillions of infidels." He acquired the habit of wonder, the habit of inquiry into commonplace things. His imagination took off from simple, everyday experience and observation, and ran free from image to image.

Like Walt Whitman, you can look for the meaning back of what you see and experience. You can acquire the habit of asking, "What's new about this?" "What's significant here?" "What's behind all this?" "What does this imply—suggest? How far can I carry this line of imagination?" "How can I associate this with other ideas, other experiences, and thus see new light?"

Will this inquisitive approach, this questing imagination, really produce ideas for you? Yes, it will. Take it this way:

The city sales manager of a good-sized oil company had three salesmen in his office for a conference. Sales had been slipping, and he was worried. "Have we lost our hold on the market in this city?" he asked aloud. "Are we at the end of the line? Have we run out of opportunities here?"

He got up from his desk and strode to the window. There,

stretching before his eyes, was the long-familiar sight—office buildings, homes, factories, traffic on the streets. This time, though, he looked at all these sights with a fresh approach. After a moment's thought he called his three salesmen to the window.

"Look at all those things out there in front of us. I see them every day. So do you. But this time let's ask ourselves what are the market potentials in what we see. Look at that taxi. It's burning gas and using oil. How long has it been since one of us called on the owner of the cab company? There's the new city hospital. I've watched it grow almost before my eyes. But I haven't even been in to see the purchasing agent about his boiler fuel. And look at that airliner overhead. Takes a lot of gas and oil and grease to keep it in the air. Have we got our fair share of that market? Would a letter to the airline's headquarters pave the way to a sale?"

The three salesmen caught on. As they stood at the window they came up with their own ideas for new sales approaches. For the next two weeks all four men—sales manager and salesmen—were kept busy following the leads they had thought of in five minutes. And the leads set in motion that day developed into profitable service contracts that lasted into the years ahead.

This habit of taking a new look at familiar things works in other ways, too—for safety directors, training directors, personnel directors, industrial relations managers, office managers, church groups, and civic committees.

Take a hospital chief administrator, for instance. He has just about run out of ideas to discuss at regular meetings of his staff. He decides he needs a fresh look at the way the hospital runs. So he leaves the building for an hour, then comes back and walks around as if he had never been in the place before. As he passes through the reception area he overhears an impatient cashier say something sharp to somebody who is checking out. He stands aside until the incident has passed, then approaches the cashier.

"Things pretty rough today?" he asks.

"Sure are," the cashier replies. "Seems everybody who comes through here has a problem. I've about run out of patience."

"I know how you feel," the chief administrator says. "But we've got to remember that we're dealing with sick people. They're our business. As our training courses put it, our patients come first— even ahead of our personal feelings."

"Yes, I remember that," the cashier says. "It's just that we talk things one way when we're together and then do them differently when we're under pressure on the job."

With that, the superintendent had his idea for the next supervisors' meeting. His theme: "We all know our rules for dealing with patients. But do our patients leave here feeling they've been treated kindly and considerately?"

3. *Challenge yourself with problems.* Problems really aren't crises. Instead, if you approach them creatively and analytically, they're idea stimulators. They challenge your ingenuity.

The imaginative approach to problems touched off the success of the purchasing agent for a large Middle Western city. One day, for example, he showed up twenty minutes late for a meeting with the mayor and the controller. "Just couldn't break away any sooner," he apologized. "Ten salesmen came into my office today—all of them wanting to sell oil and gas. I'm bushed. I'll tell you—time is my biggest problem."

"Even if you are late, I'm glad you came," the controller said. "We've been wrestling with a problem here. Our police, fire, sanitation, and welfare departments are 'way over budget on expenditures for their fleets of trucks and cars. Gas and oil are a good-sized chunk of the total. You got any ideas for cutting down?"

Now the purchasing agent had not one problem but two: tremendous pressures on his own time, and the need for cutting the cost of keeping the city's fleet operating. He simply merged the two problems into one challenge. If he hadn't had to see so many salesmen that day, he could have made it to the meeting on time. And he could have bought the same total quantities of gas and oil from fewer salesmen. Fewer salesmen to see, more gallons per order, and probably lower prices per gallon. That was the way it looked. He did a little arithmetic, then began to talk:

"Tell you what I think. We're buying gas and oil from a lot of companies. We're buying it in small lots and storing it in small underground tanks. I believe we need larger tanks. If we can buy in carload lots we can save 10 cents a gallon on gas and 50 cents a gallon on oil. Tanks would cost us about $50,000. Carload-lot purchases will save us that much the first year. In twenty years we'll save $1 million. Besides, I won't have to see so many salesmen, and I'll have a lot more time."

This same purchasing agent went after every problem just that way. He turned problems into challenges. To cut costs and simplify paper work (including his own), he standardized on certain paperwork forms, put an end to the purchase of printing from a dozen or more job shops, set up a central duplicating office and equipped it with standard machines. This way, he needed fewer machines and had fewer maintenance and repair problems. Net result: He improved output in quantity and quality, systematized and simplified communications and record keeping, and cut costs about 30 per cent.

Still not content, he faced up to the problem of 45 different departments with different types of photographic equipment. He centralized and standardized the entire operation, thus slashed costs. What's more, the problem of poor quality in microfilming records led him to cancel outside contracts and bring the entire operation together under one half-time man.

Small wonder that this man today talks centralized purchasing effectively. Small wonder, too, that he's the idol of many a municipal purchasing agent across the nation.

The most striking examples of idea creation stimulated by challenging problems appeared in military training in World War II. Take the problem of aircraft recognition, for instance. In one of the early battles in the Pacific American pilots shot down more of their own planes than enemy planes. What to do about it? The answer: visual aids to speed training in aircraft recognition. Weather analysis, another skill essential to pilots, was a problem. The answer: again, visual aids showing graphically how air masses create weather. Another problem: languages. The answer: highly accelerated training courses in which young men learned to speak a foreign language in a fraction of the time it had taken to teach it in high school or college.

4. *Pause for reflection.* The man who creates ideas is the one who sets aside some time every day for thinking. He makes it a rule of his life. Abraham Lincoln was such a man. "I'm never easy when I'm handling a thought," he said, "until I've bounded it north, bounded it south, bounded it east, and bounded it west." And Henry C. Whitney, a friend of Lincoln, tells in these words how he once came upon him: "I saw Lincoln sitting, remote from anyone, wrapped in abstraction. He seemed to be pursuing some specific subject . . . regularly and systematically."

It takes time to think this way—specific, regularly scheduled time. Take a look at your desk calendar. If it's like most calendars it reads something like this:

9 A.M.   See Pete.
9:30 A.M.   Take Pete over to meet Smith.
10:30 A.M.   Nickel in parking meter.
12 noon   Lunch with Mr. Dall.
2 P.M.   Call Horace Brown on specifications.
5 P.M.   Pick up at bakery on way home.

What's wrong with that schedule? There's no time set aside for thinking. Somewhere in that schedule there should be a notation like this:

10:35—11:30 A.M.   Think up ways to attract young engineers. Or . . .
Plan remarks for June 5 meeting. Or . . .
Sketch ideas for new package design. Or . . .
Outline ideas for budget presentation. Or . . .
Plan conversation with department head.

Not long ago an advertisement that ran in some business magazines stated this very theme. The advertisement pictured a businessman standing at his office window and looking out over the buildings and driveways of his plant. He seemed motionless—at first glance, idle. But the text of the advertisement told what this man was doing. He was thinking—creating ideas. "That's what we pay him for," the advertisement said in substance. "We pay him to take some part of every busy day and dream of better ways to make and market our products."

5. *Grasp the "magic moment."* By this time in your life you've probably learned something about how your mind works. Maybe there's no pattern at all. Maybe ideas just pop into your head almost anywhere, any time, when you least expect them—during a coffee break, for example, or when you read a newspaper story or hear a sermon or take a train ride or see a quiet landscape. That's fine. You're lucky.

For lots of people, though, the idea machine works best under given conditions. Of course, these given conditions vary with the individual. Maybe your mental impulses come fastest in conversation with other people, maybe in solitude. Maybe during a walk before breakfast, maybe in the midnight hours. Maybe background music helps, or the sound of a running brook, or utter quiet. Maybe the city's stir and bustle keeps your mental wheels spinning. Or you may feel you must retreat to the country before ideas begin to flow.

Doesn't matter how these mental impulses, these "magic moments" of creativity, come to you—whether you have to create the setting for them, or whether they come without your planning for them. The important thing is to be ready for them when they do come—ready to grasp them and hold them. They're elusive, but precious. They're the root of creativity. As Scotland's cherished poet Robert Burns said of himself, "I have two or three times in my life composed from the wish rather than the impulse, but I never succeeded to any purpose."

So be ready for these "magic moments" when they come. Keep pencil and paper close at hand—in your pocket, at your bedside, in the glove compartment of your car, in your purse, on your living room table. Don't trust your memory. It's frail at best, and ideas, especially at their birth, are often no more than a faint glimmer. Capture them at birth. Write them down. You can develop them later, at leisure.

Whatever you do, don't tolerate obstacles to your creativity, even at the expense of seeking an entirely new climate. For instance, a bright young woman some years ago found the idea climate so stuffy at the bank where she worked that she quit. She gave up pension rights, earned vacation, and other fringe benefits, and gambled on finding another job soon. She did get a job in another bank where the people for whom she worked stimulated and welcomed ideas. In a few short years she became a vice president. She had sought and found a place in which her "magic moments" came often, a climate in which she could grow ideas.

6. *Project yourself into conversations, discussions, debates.* You'll strike sparks in your own mind when you bump against the views, the information, the experiences, and even the questions and doubts of other people. It doesn't matter whether it's in a business or a social situation—a policy discussion, a sales meeting, a luncheon conference, or an after-dinner conversation in the home of a friend. And, as far as idea creation is concerned, it doesn't matter whether you agree or disagree, broaden or narrow down the scope of the subject at hand. The important thing is that you involve yourself in what's going on—project yourself into idea-creating situations. Throw yourself in with people who will strike sparks in your mind.

Take the story of a certain advertising manager. He was preparing a new campaign for a special-purpose machine tool. He envisioned a narrow but profitable market if he could go after it the right way. He had prepared a tentative outline for the campaign. But he had an uneasy feeling that something about it was weak— something he couldn't put his finger on. He called in the sales manager and the account executive from the advertising agency. He gave them a copy of his tentative outline and asked for their reactions.

"Seems to me you're off to a good start," the agency man said. "It will hit the engineer right between the eyes. There are lots of engineers who'd want to fit this machine into their production lines."

"I'll grant you that," said the sales manager. "They're important to us. They've got the background to understand what this machine will do. And some of them are high enough in their organization to make the decision to buy it. They've got the technical knowledge, and they've got the authority, too."

"You two men have given me an idea," the advertising manager said. "I believe we're thinking about these engineers in the wrong framework. Sure they're engineers. But we've got to narrow our thinking to the engineers who are executives as well. They're the ones who are going to make the decision to buy. In short, they're engineers-turned-managers. And I think that's what this tentative outline lacked. It lacked a clear focus on our market. Now that we've got that in sight, I think we can frame this campaign better. Many thanks to both of you."

So, if you want to generate ideas, don't shrink from conversations and discussions. Invite them. Get into them. And speak up every time you get a glimmer of an idea. Maybe it won't be a fully shaped idea. But if you'll grasp it, bring it into the open, and talk about it right then, it will take on substance and form as you talk about it.

While you're seeking people to talk with, don't overlook the experts in your field. There's one nationally known marketing consultant, for instance, who travels and lectures a great deal. Whenever he's in a city or town where some other marketing expert lives, he phones the man and invites him to a shoptalk luncheon. He reports that these meetings are always stimulating and often inspiring and that some of the ideas born of these conversations have become turning points in his career.

7. *Discipline yourself.* Pick a subject or a problem. Set a goal for yourself and a time limit—say 10 ideas in an hour. Then get busy. Think. Concentrate. Force yourself. Get desperate. Grasp at every hint.

Say you're a schoolteacher like one in North Carolina some years ago. She made it a habit to begin every day with her pupils by drawing some significant comment from a commonplace incident she had witnessed or been a part of the day before. Or say you're an advertising copy writer who's expected to bring in new ideas at the weekly conference with the copy chief. Or a personnel director who has to write a folksy paragraph or two for the company newspaper every week. Or a nurse who likes to bring her patients a fresh story every morning. Or a short-story writer who has to keep grinding out stories to feed and clothe his wife and their two children.

Whatever your plight—any one of those above or some other— there come times when you feel you've run dry of ideas. That's the time when you have to discipline yourself.

Take that short-story writer. He's down to zero on ideas—and down to his last $50, too. With a wife and two children, he can't wait for "the great inspiration." He's got to get busy—right now. "I'm going for a walk," he tells his wife. "The first thing I see or hear is going to turn into a story."

The first thing he hears is the high-pitched sound of locusts in the treetops. "There's a sound. What can I do with it?"

He walks to a park, sits on a bench, and ponders. He has heard somewhere that these locusts stay in the ground for fourteen years, at the end of which, on a warm summer day, they emerge, climb to the topmost twigs of a tree, and "sing." Two weeks, and they're dead.

Fourteen years underground. Two weeks in the summer sun. In a way, it's the same with people. Nose to the grindstone fifty weeks a year. Then two weeks at a resort. Like a million clerks and stenographers. Fifty weeks working hard—for a two-week dream. In a way, pitiable. In a way, bright and cheerful. This is the thread of meaningful story. It begins to unwind. Our short-story writer has his idea.

"I think I'm set," he says to his wife when he gets home. "If I sit at the typewriter long enough, if I keep at it, it will come around and take shape."

8. *Take clues from little things, apply them to your own experience and needs, make them into big ideas.* Wilbur and Orville Wright were fascinated by kites. They pinned down their elusive ideas, developed them, and at last launched man's first airplane flight on the dunes at Kitty Hawk, N.C. Elmer Sperry's small son asked what made a spinning top stand up. Sperry's answer took shape in the gyroscope, with its thousands of applications today in air, marine, and guided-missile navigation. George Stephenson's contemplation of a commonplace kettle 150 years ago was the germ of yesterday's giant steam locomotive and today's great steam turbines that feed millions of kilowatts of electric power to our cities. A falling apple led Sir Isaac Newton to state the laws of gravitation, upon which much of today's space navigation depends. Mrs. Lane Bryant parlayed a sympathy for stout, middle-aged ladies into a thriving line of specialty clothing.

The truth is, the germs of ideas are all around you, in the every-day things you see and do. The idea-producing man is the man who looks on these everyday things with a questioning eye, captures the fleeting suggestions that grow from commonplace things, and shapes them into useful ideas.

9. *Broaden your interests.* Many of us tread our beaten paths through life—going to office, plant, or schoolroom; marketing, shop-ping, or playing bridge or golf; reading the evening newspaper and watching television; seeing the same people day after day and talk-ing about the same narrow things. Small wonder fresh ideas come seldom if ever.

If it's ideas you want, break the pattern. Go to a symphony con-cert. Turn your radio to an opera. Better still, buy a ticket to a big city and hear an opera—live. Take a trip to a new place. Buy a first-class book of famous paintings and study them—or visit your local art gallery and study a painting that appeals to you. Read a good book. Join your local Great Books Club. Or lay out a reading program of your own. One sympathetic reading of a great classic will yield a thousand ideas—Shakespeare's *Hamlet,* Solomon's *Prov-erbs,* Emerson's *Essays,* Sandburg's *Abraham Lincoln,* or Frost's *North of Boston.* Any one of these, or some other, will do for a start.

When you do things like these, something happens to you. You get off your well-worn track. You begin to respond to stimuli. You get caught up in the same current that moved the great idea pro-ducers. Your own ideas begin to flow—ideas that you can relate to your own experience, your own needs, your own fulfillment. This is the way Keats got the idea for his inspired sonnet "On First Look-ing into Chapman's Homer." The medieval legend of Dr. Faustus inspired Berlioz and Gounod to compose their great operas. Mous-sorgsky's piano suite *Pictures at an Exhibition* got its start in a walk through a gallery. A journey to a new place inspired Wordsworth's famed "Tintern Abbey," Byron's *Prisoner of Chillon,* Irving's *The Alhambra,* Hemingway's *For Whom the Bell Tolls.* These are only the beginning of a long list of similar names and achievements.

10. *Record what comes to you.* The beginnings of an idea are slender, frail, and short-lived. One small interruption—a casual visi-

tor, a jangling phone, a diversion to some other subject—can be fatal to an embryonic idea.

That's why you should nail down every faint flicker of an idea that comes along. Time enough, later, to develop it and examine it critically. Right now, the important thing is to get it down on paper.

## Summary

The man who forges ahead in business, in industry, in community life, is the man who produces ideas.

But rare is the man to whom ideas come like magic, without conscious effort. Most of us, when the pressure is on to produce ideas, struggle feebly—and produce feebly if at all. A creeping paralysis snuffs out our imagination. We feel self-conscious and inadequate. We withdraw into our shells for lack of something meaningful to say. We go through the motions and work hard at it, but nothing comes out.

The price we pay for our failure is high. It's high in terms of disappointed ambitions and hopes, high in terms of failure to contribute constructively to our business and our associates, high in terms of missing many of the rich experiences of creative living.

Happily, you needn't be a failure at generating ideas. There are things you can do, procedures you can follow, situations you can thrust yourself into, attitudes of mind you can acquire, all of which will waken your dormant mind, sharpen your sensitivities, and deepen your perceptions. All this is detailed in the 10 tips set forth in this chapter. Follow them, and you'll create your own ideas in full measure. This way lies success in business—and in your personal life as well.

## Exercises

1. Pick out one commonplace thing in your living room or office —a doorknob, your desk, a footstool, your typewriter, a rug, a chair. Take ten minutes and see how many ideas you can produce about that one object. For a starter, consider it from the standpoint of

shape, material, color, improvements. Go on from there. Par for the course: about 50 ideas.

2. Ask your wife (or husband), a good friend, or an understanding business associate to tell you about one simple problem that's worrisome. Then ask your partner to note down every idea you can produce in five minutes that will help solve that problem. Par for the course: about 15 ideas.

3. Read your evening newspaper with special care tonight. Tomorrow, with pencil and paper close at hand, note every occasion (conversation, business conference, preparation of a report) to which you find it possible to apply something you read in the newspaper. Count up these occasions at the end of the day. Par for the course: about 10.

*How can I keep people from getting the wrong
idea from what I say?*

**9**

# How to Put Your Meaning Across

An ancient fable, retold by Tolstoi, goes like this:

A czar called seven blind men together and ordered them to place
their hands on his palace elephant. Then he asked, "What does my elephant feel like?"

"Like a broom," said the blind man who had felt the elephant's tail.

"Like lumps of earth," said the man who had felt the belly.

"Like a hill," said the one who had run his hand over the back.

"Like a handkerchief," said the one who had felt the ear.

"Like a strong rope," said the man who had run his hand up and **down**
the trunk.

"Like a wall," said the one who had felt the side.

"Like pillars," said the one who had felt the legs.

**129**

Why bring this fable in? Because it illustrates a troublesome problem in human communications—a problem you must solve if you want to talk successfully. All the blind men were right about the elephant. And all of them were wrong. The trouble was that all of them were specialists. By running a hand up and down the elephant's trunk one of them had become a specialist in elephant trunks. Another had become a specialist in elephant ears. Another in elephant legs. No one of them talked in terms of the experience of the others. So they failed to understand each other. They fell to bickering among themselves, and no one of them could persuade another to share his view of what an elephant is.

"Not a problem today," you say? But it is. Take the example used by the late poet Lew Sarett. Imagine four men—a farmer, an aviator, a businessman, and an engineer. Show them a meadow, then ask them what it is.

"A good place to grow corn," says the farmer. "It's rich land."

"A good spot for a forced landing," says the flyer. "It's level."

"A good piece of property for a real estate development," says the businessman. "It's close to town."

"A good place for a proving ground," says the engineer. "It's away from downtown congestion."

Each man—farmer, aviator, businessman, engineer—sees the meadow in terms of his own experience and needs. No two of them describe it in the same terms. For each of them, it summons up a different mental image. And without taking some thought, no one of them would convey his feeling about the value of the meadow in terms that would be meaningful to another. In such various and narrow frames of reference, they simply couldn't communicate with each other.

Is there a need for clear communication today? There is, indeed. Listen to Foreman X. He was an invited speaker at a recent conference of the American Society of Training Directors. In taking the training directors to task for dropping into professional jargon, he voiced his plea for clarity and help in these words:

"Now, for those of you who like to play psychiatrist: All I can say is that I'm sure psychiatry is very interesting. It's probably pretty lucrative, too, from some of the stories I've heard. But I can tell you now that if you expect me to take the time to try to find out some of the underlying reasons for Willie's actions on the job, you're barking up the wrong tree. I'm not much interested in Willie's 'ego drive' or his 'subconscious motivation.' I just want to know what the hell I do when he goofs off. And how I can get a fair day's work out of him for a fair day's pay. Seems to me there must be some good standard procedures around, if you'd give them to me. Maybe some short courses in basic psychology."

This bright foreman knew what he wanted. He wanted help— help stated in clear, simple terms—help related to his needs. Trouble was, the psychiatrists had been talking at him without communicating with him. Failing to communicate, they got an unfavorable decision from him. Foreman X decided psychiatrists couldn't help him. He decided to brush them off and go it alone.

Now one of the first aims of talking is persuasion—persuasion that leads your hearers to make decisions your way. The way the decisions of your hearers turn can determine whether you succeed or fail in sales, in policy administration, in committee work, in supervising employees, in customer relations, in civic enterprises, and in the fulfillment of your personal hopes and ambitions.

To win a favorable decision ("This man who's talking states his case clearly and winningly—I'll go along with him"), you must first lead your hearers across a plateau of fact. If you lead them right, if you make the route clear to them, you can urge them up to the higher level of decision with little fear that they'll turn off the path you want them to take. In short, in the degree to which you can put your meaning across on the factual level, your chances of winning at the decision level will improve. And that's what this chapter is about—putting your meaning across at the factual level.

## Six Guides to Putting Your Meaning Across

Here are six suggestions that will help you make your meaning clear to your hearers:

1. *Tune your language to the experience of your hearers.* The

trouble with the blind men in the fable at the beginning of this chapter was that no one of them shared the experience of the others. What each of them reported about his own experience with the elephant was meaningless to the others—and therefore a source of dispute. Same was true of the training directors turned psychologists. They had taxed the patience of our articulate Foreman X above. They had made no effort to understand his everyday experience in the plant. Without such understanding they couldn't communicate with him.

This failure to communicate is where many of us fail. We don't cross the bridge of understanding between ourselves and others. The result is that we fight and argue across a chasm a dozen times a day, curse our neighbors, hate institutions, lose out to competitors, break marriage engagements, fire people (or get fired ourselves), get arrested, seek divorces, go bankrupt, or take to the bottle.

Such communication failures happen all the time in business. They're responsible for many a lost sale, many an offended customer, many a puzzled client. For example, look at banking. How can a bank teller sell services like budget checking accounts, retail-credit plans, travelers' checks, personal loans, safe deposit boxes, money orders, sight drafts, and the like if he doesn't use words that flow easily into the mind and background of his hearer? Take just one word, for instance: the word *draw*. To the teller it usually means one thing—a customer *draws* a check. To a farmer a *draw* is a gulley he must fill. To a dentist it's what he does to a bad tooth. To an artist it's what he does with pencil or brush. A soldier *draws* his side arm. A preacher *draws* a moral. A laborer *draws* his pay. A lawyer *draws* a contract. A referee calls a wrestling match a *draw*.

The point is this: The successful talker is the one who is more concerned with experience definitions than dictionary definitions. Unless he can tune his words to the experience of his hearers, even the simplest words can become stumbling blocks in the way of understanding. Why? Because a single word can have as many meanings as there are people listening.

The late Professor Irving Lee, of Northwestern University, had a way of demonstrating this problem of multiple meaning in his course in general semantics. He would hold aloft an ordinary blackboard eraser and ask, "What's this?" Then he'd point to various students for their answers.

"A 2- by 5-in. piece of felt with chalk dust on it," one student would say.

"Something to clear off a blackboard with," another would say.

"A dusty job for the janitor," a third would reply.

"It's what I once saw an exasperated teacher throw at a young roughneck in high school," a fourth would say.

Then Professor Lee would say: "This is whatever your individual background is bringing to this eraser at this moment. It's 25 different things to 25 different people."

The professor was right. Words do have meanings peculiar to each person. They take on the color of individual experience. And they even take on the color of what a person may be doing at the moment. For instance, the word *security* may mean different things to a banker, depending on what he happens to be doing or thinking about at the moment. If he's buying stocks for a trust fund, *security* means one thing. If he's locking up the vault for the night, it means another thing. If he's figuring retirement income, including social security, for a customer, it means something else. If he's making a loan, it means quite another thing. And if that word has various meanings for him, think how many meanings it has for people who may come into his bank in the course of a day's business. To a labor leader in the midst of contract negotiations it means one thing. To a man approaching retirement it means another thing. To a man who has access to secret military information it means something else still.

If the examples thus far have led you to believe that bankers are the only people who have trouble with words whose meaning changes with experience, take a look at just a few more examples. To a soldier, for instance, the word *protection* means national defense; to a wealthy old lady it may mean a companion or bodyguard; to a laborer, his union; to a college professor, academic tenure; to a football player, shoulder pads; to an insurance man, repayment of losses; to an airline pilot, airway controls. In a hospital the word *soak* can mean to saturate something (like a bandage) in a liquid, to immerse a patient in a bath, or to soften a food such as tapioca. But in a steel mill to soak is to anneal metal in a furnace. Suppose a doctor told a steelworker to soak himself. What would the steelworker do? Sit in a tub of water for an hour? Or get under a heat lamp?

What the successful talker needs, of course, is to project himself into the experience and needs of his listeners. This way, he will place his key words against the background of his listeners. He will use these words in the sense in which his listeners are most likely to understand them.

How do you project yourself into the experience of other people? It's really not hard to do.

If you already know your listeners (or your listener), look at them in the light of their background and purposes. Are they youngsters with a cause—4-H Club members, for example? Are they troubled oldsters facing retirement? Are they a pressure group with an axe to grind? Is your listener a sailor, seamstress, banker, baker, lawyer, layman, housewife, huckster? Is he lonely, frightened, excitable, stubborn, grieving, easygoing, good-humored, angry? Does he have problems? Prejudices? Has he already taken a position on an issue? Or is he open to persuasion?

Where do your listeners live? City? Town? Country? What do they read? How do they entertain themselves? Make their living? Educate their children? Are they rich, poor, or (like most of us) worried about making ends meet? What's their level of sophistication? Their education? Grammar school? High school? University? Is it a mixed group, or homogeneous? What binds the group together? What are the answers to a hundred other questions you could ask about them?

If you don't know your listeners (or your listener), probe for answers to questions like these before you plunge into your remarks. Feel your way. Seek the bond between yourself and them. Once you find this bond (and there is one somewhere if you can only hit on it), you can talk to them in meaningful words. You can see what their experience is—what their problems are—what their wants, needs, and motives are. And you can frame your facts and persuasions in language and imagery with which they're familiar and to which they'll respond.

In short, the key question you should ask yourself is this: "What does this word mean to my listeners? Am I using it his way, or mine?"

2. *Avoid specialized or professional language.* Unless, of course, you're a specialist talking to another specialist or a group of specialists like yourself. If that's the situation, go ahead and use your special language. Your hearers will understand you.

For most people, though, specialized professional language is puzzling and often quite meaningless. That's why ability or failure to talk in simple, commonplace terms about complex matters can make or break your efforts to persuade and convince.

Apply this principle to insurance, for example. An insurance salesman can loose a torrent of words about term insurance, annuities, straight life, endowment policies, decedents, beneficiaries, actuarial forecasts, dividends, premiums, commuted values, conversion options, additional indemnity, and similar matters. He can do all this and still sell no insurance. Why? Because few of his prospective customers will get more than a spinning head from what he says. Mostly, he'll be talking only to himself.

Not so with insurance salesman John J. Lansing. In one year he sold 168 life insurance policies with a total value of $1,049,000. His record made him president of an organization of his company's agents who sold more than 100 policies in a year. Lansing made his record in spite of the fact that he lived in a town of only 2,300 people and worked in an area with only 12,000 people. He explained his success this way: He felt the most important thing an insurance man had to do was to explain simply and clearly, in layman's language, what an insurance policy is and what it will do. No talk about indemnities, commuted values, or decedents. Just plain talk, and nothing else.

Insurance is by no means the only field in which professional jargon can be a barrier to successful communication. A doctor may use technical language to describe a course of treatment to his local medical society, but he'll have to speak a simple language if he expects his patient to follow instructions. For instance, a famed surgeon recently performed a long and serious operation on a patient. The operation was successful. When the time came for the patient to leave the hospital and continue his recovery at home, the doctor came into the hospital room. "You've had a tough operation," he said, "but you're doing fine. Now I could tell you in doctor's language what I've done to you and how to take care of yourself. But you're not a doctor, and I think I'd better talk in plain language. So think of yourself as a house. I went inside and took out the furniture, rolled up the rugs, took the pictures off the walls, and pulled down the wallpaper. It will take your system a while to get used to this rather barren way of living. But slowly it will refurnish itself. Meantime, don't throw any parties in the house. You might scratch the floors or jab a hole in the wall."

Similarly an engineer can talk about stresses, alloys, and mathematical formulas to his fellow engineers, but he needs a different language to win the city fathers' approval for building a new bridge. A tool designer can talk electronic gauging and millionths-of-an-inch tolerances, but he must choose other words for the operator who will run the tool out in the shop. A legislator (or his legal assistant) can write a tax bill that accountants and the courts will understand, but he'll have to talk in a familiar language when he's telling the folks back home about it.

And so it goes. You can sound very smart to yourself when you dress your thoughts up in specialized, professional language. But the words of that language won't put your meaning across to your listener. They won't connect you with him. They're your words, not his. If you want to tighten the connection between yourself and your listener, use his words.

3. *Frame your talk in contexts that will make your hearers want to grasp your meaning.* Put yourself in their position. What can you say (or do) that will make them respond: "That man talking understands me—and what I want. I'll do the best I can to understand him"?

William Oncken tells the story of men aboard a battleship in World War II. At the height of battle the captain asked for an extra five knots of speed. Back came the reply from the engine room: "Engine ratings and specifications don't allow another five knots, Sir. Besides, we've got boiler scale."

The captain was puzzled. He knew the engine ratings. And he knew all about boiler scale. But he also knew that other warships squeezed out extra speed when they needed it. A matter of morale, he decided. He investigated. He found that working conditions were good, the men knew their jobs and responsibilities, orders were given clearly, coffee breaks and rest periods ran according to the textbooks. No clue there.

But the chaplain had a clue. At mess the topside men shouted and slapped each other on the back over the day's battle. But the below-decks men ate in silence. It was clear to the chaplain that the engine-room men felt they weren't in the act. They didn't share the excitement of battle, had no way of knowing how important their work was.

The chaplain thought out a plan. He found an officer who had been a sports broadcaster in peacetime. With the captain's permission, he asked the sports announcer to take over a microphone on the bridge during the next engagement and give a blow-by-blow account, over the ship's public-address system, of the battle—especially the part that his own ship played.

The plan went well. In fact, it went even better when the captain himself grabbed the mike. "Great, men! Great!" he shouted. "Here's the box score so far." He didn't stop with the box score. He went on: "But this is peanuts compared to how we could clobber them if we could reach those enemy destroyers to the west. All we need is 5 knots more." Immediately the engines deep down in the ship turned up faster. And the captain got his extra 5 knots.

What's the moral here? Just this: The men above decks could see the battle, shot by shot. Orders came to them in the context of visible tactics and measurable results. Every order was meaningful to them. Not so with the men in the engine room. All they had to go on was the captain's order for five extra knots. Now the captain didn't really mean this to be an order. It was, instead, a statement of need; a hope rather than a command, because he knew the engine ratings and he knew how boiler scale trims efficiency. But the men below decks took it as an order. They became resentful and threw up obstacles. At last, when the captain made the need clear, when he gave them a motive for understanding his real meaning, they came through magnificently.

What does this mean in terms of successful communicating? It means you may run into resistance unless you can give your hearers a motive for understanding your meaning—unless you can impart to them the same urgency you feel.

For example, if you're a safety director, it means you'll find yourself saying to a new worker, "Look, you've simply got to understand how this machine works if you don't want to lose a couple of fingers." Or if you're a sales manager, it means you may tell one of your salesmen, "You've got to get this new discount rate clear in your own mind. If you do, it can easily double your sales."

4. *Make the facts clear.* Talk to somebody who doesn't know much about your work. Tell him about the tough, complex problems you have to face. But don't explain the important terms you use in your work and don't give him the basic facts as you go along. Then ask him to help you make a critical decision on a worrisome problem.

Chances are your friend will do one of two things. (*a*) He'll back away from decision and give you a reply like this: "You want my advice when I don't even understand what you're talking about." Or (*b*) he'll plunge brashly ahead and give you an off-the-cuff solution. If he does the former you will have spent your breath to no purpose without getting help from your hearer. In fact, you will have puzzled him—possibly antagonized him. If he does the latter, you'd better beware of his advice. It may hurt more than it helps. Whichever he does, you'll soon realize your mistake: You've thrust him up to a decision level without first giving him the facts he needs to make a sound decision.

People are like that. Either they back away from decision for want of facts. Or they run ahead of the facts and come to decision without them. The task of the successful talker is the same in either event. While he leads his indecisive hearers gently but surely up to the decision level, and while he holds headlong decision makers in check, he must make the facts clear and bring them to bear on the issue. Otherwise he'll lose control of his listeners' decision making.

Case in point? Think back to 1952, when Richard Nixon was the Republican candidate for the Vice Presidency. A great clamor arose over some revelations about his financial affairs. Most Democrats —and many a Republican into the bargain—demanded that he withdraw from the race. Yet many people, like Mr. Eisenhower, waited for the facts. Nixon moved swiftly. In remarkably short time after the storm broke he appeared on television. "Hear the facts," he urged his listeners. Patiently and clearly he explained them, set them into the framework of politics, stated them in terms his hearers would understand and be sympathetic to, then asked for favorable decision and rested his case. The outcome is history.

You don't have to run for the Vice Presidency to have this kind of problem. Lots of people have it. Suppose you're a member of the local school board. An architect submits plans for a new school. His design is simple, functional, contemporary. But one member of the board can't make up his mind about it. "Looks pretty extreme to me," he says. "Doesn't seem to fit our neighborhood."

Can you swing him to your side? Not if you plunge ahead, race him up to the decision level without first giving him facts. To decide your way, he needs facts on construction costs. Facts on savings in heating costs. Facts on natural lighting. On play areas. On student traffic flow. Facts also on new trends in residential design, the changing look of the neighborhood, the need to serve the future as well as the present. If you give him these facts, patiently and clearly, you'll stand a good chance of winning him over to your side of the question.

How bad can it be if you don't state the facts as you go along? Pretty bad. Not very long ago, for instance, a preacher who had just moved into a new town was invited to speak to a local civic club. Thoughtlessly, he let go with this statement: "There are a great many elderly people in my church. They'll be a problem." He might as well have thrown a rock at a hornets' nest. His parishioners were indignant. The newspaper picked up his statement and spread it through the town. It was several months before the startled preacher could soothe ruffled feathers and go about his job.

How much better it would have been if this preacher had laid a groundwork of fact before jolting his listeners with the statement that older people would be a problem. What facts? Facts that would have put his conclusion in perspective and on solid ground. Are there more oldsters in this present church than in his former parish? How many more? Enough to make a significant difference? Are there ways to make use of the experience of these older people? What are their peculiar needs? Are there any new ideas for keeping in touch with shut-ins? Will the subject matter of his sermons be different? Are there young people in the community who can be attracted into the church? If he had given facts in answer to these questions, he doubtless could have won his hearers to a sympathetic understanding of his purpose in coming to this church and could have enlisted their support for his work. As it was, he very nearly lost them.

5. *Speak in simple words and short sentences.* You'll find guides for this in earlier parts of this book (Chapters 5 and 7). Suffice it here to say that garnishing your thoughts with fancy, unfamiliar words seldom will add to your stature or reputation as an effective communicator—and nearly always will build a barrier between you and your listeners. High-sounding language is no way to put your meaning across.

6. *Approach the complex by way of the simple.* Sometimes you just have to lead your hearers by the hand. You have a professional or special knowledge about something that they know little about. You want to make it clear to them so they'll want to do what you ask them to do. Your problem: Communicate with them. Solution: Take something they're all familiar with, show its relation to what you want them to understand, and thus lead them from simple to complex.

Suppose, for instance, you're an eye specialist. It falls to your lot to talk to a small group of people about eye care. In doing so, you have to tell them something about how the human eye responds to images on the television screen. You take an easy, familiar starting point—something most people in your audience will remember. You recall those childish cartoons you used to draw on successive pages of a tablet—how you'd flex the edge of the tablet and let the pages run on top of one another, very fast. If you had drawn them right, the successive cartoons seemed to make a moving picture—somewhat jerky, to be sure, but still a moving picture. So far, so good. Everybody in the group is with you.

Next you tell your audience how these childish cartoons are like motion pictures—a succession of still images that pass before the eye so fast that movement seems smooth and unbroken. Still good. Your hearers are still with you.

Finally, you move to today's TV screen, which presents the human eye with some 60 images per second and thus gives a perfect illusion of sustained, uninterrupted movement. Because you've led your hearers from simple to complex, they now understand the complex.

Or maybe you're a salesman with a brokerage firm. A widow comes into your office with some money she wants to invest. She asks you some questions—questions that show she knows little or nothing about the difference between bonds and stocks. You decide you'd better explain. Here's how you might do it:

"Suppose I want to open a small candy store, Mrs. West, but don't have quite enough money. I could do either of two things. First, I could ask you to lend me $50 for three years. I'd promise to pay you 5 per cent interest per year. At the end of three years I'd repay you your $50. All the while, though, as long as I held your $50, I'd keep on paying you interest every year. But your loan to me wouldn't entitle you to any ownership in my store. No matter how much profit I might make, I'd have to pay you only $50 plus interest. You'd have nothing to say about how I ran the store.

"That's the way bonds work. The bond is a certificate saying you have made a loan of a certain sum of money to a corporation (or to the government), for a certain length of time, for a certain rate of interest. It doesn't give you any ownership of the corporation or any voice in how it's managed. It pays you a fixed income (interest). It's not likely to fluctuate much in basic value. It gives you dependable though modest income, little or no capital growth, and minimum risk.

"Or second, I could offer to sell you a share of my candy-store business for $50. I wouldn't pay you any interest at all. Instead, I'd pay you a part of the profits at regular intervals. These payments would be dividends. If our store prospered, your dividends would increase. If our store made no profits, there'd be nothing to divide up, and you'd get no dividends. In other words, you'd be part owner of our candy store, and you'd have a voice in its management. If dividends increased, your share of the business might become so attractive to somebody else that he'd offer you $100 for your part ownership. If dividends decreased or vanished, your share of ownership would become less attractive to others, and if you wanted to sell it you might not be able to get even $20 for it.

"That's the way stocks differ from bonds. If you're a stockholder you own part of the business and, through dividends, you share its ups and downs. You have a say in its management. Your capital may grow, or it may shrink to the vanishing point, depending on what other people think your stock is worth. Stock ownership involves substantial risk, fluctuating dividends, and fluctuating capital value."

Here, as in the oculist's explanation above, the communicator put his meaning across by advancing from something that's simple and familiar—the financing of a small candy store—to something that's unfamiliar and hard to grasp. He now can lead Widow West to a wiser decision on investing her money.

## Summary

In today's complex society clear communication is a "must," because breakdown of communication can be disastrous to others as well as to ourselves in our business, professional, social, and civic relationships. Yet many of us confront our associates, our customers, and our friends with a request for action or decision without first making ourselves clear. We speak our own unique language, colored by our professional and personal experiences, instead of the language of our hearers. We don't place our thoughts against the backgrounds, the needs, and the wishes of others. We don't give our listeners a motive for sympathetic understanding of our purposes. We don't make our facts clear. We clutter our thoughts with fancy, high-sounding words. And we plunge ahead with matters that are simple to us because they're part of our everyday patterns of living, but sound complex to people whose activities follow other lines.

This failure to make ourselves clear is usually the product of our failure to project ourselves into the experience and needs of our listeners. The successful communicator, on the other hand, does probe into the experience and needs of his hearers. He seeks for their motives, clothes his thoughts in words that are familiar to them, and lays his facts into a framework that's meaningful to them. His guides are the six rules above for putting his meaning across.

## Exercises

1. Prepare a two-minute talk in which you explain the toughest, most complex problem in your job to your immediate superior. When you have finished that, adapt your explanation so it will be clear to somebody who knows little or nothing about your job (for instance, your wife, your next-door neighbor, your father-in-law, your twelve-year-old son).

2. Most of us have something to "sell"—sewing machines, accident insurance, banking services, the reputation of a hospital or some other institution, our personal needs and skills, our ideas. For whatever it is you "sell," prepare a two-minute sales talk for any two people in the following list, adapting your talk to the experience, the needs, and the special interests of each of the two you choose below:

A policeman's wife.
The father of four children.
A plant superintendent.
Your pastor, priest, or rabbi.
A railroad conductor.
A bank officer.
An attorney.
Your filling-station attendant.
A newspaper reporter.
A recent high school graduate.

*Even when I have the facts I run into trouble.*
*I want to know how to convince people.*

# 10

# How to Argue Convincingly— and Prove Your Point

"We've got an opportunity now to change the layout of our hospital. In this connection I'd like to propose a new plan for the physical-therapy clinic. Some of us feel it would be a good thing to change the location of this clinic."

That's the way a hospital chief administrator not long ago gave a good start to a new plan. He was talking to his board of directors. It was a policy conference.

"By change of location I mean bringing it from far out in the north wing and putting it in Rooms 101 and 102, near the center of things.

Some of us feel there's a drastic need for this change. The way things are now, physical therapy is way out in the north wing, close to the doctors' offices. That's convenient for our doctors. Fine. The location is also good for our budget. It's close to the boiler plant, so we save money on water and steam piping and on electrical conduit and wiring.

"But in the past two years we've averaged 20 physical-therapy inpatients per day and 15 outpatients. We don't like to move those 20 inpatients—their number is now increasing—back and forth through our narrow hallways every day—a trip of some 250 to 300 feet. As for our outpatients (they, too, are increasing), there's no place for them to park anywhere near the north wing. They have to come in through the entrance on the west and make a long walk to the north wing. Many of them need orderlies or porters to help them.

"It seems to some of us that this system has little that's good for our patients. That's not the way we'd like to see things. We want our patients to come first. Let's take a look, and see what this new plan will do for them."

This hospital administrator knows how to be convincing in a policy conference. He has the right approach to controversy, and he structures his argument clearly and systematically. This is an important technique for all of us when we have to sell or defend our plans, our ideas, or our products. To see how you can master the technique, read on.

## The Right Approach to Argument

Let's see how our hospital chief administrator looks at the art of convincing. What lies at the root of this useful skill? Four things, as follows:

1. *He knows when* not *to argue.* This is no trifling matter he's talking about. He isn't arguing just for the sake of argument. He isn't being a chronic "aginner." He isn't finding fault just so he can feel a temporary sense of superiority. He's not out to wound anybody's

pride. He wouldn't argue at all unless he felt the issue was more important than the pride of his hearers. This issue, he feels, is important. He knows he'll meet opposition, but that doesn't deter him.

Knowing when not to argue is one of the marks of the skillful communicator. Yet many of us fall short of success on just that score. We sometimes go among our associates and acquaintances with a chip-on-the-shoulder attitude. We argue over trifles, in the mistaken belief that we're displaying our high moral character or our strong intellect. Granted, we may be brilliant. And we may often be right. But if we go about our relationships that way, we're doomed to be disliked. What's more, as our reputation for taking the dissident view flourishes, our hearers will begin to discount our views. Result: Having pressed them so often and so violently in behalf of trifles, we'll find our hearers turning aside from us when we seek their support on major issues.

2. *He recognizes the right time for argument.* Our hospital administrator knows, as other effective talkers know, that there come times when he can't avoid an honest clash of opinion. When he recognizes these situations—when he feels compelled to oppose some idea or to convince somebody in the interest of a good cause—he speaks out.

It's important for us to recognize these argument situations. It's equally important that we be not led into argument that really isn't argument at all, but bickering. We bicker when we get into heated exchanges over interests and matters that call for explanation, or description, or problem-solving discussion, rather than for argument. We don't argue "tank-car heater," for example. We describe it or explain it. But we *can* argue over what kind of tank-car heater is best for a given situation. We don't argue over whether the men are taking off early at quitting time. We find the facts—and discuss them. Once the facts are clarified—and if two plausible interpretations of the facts emerge—then we can argue about which is the better interpretation and what action should follow.

In short, we argue propositions—not facts. A proposition is a formulated conclusion—an assertion that can be believed, proved, doubted, or denied. We identify an argument situation when we see in it a genuine *pro* or *con*. We ask ourselves, "Is this debatable?" If the answer is "Yes," then argument is appropriate.

3. *He defines his terms.* The hospital administrator does that right away: "By change of location I mean bringing it from far out in the north wing." That definition provides a frame of reference for the points of his plan.

Not every issue is as simply stated and easily explained as this one. One reason, as we have seen in the previous chapter, is that the connotations of words, their associations, and the images they summon up in the minds of our hearers differ with nearly every individual. That's why it's important that we and our hearers understand our words the same way. Right here is where many a potentially gainful argument bogs down in bickering and misunderstanding. It's the source of much unwanted and fruitless ill will.

Not long ago, for instance, an organ builder and a church committee met to discuss a new pipe organ.

"The trend in church organs today is toward austerity," the organ builder said. "That's what we should aim for in drawing up our specifications."

"We don't want an austere organ," the committee chairman said. "An organ with grandeur is what our church needs."

Tempers flared and disagreement blocked progress for an hour or more, until it dawned on the organ builder that he and the chairman were talking about the same quality in an organ but were using different words to describe it. Once that was settled, they were in a position to argue constructively over the builder's proposals.

Take another situation. Two officials of a seed-packing company came to bitter words over a "ten-minute morning coffee break" for secretaries and clerks. To one of the officials it meant fourteen minutes—ten for the coffee, two from desk to hot plate, and two from hot plate to desk. To the other official it meant ten minutes—no more, no less. If the meaning had been clear on both sides, there would have been no harsh words. The issue would have been clear: Is exactly ten minutes long enough for a coffee break? That's something they could have argued rationally and constructively.

4. *He avoids personalities.* The hospital administrator is nothing if not direct. He's even blunt. "I'm going to vote 'Yes,'" he announces. And he says, bluntly, "We must design this not for our doctors and ourselves, but for our patients. This is the only right thing to do."

Now directness is all right. In fact, it often carries a strong appeal. But the trouble comes when you intrude on the personal feelings of those you want to convince—when you bruise their self-respect—when you argue personalities instead of issues—when you treat your hearers with scorn, or sarcasm, or even indifference.

Suppose, for instance, the hospital administrator had said: "You doctors are responsible for this poor plan we've had for so long, and you're thinking selfishly when you oppose the change some of us want." Or suppose he had said: "If our controller weren't a penny pincher, we never would have placed our physical-therapy clinic way out in the north wing to begin with." Such a misguided approach would have put our administrator in deep trouble. Why? Because debate based on personalities impairs the effectiveness of argument three ways, as follows:

• *It gives your hearers nothing solid to go on.* It's based on feelings, not facts. Feelings are personal and subjective, and they may change from day to day. But facts are objective and unchanging. If you convince your hearers with facts, they're far more likely to stay convinced.

• *It makes enemies of the people you attack.* It's bad enough to lose their support in the present argument. It's even worse to lose all hope of their support in future arguments.

• *It often boomerangs.* Other hearers, their sympathies stirred, may rally to the defense of the person you attack and, in simple kindness, take his side in the argument. What you may gain in strength of logic you may well lose to psychological reaction.

Many a potentially constructive argument in business, professional, social, and political life founders on this rock of personalities and breaks up in bitter words, shattered friendships, sagging morale, political wrangling, and failure to put worthwhile ideas across. Your attitude toward the person on the other side of the argument counts for a great deal. Make it clear to him—and everybody else—that you're not fighting him, but you are fighting the issue. That approach is the mark of the effective communicator.

## Six Steps in Shaping Successful Argument

In most argument situations effective debate follows a well-defined six-step pattern, as follows:

• You make sure the proposition (what you intend to prove) is clearly stated and defined.

• You identify the main issue (or issues).

• You state the evidence.

• You relate the evidence to the main issue (or issues).

• You state your conclusion (same as the proposition you started with).

• You prepare to rebut.

Now go back and see how well our hospital chief administrator followed this six-step pattern.

Step 1. *State the proposition.* The administrator leaves no doubt about what he intends to prove. He intends to prove that it would be a good thing to change the location of the physical-therapy clinic. A good thing in terms of the patients, for whom the hospital is run.

Step 2. *Identify the main issue (or issues).* The administrator doesn't stray into bypaths. At this stage in the development of the clinic, decorator's colors aren't important, nor is architectural design, nor is cost (though he does touch on cost in the course of his argument). The important thing, in his view, is the need for a complete change in approach—a deemphasis of the needs of the doctors and new stress on the needs of patients. The administrator fixes on that issue, and that issue alone. It becomes the theme of his argument.

Finding the main issue may not always be as easy as that. Business problems can be pretty complex. So can social and civic problems. And so can personal problems. Simple or complex, however, if your proposition is one of policy, one that changes the *status quo,* you can nearly always pinpoint the issue (and thus state your proposition) by asking yourself these five questions:

• Is there need for action?

- Is this the correct action to take?
- Is it theoretically sound?
- Is it practically sound?
- Do the advantages outweigh the disadvantages?

If you ask yourself these five questions, it's pretty hard not to put your finger on the main issue at stake. For the hospital administrator the first question immediately isolated the real issue. He saw an urgent need for change. In different circumstances—say, a question of the hospital's operating budget—the second question might have given him quite another proposition to argue: "We should seek more money from the city rather than from Blue Cross."

These five issue-defining questions are already familiar to most people. You probably go through them, consciously or unconsciously, when you debate your personal and individual problems: whether to buy a new car, take a new position, go on a midwinter vacation, hire Jones, or marry Mary. Likewise, you should use them when you fall into argument situations in business or community affairs—whether to increase production in the plant, invest in new machinery, enlarge the personnel department, launch a new school-bond issue, increase an insurance estate, tighten up the loan policy in a bank, move a downtown church to the suburbs. In almost any debate, within yourself or with others, one or another of the five key issue-finding questions will stand out as the vital question—the one question that will provide the proposition that must be proved before sound decision takes shape.

But if these five key questions seem simple, don't overlook their importance. If you settle on one without going through the entire list of five you may turn up with a faulty proposition or a weak one. This way, you'll find yourself arguing for an unsound decision—or even losing out to an opponent who has hit on a stronger proposition than yours.

Step 3. *State the evidence.* That's just what our hospital administrator did. He cited facts and figures on physical-therapy patients, distances they would have to travel, and absence of parking space for them. Nobody could refute such tangible evidence. It left no loopholes.

And that's not all. The administrator's facts were right on target.

They were correct, they were adequate, and they carried the authority of his position. He didn't distract his hearers or dilute his argument with costs, employment problems, or architectural design. Such facts would have been irrelevant in this situation. Instead, from the thousands of facts available about hospital operations, he selected only those that bore directly on the issue.

Not all of us are as careful as the hospital administrator in sifting out the facts to use in an argument. We sometimes seek to win by sheer bulk of evidence rather than impact of evidence. That's why the hearer who protests, "Don't try to confuse me with facts," is probably not joking at all. His protest is really a plea for believable evidence in digestible quantities. An insurance salesman, for example, may have a dozen ways of proving that insurance is a good thing and that every client ought to be well covered. But the successful insurance salesman is usually the one who proves his point just one way—the way that will have greatest impact on the one customer he is talking with at the time. He selects his facts accordingly. For his next client he may use an entirely different set of facts.

There's nothing wrong about selecting facts this way. If you can prove your point with a dozen different sets of facts, what's wrong with selecting just one set of facts? There's no deception or trickery involved. The trickery comes if you select only the facts that support your view while you conceal the damaging facts from your hearers. Such deception is not only immoral. It's also dangerous, because you run the risk that some hearer will know the facts that you're concealing and that he'll rise to his feet, demolish your argument, and show you up for the deceiver you are.

Step 4. *Relate the evidence to the main issue.* That's just what our hospital administrator did. Remember, his proposition was that the board must take a new approach to the question of locating the new physical-therapy clinic. The facts showed that the old arrangement was (*a*) loaded in favor of the doctors and the treasury, (*b*) neglectful of the needs of patients, and therefore (*c*) indicative of the need for a new location. The evidence supports the proposition.

What's more, the administrator makes this relationship between evidence and proposition clear to his hearers. That's more than some communicators do. In their own minds this relationship is clear enough. They assume, therefore, that it's also clear to their listeners. All too often that assumption is false. Recall your own listening experiences. How many times have you listened anxiously to a talker who was advocating a course you supported—anxiously because you felt he needed just a little nudge to push him over the line and into an area of perfect clarity? Just a little bridging of the gap between evidence and proposition? Just a little more awareness of the need of his hearers for some leading by the hand? Just a little more effort to fit the pieces of an argument together?

The danger is that the spoken language moves swiftly, leaving only fragmentary phrases and clauses behind. You can't expect your hearer to piece the fragments together while you move on ahead of him. You must take him with you all the way, piecing the fragments together for him as you go and thus bringing evidence and proposition together into a clear, logical relationship.

Step 5. *State your conclusion.* You have shaped it, strengthened it, made it meaningful by evidence and reasoning. Make it clear and straightforward. That's what our hospital administrator has done. No trailing off into generalities. No backing and filling. A simple restatement of his original proposition, now made strong enough, by fact and logic, to stand on its merits as a conclusion.

How can you state your conclusions clearly and crisply? How can you give your conclusions the definition, the impact that you want them to have? How can you tell your hearers that this—and this alone—is what you've been driving at all the while? How can you tell them, "This is the end. This is the most important thing I've said in this talk"?

You can invent some devices of your own to serve as flags for these conclusions. In fact, maybe you have some already. A distinguished Southern preacher, not long since retired, used to mark the beginning of his conclusion by closing the large pulpit Bible that had lain open before him all through his sermon. A banker in a large Eastern city sits with his right leg folded beneath him as long as he presents his side of an argument. When he's ready to state his conclusion, he unfolds that right leg and places his right foot on the floor. The general manager of a manufacturing plant in New England leans back in his chair while he's developing his argument, but when he's ready to announce his conclusion he leans forward and places both hands, palms up on his glass-topped desk, as if to say, "Now there it is, plain as a pikestaff."

These, of course, are personal quirks. Even so, you don't have to know the men involved to understand what's going on. In each instance, there's a new vigor, a new directness, that marks the start of something important and rouses the attention of listeners.

Stock phrases, too, will help you mark your conclusion. The list is endless. But here are a few samples:

"Now, this is what I've been coming to all this time. . . ."

"The evidence points to this conclusion. . . ."

"Here's what I hope you'll take home with you. . . ."

"This is what I want you to remember as you cast your vote. . . ."

"Where do these facts lead us? To this, and nothing else. . . ."

Step 6. *Prepare to rebut.* Our hospital administrator didn't get into rebuttal. But if he's intelligent enough to devise the argument he presented, you can be sure he's also intelligent enough to make effective rejoinder to anybody who takes the opposing view. In fact, you can be pretty sure he knows the other side of the question as well as he knows his own side. He has the facts on both sides at his fingertips. Indeed, with a sincerely conciliatory attitude he has deliberately revealed some of the facts on the other side, thus conceding a little something to his opponents but not enough to damage his own cause.

Have you ever been in the frustrating position of a certain Middle Westerner who attended a realtors' convention? During a speech by a Chicago lawyer this Middle Westerner kept shifting around in his seat and whispering to his friend, "He's wrong there." But after the speech, when the time came for discussion, he couldn't say a word. He wanted to rebut the speaker, but he didn't know how to go about it.

You can be sure our hospital administrator wouldn't be speechless in such a situation. Why? Because he holds at his command the five key issue-finding questions (Step 1, above) that enabled him to find and evaluate the issue. With those same five key questions he can also isolate the real issues in his opponents' arguments and develop appropriate arguments with strength and clarity.

The successful talker holds himself ready for rebuttal. He's always on guard against opponents or contenders who throw their facts around carelessly or credit their evidence to unacceptable or questionable authorities or experts. Why on guard? Because fact, authority, and testimony, however convincing they sound, can sometimes be wide of the mark. You should check the data and the testimony your opponents muster against you. Are the data correct? Are they related to the matter at issue? Are there other authorities whose word carries equal weight and whose data and interpretations differ?

Finally, the successful rebutter develops the habit of questioning general statements. "Some members of the committee call this a good plan," you might say. "Good for whom?" It's the kind of probing, pointed question every businessman should throw at such statements as the following:

"The experts are saying . . ."

"It has been proved conclusively . . ."

"Statistics show us . . ."

"We have ample authority . . ."

"Other companies say . . ."

"Top management agrees . . ."

"Everything points in the direction of . . ."

"All the material we read declares . . ."

"Exhaustive case studies show . . ."

It's important to form the habit of questioning such statements as these before you let them impress you or before you rely on them for decision. But it's equally important that you do such questioning sincerely and constructively, seriously yet pleasantly. If you let impatience or arrogance color your questions, you may lose a cause while you're winning an argument.

## Three Traps to Avoid in Controversy

Controversy is full of booby traps for the unwary, the shy, the overconfident, the careless, the unthinking talker. They include simple slips of the tongue, overlooking basic facts, plain ignorance of the subject under debate, and the like. But these traps are easy to avoid. You can usually back up and correct a slip of the tongue. You can often explain away your unintentional omission of facts. And you can keep your mouth shut when opening it would reveal your ignorance.

But there are subtler and more dangerous traps in arguments. And the insidious thing about them is that your sharp-witted listeners may spot them before you do. You can talk blithely on, confident of your eloquence, sure of sound logic at your command, almost swept away with the power of your own persuasion—and all of a sudden stumble ingloriously into one of these traps. They are the hasty generalization, the false analogy, and the weak cause-and-effect relationship. They are the reason why the skillful debater, like his smartest hearers, observes three good rules, as follows:

• *Shy away from overgeneralization.* Generalization is the process of drawing broad conclusions from representative facts. For instance, our Federal government draws generalizations about rising national income and our improving standard of living from facts that are scientifically collected and weighted. These are sound generalizations because there are enough facts to support broad conclusions, though the generalizations do not reveal particular instances of joblessness or hardship.

In the same way you could generalize like this: "As a general rule, large malting companies of the Middle West produce better malt than small malting companies." But you would need enough facts to show that any small company that produced better malt than the big companies was the exception.

The trouble with generalization comes when you draw broad conclusions without enough facts—or when you overlook or ignore a substantial mass of facts that would invalidate your conclusion.

Suppose, for instance, you were to argue this way: "My father was an elevator operator during the Depression. The union roughed him up and caused his death. Therefore all unions are bad." However much you loved your father and however much you may hate unions, your argument is still pretty thin. From just one fact—your father's death at the hands of one union—you take a long leap and indict all unions. What are the facts about other unions? How have unions changed since the Depression? How common were union strong-arm tactics in those days? How common are they today? You see, the generalization just won't stand up on one fact alone. You've got to have more facts.

Or suppose you made this report to your boss: "Mary had too much to drink at the office party. Therefore she's an alcoholic." Maybe Mary did drink too much at the party. Maybe that's all you need to have her fired. But getting her fired is one thing. Accusing her of alcoholism, on the basis of just one incident, is quite another thing. Your charge certainly wouldn't stand up if the union challenged it.

So be cautious about generalizations. When they're sound, when you've got facts to back them up, go ahead. But beware of too long a jump from a narrow base of fact to a sweeping conclusion. You'll be fairly safe if you use such qualifiers as "in most instances," "usually," and "from the evidence before us."

• *Be careful with analogies.* When you use analogy you're saying, in effect, "Compare these two things (or situations). They're alike in some respects. Since they're alike in these respects, they're alike in other significant respects."

Suppose, for instance, you're an official of a manufacturing plant that makes thumpits, whoppits, and whammits. One member of the management group sees new market opportunities if the company can broaden its market to include fixits as well. You don't see it that way. Your argument goes like this:

"This proposal to add a new product line would stretch our resources too far. We couldn't cover a new market except at the expense of some part of our present market. It would be like moving a child from a single bed to a double bed, and sending his single-bed blanket along with him. Sleeping alone in that double bed, he'd stay warm and comfortable under a single-bed blanket. But if another child moved in with him, there wouldn't be enough blanket to cover both children. The feet or back or shoulders of one or the other would get cold. As I see it, that's our situation. If we add fixits to our line, we won't be able to cover our markets."

On the face of it, that sounds like a pretty good argument from analogy. But a sharp-eyed member of the manufacturing group would spot the flaws right away. "Let's go along with Smith's analogy," he would say. "First of all, our bed wouldn't be any wider if we added fixits to our product line. It would just be deeper. In other words, the same people who use our thumpits, whammits, and whoppits would also use our fixits. Our salesmen would make the same number of calls they've been making—and they'd call on the same people. We wouldn't have a wider market. We'd just penetrate deeper into the market we already have.

"In the second place, one child is now sleeping in this bed. He has warmed it up. If another child climbs in, he'll benefit by this already generated warmth. Sleeping together under the same blanket, they just won't need as much blanket. In other words, the acceptance we've won over the years for our thumpits, whoppits, and whammits will make it easier to introduce our fixits. With this in mind, I urge that we get into the fixit business as soon as we can."

That's the hazard in arguing by analogy. An analogy can be colorful, attention-getting—a great help in illustrating argument. But there must be logic to back it up, because an analogy is never a proof absolute. So when you use analogy in argument, be sure your comparison isn't full of holes (like the analogy of the blanket above). Also, when an opponent brings in an analogy, think through it critically and search it for some fatal flaw.

What tests can you apply to see whether your analogy—or your opponent's—stands up? There are four, as follows:

1. Does the analogy cover all the points of likeness?

2. Does the analogy take points of difference into account as well as points of likeness?

3. Do the points of likeness outweigh the points of difference?

4. Are all the facts used in the analogy true?

• *Don't rely solely on cause-and-effect relationships.* The process of reasoning, which is the basis of argument, assumes a causal relationship between one point and the next. You advance from cause to effect or from effect to cause. If cause is known, you reason forward to effect. You predict what will happen. And if effect is known, you reason back to cause. But neither procedure is proof positive and absolute in every instance.

Take the cause-to-effect approach. You're on pretty safe ground when, for example, you state that gravity (cause) will eventually draw a long fly ball back toward the earth's surface and put it within Willie Mays' reach. In this instance, you're reasoning from well-established natural law (cause) to universally observed fact (effect). But when you argue that Willie Mays' skill (cause) makes it dead sure that he will field the ball perfectly (effect), you overlook factors that might make the effect quite different—the glare of the sun, collision with another outfielder, a rough spot in the turf, a sudden gust of wind. You're arguing from Mays' known skill to an effect that's probable but by no means certain.

The effect-to-cause argument has much the same sort of weakness. Granted, it often stands up, as when a stamping-machine operator, noting a recurring crimp in parts that come from his machine (effect), traces the flaw back to a maladjustment in the feeder mechanism (cause). But effect-to-cause is not always as clear and certain as that.

Suppose, for example, you're an insurance claims adjuster. If you try to prove that a subsurface explosion (effect) was the fault of the local gas utility (cause), you'll need more to rely on than the simple fact that the gas company has pipelines beneath the street. Maybe a street construction job caused the trouble. Maybe it was an excavation shovel or a blast of dynamite in connection with a new building close by. Maybe some children found their way into a basement and had an afternoon's fun with some valves.

The point is, when you're arguing from effect back to cause, you should be sure that the cause you state is more probable than any cause your opponent might hit upon.

In any event, whether you argue from cause to effect or from effect to cause, don't pin your entire case on this kind of approach to persuasion and conviction. As a helper-out in argument, fine. As your sole support, usually risky.

## Summary

Winning your point in constructive controversy or swinging others to your point of view can give you a high mark for your talking skill. You'll get even higher marks if you can convince your opposing listeners without leaving a trail of wounded egos and broken friendships behind you.

Much of your success depends on your approach. If you set out to demolish every tiny issue, if you leap at every opportunity to debate, if you jump into an issue just because you like a rough-and-tumble fracas, you'll wind up as a pretty unpopular character with a chip on his shoulder. If you let your personal likes and dislikes sway you, if you speak unkindly or insolently of your opponents, if you argue people and personalities instead of facts and issues, you're more than likely to come up with the short end of the vote when the issue comes to a decision.

Those are the reasons why successful talkers make sure the issue is worth talking and arguing about before they get into it. Once they decide to get into it, they choose evidence and reason, not personalities, as their weapons.

The art of convincing usually follows a logical pattern. It begins with a clear statement of the proposition and a definition of terms. (Most argument bogs down right here.) Then, in succession, come the identification of the main issue (or issues), the presentation of evidence, the explanation of how the evidence bears on the issue and, finally, the statement of the conclusion (same as the original proposition, but now strengthened by evidence and reasoning).

Mastery of this pattern is the key to success in argument. It's also the key to success in rebuttal. With this key at your command you can isolate the significant issue in your opponent's position and close in on the fatal weakness in his argument.

Of course, there are traps in argument. The most dangerous ones are unsupported generalization, in which you draw sweeping conclusions from too few facts; weak analogy, in which you press too far with likenesses between situations that are really quite different, or mistake illustration for absolute proof; and unreliable cause-and-effect relationships, in which you state as fact something that is really only a speculation. The skillful talker avoids these traps himself—and is alert to spot them in the arguments of his opponents.

## Exercise

Imagine yourself in a group that's seated around a table for a policy conference. You're going to propose a change in policy—a change that will benefit you in your job and make your work more effective and productive for the company. From the following list, select the proposition you will offer and argue for:

• We should broaden our search for skilled employees.
• We should begin planning now for markets five years from now.
• We should set up an equipment-replacement schedule on a five-year basis.
• We should float a bond issue to build a new school.
• We should relax our city zoning restrictions in the downtown area.
• We should strengthen our competitive selling.
• We should encourage small accounts in our bank.

If none of these propositions suits you, choose one of your own —maybe something that's closer to your work. Then, having selected your proposition, develop your argument according to the following outline:

1. State your proposition clearly; define your terms.
2. Identify the main issue (or issues). You'll find the issue in the answer to one (or several) of the following questions:

Is there need for a change?
Is this the best change to make?
Is it practical?
Is it sound in theory?

Do the advantages outweigh the disadvantages?

3. State your evidence in support of the proposition (facts, expert opinion, quotes, documents, photographs, and the like).

4. Relate your evidence to the issue (or issues).

5. State your conclusion (the proposition that you have now proved).

6. Prepare a brief rebuttal that will defend the weakest point in your argument.

*I have trouble when I try to wind things up.*

# How to Wind Up Your Talk

"Say what you've got to say. Then stop."

That's one of the first rules a budding speaker learns. It's an equally good rule to learn—and to put into practice—in business talking and conversation. It will keep your talk short, as a good talk should be. It will keep you traveling down the main line as you develop your thoughts—keep you from woolgathering. And it will spare you from the unhappy fate that inevitably overtakes every talker who taxes the patience of his hearers beyond endurance.

Even so, successful talkers take this rule with a grain of salt. They know the difference between an abrupt halt and a planned, effective ending. They know, as you will learn in this chapter, how to pull all the strings of a talk together at the end. And they use this

163

skill every time they talk—whether they talk to one or two people in an office or to a thousand in a convention—whether they read a report or lead a conference—whether they talk safety to a group of employees, or sell a product, or urge some action on a board of trustees.

The ending can be (and often is) the most effective part of your communication. If you neglect your ending, your talk will be as pointless as a trial in which the jury, instead of rendering a verdict of innocence or guilt, simply recites the evidence it has heard and thus leaves judge, attorneys, and the prisoner in a state of bewilderment.

What will a strong ending do for you? Two big things:

• *Create the impression you want to linger longest.* The way you act, and look, and talk as you draw to an end is the way your hearers will remember you most vividly. The ending is therefore your most crucial moment and your most telling opportunity to convince or motivate your hearers. It's your best chance to create the image of yourself that you want your listeners to remember— as a man of quiet confidence, a man of sound views and genuine ability—as a man of earnest conviction, dedication, indignation, or sympathetic affection—as a man with an urgent cause and a sense of mission—as a reasonable man whose views have their roots in understanding and forbearance.

• *Drive home your main point.* If the closing moments of your talk determine how your hearers will remember you as a person, they also determine the words and thoughts your listeners will remember longest. That's why you'll want to sum up and state your conclusion, as forcibly and clearly as you can, at the end of your talk. It's the climax you've been leading up to all the time. It's as if you were an artillery commander. Up to now you've been drawing up your field pieces (stating your evidence, your facts, your illustrations), massing them for greatest power (relating your facts to each other), and training them on your target (organizing them for impact on your hearers). Now's the time to hit your target with all the concentrated fire power you have massed. This is your conclusion. It's positive, it's decisive, it's direct.

## What Makes a Good Ending

Four things make a good, strong ending. Here they are:

1. *Quick summary of evidence and supporting points.* Your conclusion is the time for summarizing briefly—very briefly—the gist of your evidence and your main points. It's the time when you pull together all the loose threads—when you refresh the memory of your hearers about what you've said and reveal, swiftly and clearly, the structural pattern of your talk. From this your conclusion emerges surely and inevitably.

How do you fashion such a summary? You eliminate the details that bulk large in the main body of your talk and repeat only the details that carry greatest impact and conviction. You eliminate the intricate steps by which you developed your points or explanation and repeat only the main points. In other words, your summary should bear the same relationship to the main body of your talk as a large-scale map of your state bears to a series of county maps. The county maps (like the main body of your talk) show details— small streams, individual hills and mountains, county roads and highways, fishing ponds, villages, and cities. The state map (like your summary) eliminates much of the detail. Instead, it shows whole mountain ranges, great rivers and lakes, a network of highways joining cities and towns—and shows them all in relation to the whole.

How do you move into such a summary? There are a good many commonly used sentences that will lead you right in. The following are typical; others of your own invention will come to you:

"Now, let's see where we stand."

"To wind things up, let's say it this way."

"Now for the wrap-up. Let's summarize."

2. *Orientation of your comments to the experience and motivation of your hearers.* There's nothing difficult about this. In fact, it should be easy for you. Why? Because, if you've developed the main body of your talk in line with the principles outlined earlier, you've

already established a bond between yourself and your subject on the one hand and, on the other hand, your hearers. It's easy (and important) to reinvite attention to this bond in your summary.

Suppose, for instance, you're the treasurer of a club. It's a private club. It owns the building, serves meals, is a quiet place to entertain guests for lunch or dinner. But the cost of building maintenance, food, and service, like everything else, has gone up. The club faces drastic change—or bankruptcy. You believe an increase in dues is the best answer—and the only practicable answer. You develop this thesis thoroughly in the main body of your talk—bring up your evidence, cite your examples and illustrations, make all your points clearly.

Now comes the end of your talk. How do you orient your views to the interests of your hearers—the board of directors? You can do it by touching briefly on the shared experiences that make your main points meaningful to the directors—special assessments that have become a nuisance, poor service, and a noisy, crowded dining room (because the club has had to seek new members to spread the cost of operating). This way, you relate the experience of your listeners to the problem under discussion and enlist their sympathy for your views.

3. *Clear restatement of purpose and conclusion.* If you didn't have some clear purpose in speaking up (or in otherwise asking for attention), you and your hearers would have been much better off if you had sat still and held your tongue. If you did have a purpose —to ask for action, to explain a process or a situation, to rouse sympathy for a cause or a point of view—you owe it to yourself, your hearers, and your purpose to leave no shred of doubt about why you have spoken up and what you want to happen as a result of your talking.

Suppose again you're the club treasurer described above. As you see it, the only workable solution to the financial problem is higher dues. You've said so at the beginning of your talk, when you stated your purpose. And you've summoned up many a fact, many a detail, about the perilous situation the club faces. But it's not enough for you to stop there. You need to do more than recite

the facts of impending bankruptcy and then sit down. You really
want to save the club—keep it going. That's why you spoke up in
the first place. That's why you recited the facts and wove your
fabric of evidence. All this must point to some conclusion—some
one conclusion. What is it? Should the club disband? Should it
relax its rules of admittance and campaign for new members?
Should it merge with another club? Should it rent its facilities to
outside organizations from time to time?

Without your firm guidance your hearers might settle on any one
of these questionable possibilities as the answer to the problem
your facts reveal. Granted, you stated your purpose and your
proposition at the outset—to save the club by increasing the dues.
But that was a long time ago (measured by the attention span of
the average listener). How do you know your hearers remember
what you started out to prove? Unless you remind them now—
firmly and clearly—they might tear off on some tangent, quite different from the action you want them to take. That's why you must
restate your proposition—that dues must be raised—as the conclusion to which the evidence inescapably points. This way, you
erase every trace of uncertainty about your purpose, you refocus
the attention of your listeners on the action you want, and you leave
your closing words on the top level of their consciousness.

4. *A memorable impression of your personality and your conviction.* The closing moments of your talk offer you your last chance—
and your best chance—to show yourself in the most favorable light.
How can you achieve this effect? Three ways, as follows:

• *By being constructive.* Go back to the club treasurer. Assume
he knows the principles of persuasive talking. Those principles will
steer him away from using these closing minutes for a frontal attack on somebody else's proposal. Nor will he propose anything
as unconstructive as disbanding the club. That would be an evasion
of the problem rather than a solution for it. Instead, he concludes
with his own proposal for positive, constructive action—an increase
in dues that will put the club once more on a sound operating basis.

• *By expressing appropriate feelings.* Appropriate to the subject
under discussion, that is, and to the state of mind you want to create

among your hearers. Take our club treasurer again. As long as he talks with the purpose of raising dues, it's appropriate for him to be straightforward and serious. But put him in other roles. Suppose his purpose is to defeat a proposal to break up the club. In that instance the appropriate feeling would be nostalgic sentiment; he would recall the good old days and the grand old men of the club. If his purpose is to resist a special assessment, dead seriousness is appropriate—not opposition to the member who proposed the special assessment but to the proposal itself. If his purpose is to reconcile two factions—members who favor merger with another club and members who want to rent facilities to outside groups— reasonableness and good humor will be appropriate. And if his purpose is to put an end to repeated infractions of club rules, he might well let his righteous anger show through. The occasion, the issue, the group he talks to, and his own good judgment and sincerity must be his guides.

Just one word of warning: Control and restraint are essential, especially when you're dealing with people and their feelings. The feelings that you inspire among your listeners—tender sentiment, anger, and even humor—can get out of hand easily. Uncontrolled, they'll do more harm than good to you and your cause.

• *By being self-confident.* Self-confidence will come naturally if the facts you've summoned up have convinced you that your cause is right. In general, your listeners will follow you if you show that you know where you stand and where you're going. Conviction is contagious.

## Seven Techniques for Ending Your Talk

Just as there are various ways of developing your talk, so there are various ways of ending it. Here are seven tested techniques:

1. *Sum up, then state your conclusion.* Take that club treasurer once more. Remember, he wants dues increased to avoid bankruptcy or merger with another club. His summing up might go this way:

"I've stated all the statistics. I needn't restate them for you. But

I do want to touch the high spots again and summarize very briefly what those statistics mean to us. They mean four things. First, our over-all building maintenance costs are 12 per cent higher than they were three years ago. Second, our new kitchen staff and higher food prices mean we're now losing money on every meal we serve. Third, we've invested a substantial sum in enlarging our library so it will be more useful to us. Fourth, our accommodations are so much more gracious, and therefore so much more expensive, that I'm confident we could not persuade members of another club to merge with us. For me, these four facts lead to just one conclusion: We must increase our dues."

Note how this treasurer's summary takes shape. It's brief and straight to the point. It omits the detailed statistics and the illustrative material that made up the body of his talk. With telling effect, the summary states, cleanly and swiftly, the four main points. Finally, it shows how the now-proven proposition ("We must increase our dues") grows directly and inevitably from the evidence.

2. *Simplify a complex subject.* Suppose you're the director of personnel for a middle-size manufacturing company. Labor contract negotiations are just ahead. The board of directors of your company asks you to attend its meeting and offer your recommendations on bargaining. After studying the situation you decide what your main recommendation will be—a modest wage increase for employees in exchange for some concessions on working rules.

So you develop your evidence. It's pretty intricate. Some of the directors (most likely those who are also executives of your company and are therefore close to its everyday problems) will grasp much of your evidence right away. Other directors (those whose principal connection with your company is the monthly directors' meeting) will find it somewhat harder to grasp. Even so, neither group is as close to local labor problems as you are. You feel you must simplify the facts and the issues for both groups at once. Here's how you might do it:

"Now I've laid out a big array of statistics on shift schedules, pay differentials, and seniority rules. I've told you about our problem of work assignments for craftsmen. I've gone into our productivity record in three major manufacturing departments. And I've showed you in detail how work rules on machine operation, lubrication, painting, inside and outside construction, sick leave, and other matters complicate our lives and run our costs up. I work with these details every day, and if they sound to you like an intricate mass of facts, they're the facts of life to me.

"What these statistics come down to is simply this: Increases in wages have outrun increases in output per man-hour among our employees. The main reason for this is that rigid work rules, won by the union mostly because management simply defaulted in prosperous times, are now tying the hands of our foremen in directing work in the plant. If we could gain some relaxation of work rules, we could raise output per man-hour, cut our manufacturing costs per unit, and have enough left over to grant a modest wage boost to our employees. It's as simple as that. And that's what I recommend as our goal in this year's negotiations."

Take it another way. Maybe you're the public relations official of the local electric utility. You try to explain to an irate customer why the fuses in his home keep blowing out, plunging his home in darkness, shutting down his refrigerator and electric clocks, interrupting his favorite television program, and cutting off his furnace or his air conditioner. You could simplify your complex explanation this way:

"Now I've showed you the arithmetic on amperes and watts and voltages and ohms in your home and on the appliances you have. Let me wind up by putting it all in simpler terms. Your fuse is a bridge from the outside power line to the inside of your house. That bridge has a stated capacity. That capacity is the same as the safe capacity of the wiring system in your house. If any load too heavy for the safety of your house starts across the bridge, the bridge will collapse. The bridge insures you against fire and against damaged appliances.

"The truth is, you're trying to bring too heavy a load across the bridge—the fuse. In your situation you can do either of two things. You can leave the bridge (your fuse) as it is and lighten the load you're trying to bring into your house (cut off your air conditioner, for example). Or you can build up the load-carrying capacity of your wiring system and thus make it safe to install a stronger bridge —a larger-capacity fuse. With more hot weather like this yet to come, I think you ought to do the latter."

3. *Capsulize your main thought in a witty, colorful sentence or phrase.* If not an epigram, then something much like an epigram.

Examples? Here are a few:

"People's judgments, like their watches, never run exactly alike, yet each person trusts his own."

"Some people just aren't smart enough to make mistakes."

"The nations of the world must choose between Christ and the Kremlin."

What do these three examples have in common? Just this: They're succinct, brief, and witty. Not funny, but witty. They're epigrammatic. As the wind-up of a talk, they'll leave a lasting impression.

For some people these pithy ways of summarizing their thoughts come easily and naturally. Ralph Waldo Emerson was full of epigrammatic sentences ("A foolish consistency is the hobgoblin of little minds"). So was Benjamin Franklin ("We must all hang together, or assuredly we shall all hang separately"). So was Abraham Lincoln ("God must love the common people—He made so many of them"). So was Franklin D. Roosevelt ("The only thing we have to fear is fear itself").

But not everybody has the gift of manufacturing such pointed endings to fit his talks. If it's hard for you (as it is for most people), what can you do?

You can do two things:

• *Give thought to being original and imaginative.* Take our club treasurer once more. Say he's still talking about dues. He might wind up something like this:

"I believe we all agree that our dues must go up. But not too high. Somewhere there's a happy medium, as there is in women's clothes. A woman's clothes should be tight enough to reveal that she's a woman—and loose enough to prove she's a lady."

Such an ending takes a little work, a little thought, a little imagination. It means you've got to be alert to the little dramas in the passing scene—the ironies, the paradoxes, the unconscious displays of human foibles and vanities, the day-by-day revelations of kindness, love, courage, and whimsy. They're the materials from which good talkers build their witticisms, their epigrams, their shrewd observations on human nature.

• *Study the masters of epigram.* They run the range of sophistication and literary merit—Samuel Butler ("Notebooks") and Ralph W. Emerson, Oscar Wilde and Benjamin Franklin, Aesop and Joseph Addison, Martial, Alexander Pope, and Carl Sandburg. In these writers—and others like them—you'll see the gift of wit and grace and shrewd observation at work. If familiarity with these men doesn't teach you the gift of capsulizing your thoughts effectively, at least it will store your memory with a stock of ready-made epigrams on which you can draw for your own needs at appropriate times.

4. *Gear your ending to basic human drives.* These are self-esteem, security, love, curiosity, the need for a cause or a mission, and the like (Chapter 3). This kind of ending will appeal mostly to emotion. For that very reason it's sometimes especially suitable for winding up a talk that has relied mostly on logic or statistics. It changes the pace dramatically—and reveals the human values that lie beneath the cold statistics and the impersonal arithmetic.

Suppose, for instance, you're a social worker. You're asking a neighborhood group, meeting informally, to support your quest for a playground for underprivileged children. You take ten minutes or so to present statistics on juvenile delinquency—so many youngsters involved, so many misdemeanors committed, so much property damage recorded, so many people eating and sleeping in so many square feet of living area. Now comes your ending:

"These are cold statistics. But life breathes in every number I've given you. Behind every street fight and every broken window and every insolent teen-ager lies a broken home, a jobless father, or the frustrations of cramped, marginal living without sunlight, air, or room to stretch young muscles. The victims of these conditions will be the citizens of tomorrow—and your neighbors as well. To keep yourselves and your own children safe in this free land, you must make it possible for youngsters less privileged than yours to enjoy sunlight and air and the freedom of space. These children need a place where, under creative leadership, they can release their tensions and escape their frustrations. I lay it on your hearts to provide this place."

5. *Seek impact with a suitable quotation.* This way, you'll bring into your talk, at the place where it will count most, a better brain than your own—or a happier choice of words—or the prestige of a recognized authority.

Where do you find such quotations? You'll find them in the Bible. You'll find them in the writings of such men as Emerson, Whitman, Shakespeare, Wordsworth—in fact, in any truly great work of prose or poetry. Bartlett's *Familiar Quotations* will provide you with a brilliant array of appropriate quotations on almost any subject.

For quotations in specialized fields of knowledge or activity, you'll turn naturally to the experts in those fields. Suppose, for instance, you're talking informally to a group of foremen in a manufacturing plant. Your topic is employee suggestions and work simplification. You might end like this:

"Dr. Herbert True, you know, is a recognized authority on the art of creating ideas. I think he summarizes pretty well what I've been trying to say. Dr. True puts it this way:

" 'Creativity has no norm. It can appear anywhere at any time ... There are still many unsolved problems in the world ... We must give people the opportunity to be creative—and allow them the luxury of failure. Instead of emphasizing the million-dollar idea, we must encourage a million one-dollar ideas to originate and grow.' "

6. *Use a narrative.* It should illustrate your main point or state it in another frame of reference. This kind of ending will do two things for you. It will personalize your talk—give it warmth and reality. And it will bring story interest—narrative, suspense, and climax—to your closing moments.

Maybe you're a high school teacher. You're worried (and so are some of your students) by a few noisy, high-spirited youngsters who thoughtlessly disturb their classmates. They bang their books around, slam their desks shut, talk in audible whispers. So you give them a little talk on respect for the rights of others. You might end with a story like this:

"When I was six or seven years old I had a dog. I was glad for him to follow me around to most places. But I didn't want him to follow me to school, and I didn't want to take him to parties with me. I needed a chain, so I could sometimes tie him up and make him stay at home.

"On my way home from school one afternoon I saw just what I wanted at the edge of a neighbor's lawn—a good, strong chain. There was no dog tied to it, and it had nobody's name on it. I picked it up and took it home.

"My father asked me where I had picked up the chain. I told him. Gently but firmly he told me that I must return it to our neighbor. 'There are things that belong to other people,' he said, 'even though they're not locked up or marked private or fenced in. You must learn to respect such ownership.'

"Now," you might conclude, "we've got some private ownership rights here in our classroom. You can't see any signs marking them, but they're private nevertheless. I'm talking about the right to study, the right to listen, the right to learn, the right to think in quiet—without interruption or distraction by others. We must all respect those rights."

That's a simple illustration of the narrative ending. You'll find a more sophisticated example at the close of a lecture by Dr. S. I. Hayakawa, the renowned semanticist. The lecture is about the self-concept and its role in human communication. Near the end, Dr. Hayakawa summarizes this way:

"The other fellow has goals that make sense to him in terms of his environment as he sees it. You have goals that make sense to you in terms of your environment as you see it ... If you try to force or superimpose your perceptions and goals on the other fellow, he feels threatened ... He increases his resistance. This is not an instance of cussedness on his part. This is an instance of a fundamental biological mechanism he has; namely, the preservation and enhancement of the self-concept.

"Here is a goldfish bowl with goldfish in it. It is inadequate. There is not enough room for the goldfish. The water is stale. Here is a brand-new aquarium you just brought home—with running water, air conditioning, and everything. For their own good you would like to transfer those fish. But when you try to catch the darn things they try to get away from you . . . They see your hand with the net as a threat, although you intend it to help . . . When goldfish resist like this we don't cuss them out for their stupidity, because we accept as a fact about goldfish that you can't reason with them . . .

"When human beings refuse to do something for their own good, we sometimes cuss them out for their stupidity, sometimes treat them as if they were goldfish, force something upon them and then get mad if they resist. But notice that we ourselves are stupid very often, because of a failure in our techniques of communication."

7. *Ask for action.* If action is the aim of your talk, and if your material has put your listeners in the mood for action, then ask for it. Be as definite, as clear, as concrete as you can about the action you want. Make it easy for your listeners to understand what you want them to do. Follow the lead of the lawyer who prosecutes a case before a jury. His closing sentence is a straightforward request: "I ask you, ladies and gentlemen of the jury, to bring in a verdict of guilty." That's a clear, direct request for action. There's no mistaking what the prosecutor wants the jury to do.

Imagine yourself a member of the program committee of your local civic club. Recently your club has heard luncheon speeches by the mayor, the chief of police, the commissioner of sanitation, and the chief of welfare. You feel these programs have followed a pretty unimaginative pattern and have accomplished little or nothing. You want a change. So you express your feeling in a program committee meeting. You review what's happened, then lead up to the need for a change. Now comes your ending—the time when you want to leave no doubt about the action you want:

"I ask you," you say, "to act on this need for change. I ask you to invite these same men back to our club. But not as speakers again. Ask them back as listeners, question answerers, and problem solvers. Meanwhile, let's poll our members for their questions about our city management—for their problems, puzzles, gripes, and suggestions. We'll throw these problems and suggestions at our city officials. This way, we won't be just sitting and listening passively. We'll be making some positive moves in city affairs. I ask this committee to take the first step now: Start polling our members."

That's a clear call for action. It's straightforward. It has the impact that a good ending should have.

## Summary

Social conversation is one thing. When you talk socially, in somebody's living room or at the dining table, your aim usually is to be pleasant, agreeable, entertaining. Sometimes, desperately trying to fill a void in the conversation, you may even say things that are nearly meaningless. Your social talk almost always dovetails into what somebody has said before you, and the person who follows you usually picks up the thread of the talk where you have let it drop. You don't have to worry about how you end your part—or parts—of the conversation.

But business talking is different. It's purposeful. You have an aim in saying whatever you say. You want to put a point across, explain a situation or a procedure, win somebody to your view, persuade somebody to act. When you're talking this way, purposefully, your ending is important. You've got something at stake.

That's why, when you're talking in business, you must shape your closing remarks thoughtfully. It's not enough to halt, in the hope that somebody else will pick up where you left off. You've got to design and calculate your ending. Why? Because your ending is the part of your talk that will linger longest in the memory of your hearers. It's your last shot at your hearers. You must make it a telling shot.

This is not to say that a good, strong ending is hard to achieve. There's really no mystery about it. It's a simple matter of picking the meat (your main point, your purpose in talking) out of the nut (your evidence, illustration, explanation, the twists and turns of your reasoning, the main body of your talk), and then serving the meat to your listeners in such an inviting form that they will accept it—even reach for it eagerly.

How to do that—how to bring your talk to an effective, efficient, persuasive, and therefore successful end—is the theme of this chapter. How well you turn out as a talk ender will depend on how well you master the principles and techniques described in these pages.

*Exercise*

Below are five subjects. Choose any one of them (or, if you're ambitious, as many as you like). Imagine that you've just finished a ten- to twelve-minute talk on the subject you picked. Now you're ready to bring your talk to an end. Bearing in mind the principles and practical helps in this chapter, sum up (in thirty seconds) what you've said in the main body of your talk, then give your conclusion (ten seconds). Practice on any willing victim you can find—your public-speaking instructor, your luncheon guest, your college-age son or daughter, your next-door neighbor, your classmates, your understanding wife.

Here are your subjects to choose from:

1. What a hobby will do for you.

2. Why you should know your bank better (or your church, newspaper, Red Cross, or hospital).

3. Why people should think well of your company (or organization, institution, profession, or skill).

4. What's needed to make your community better.

5. Why I support the Democratic (or Republican) party.

*I get jumpy when I have to talk to important people or groups. How can I overcome this nervousness?*

**12**

# How to Overcome
# Common Handicaps in Talking

Whatever your business is, and in whatever relationships you meet groups and individuals, there come times when your personal success hinges on your success in communicating—talking convincingly, persuasively, winningly to individuals as well as groups.

This is true whether you're a foreman or plant manager, department head or organization president, sales manager or industrial relations director, training director or safety manager, bank teller or cashier, chief of a hospital admitting office or head nurse, insurance salesman or managing editor, doctor or dentist, research scientist or professor. For all these people (and others as well, including you), every opportunity to talk to groups and to key individuals is an opportunity to score a success. Not always a victory, to be sure, because not even the best communicators score a victory every time they talk. But a success, yes—from the standpoint of clear, purposeful statement of thoughts. Measured that way, every talk you make can be a success even if you don't win your point every time. And each success you have, measured in those terms, will bring victory a little closer next time you talk.

The trouble with many of us is that we shy away from these opportunities to talk—these opportunities for success. We feel we can't match others in wit or words. We grow nervous. We're afraid of sounding foolish—or looking foolish. We become self-conscious —too much aware of our little shortcomings and weaknesses, as if we were the only people who bore such handicaps.

If you feel like this when opportunities to talk come your way, cheer up. These are common handicaps. Like other people who have acquired the art of successful talking, you can master these small shortcomings. This chapter will help you.

## How to Talk Well Even If You Are Nervous

Keep this fact uppermost in your mind: Every speaker, even the man who makes a profession of talking, gets nervous when the time comes. Veteran actors get stage fright. Radio and television newscasters have their moments of dread before they go on the air. Senators and congressmen tremble before their colleagues. And a distinguished minister, who preached two sermons every Sunday for nearly fifty years before he retired, confessed in the last years of his active life that he never walked into his pulpit without damp palms and a feverish fear.

The truth is, fear is perfectly natural. It's nature's way of bracing you to meet challenges. When you quail at the thought of opening your mouth before a group of people, you're feeling the same tension a boxer feels when he steps into the ring—or a sprinter feels when he takes his place at the starting line. Your glands begin to pump adrenalin into your system, your blood pressure rises, your sweat glands work more actively. It's normal—all of it.

"Even so, I'm still uncomfortable and frightened," you say. "What can I do?"

You can learn to control your fear—indeed, convert it into an asset. Here are a few tips on how to do it:

• *Know what you want to say before you begin to talk.* If you've had time to prepare in advance, fine. You're all set. A now distinguished platform speaker confesses that as a young man he always prepared something to say before joining any discussion group or attending any meeting he was invited to. He wasn't always called on to talk—but he was prepared every time he was called on.

• *Pause before you plunge in.* The very act of presenting an unruffled front will calm you down measurably. The pause—the slow, deliberate approach—will give you time to collect your thoughts and bring your taut nerves under control.

How can you pause gracefully—without seeming to stumble for thoughts and words? Several ways. For example, make a slow business of walking to the front of the room or approaching the chairman's table. Move some books around or shuffle some papers on the table or lectern in front of you. Or, if this is an informal, sitting-down talk or business conference or discussion, move your chair around to a new vantage point, or stroll over to the window, or light a cigarette.

Whether it's formal or informal talking, standing up or sitting down, you can gain a few moments—and a little calm—by looking intently and purposefully down at your hands, at your desk, or out the window, as if gathering your thoughts. In fact, there's many another way to pause gracefully—and with dramatic effect on your hearers—while you pull yourself together. Your hearers need never suspect your anguish. They're more likely to say to themselves: "This man is thinking through his remarks. He's going to say something meaningful. But I must give him a little time."

• *Relax physically.* Let your arms and hands hang loose at your sides. When you breathe, let the air out—way out. If you're seated, put your feet flat on the floor. Relax your muscles group by group—neck, arms and hands, back and shoulder, legs and feet. All this will break the tension cycle—physical tension answering mental tension answering physical tension.

• *But don't let down altogether.* Some tension is an asset when you're talking. Being tense (as long as you keep it under control) means your nerves, your reflexes, and your sensitivities are alert and responsive. It means you'll sense the reactions and needs of your hearers. Your personality will be alive, and you'll get a fine edge on your sentences, neither of which would happen if the challenge to talk left you unmoved, unexcited, completely relaxed.

• *Be sure of your first few sentences.* If you have prepared a talk, be sure of the opening. This way, your first sentences will come out clear and strong—and in so doing they'll give you confidence to go ahead. The experience will be like plunging into a cold lake: If you go at it boldly, with assurance, staying in will come easily. You might even enjoy it.

Suppose you haven't had time to prepare. Suppose this is an informal talking situation—a meeting on sales, personnel, or policy. Even in this situation you can be pretty sure of your first few sentences. How? Well, you can usually find time to frame them while others are talking. (You can do this without being a poor listener.) Or you can pause deliberately, as described above, to shape your beginning. If this isn't enough, stall for a little time. Off the top of your mind pull a few stage-setting comments (for example, "Let me see if I can state what I mean about this matter") while the deeper layers of your mind take hold of your need for a clear opening statement. And if even this doesn't give you time enough to create your start, spend a few moments summarizing the views of preceding speakers while your own thoughts take shape in the creative recesses of your mind.

• *Talk about what you know about.* This is what people want to hear from you anyhow. It's what gives validity and personal warmth to the things you say. Your listeners will sense your authority and conviction, and you'll have the confidence that comes with mastery of facts. For example, a bank official can look silly telling a pilot how to bring a plane in for a smooth landing. But as an experienced passenger he can talk pretty convincingly about ways to improve service to airline customers. In the same way, a training director can look foolish telling department heads about the intricate details of their jobs. But he can be authoritative and convincing when he talks about the need for creativity or better human relations. In short, the more carefully you confine your remarks to the things you know about, the more reason you'll have for confidence in your ability to say something meaningful and say it well.

• *Go ahead even if you are nervous.* Maybe you'll stumble and halt and make a mess of things the first few times. But each time you speak up you'll gain experience. And experience will give you confidence for your next venture. This way, you'll develop like the veteran soldier. He fears the coming challenge just as the raw recruit does. But he has faced it before and, knowing what's coming, he knows he can handle it this time. There's not much that can surprise him.

## Why You Don't Need a Big Vocabulary

"I can't be eloquent."

"I can't put my thoughts into words."

Those are common complaints among people who shy away from opportunities to talk. These people make the mistake of thinking that multisyllabic words are the key to successful talking in business, in industry, and in community affairs. They couldn't be more wrong.

The fact of the matter is this: In speeches before learned philosophical societies, diplomats, and highly technical groups (medical, engineering, and the like), a polysyllabic and specialized vocabulary, more often than not based on Latin and Greek, can be meaningful and precise. But in most day-by-day communication such words become barriers between us and the people we want to talk with. They don't have the common-denominator value that we need for effective spoken communication. What's more, people who hear them are likely to think we're trying harder to impress them than to communicate with them.

The key to a good talking vocabulary, then, is not the heavy multi-syllabic word, which is also likely to be an abstraction. The real key is the simple, familiar word that stirs an image in the hearer's mind and is rich in association and suggestion—for example, such words as *love, home, trust, hope, life,* and *joy.*

Take a few examples from the literature that has shaped so much of our American thinking. Not counting syllables made by suffixes for plurals and verb endings, Lincoln's Gettysburg Address has only eleven words longer than two syllables; the story of the Creation, in Genesis, only eight. The Beatitudes (Matthew 5 : 3–12) have only five words of three syllables; The Lord's Prayer, only two; the Twenty-third Psalm, only one.

Shakespeare expressed his deepest thoughts in the simplest words:

He wears his faith like the fashion of his hat.
*Much Ado About Nothing*

The quality of mercy is not strained.
It droppeth as the gentle rain from heaven
Upon the place beneath.
*The Merchant of Venice*

In our own time, who proves the merits of simple, image-provoking language? In literature, Hemingway, Frost, and Sandburg. In the pulpit, Father Gannon, Bishop Sheen, Dr. Ralph W. Sockman, and the late Rabbis Jonah and Stephen Wise. On television, Raymond Gram Swing, Howard K. Smith, Charles Collingwood, Chet Huntley, David Brinkley. In business and industry, Ben Fairless and Paul Hoffman. These are specially gifted men, to be sure, each in his own way. But they're not pretentious in manner or in speech. They don't pose. They don't try to impress. They just speak out, simply and directly. So can you.

How can you get that way? How can you shape an easy-to-understand vocabulary that will carry your meaning—clear, straightforward, and colorful—to your hearers? Four things will help:

• *Accept the fact that the vocabulary you have is probably the best, after all, for talking to people.* It's probably much like the vocabulary of most people you talk to. That's good. It means they'll understand you when you talk to them. They won't puzzle over what you mean. You can communicate without effort.

• *Be firm about those big words you're tempted to use.* Rule them out. Prune them from your talking vocabulary. For some people—maybe you—this may take a little doing. If so, drill yourself this way a few times: Write as fancy a paragraph as you can on some subject of your own choosing. Fill it with words of three, four, and five syllables. Then go back through it with your pencil, ruthlessly cut out every word of more than three syllables, and for each word that you cut out substitute a one- or two-syllable word. Go through this little drill every evening for a week or so, and you'll find out how easy it is to get along without the big, elegant words you once admired.

• *Study your dictionary.* If you use it only to track down the meanings of words you don't know and to find out how to spell troublesome words, you're missing most of the fun of owning it. Reading it just for the joy of discovering new words—and new meanings for old words—is fascinating enough. Even more fascinating is the new idea, the new image, that lurks in nearly every definition. As you read your dictionary, single out the words that will make your vocabulary more colorful, more image-provoking, more down to earth. When you find these words, you'll discover that most of them come from ancient Anglo-Saxon, mother of English, and not from Latin and Greek, which tend to give us our abstract words.

• *Read as widely as you can.* Poetry as well as prose. Modern as well as classical. Watch for the graphic, lucid words the masters use—and make them your own. You'll find some of the masters already named in this chapter and others. A few more? Take John Masefield, Virginia Woolf, Governor William Bradford's *Of Plymouth Plantation,* John Woolman's *Journal,* Thoreau's *Journals,* Jack London's novels, Mark Twain, Willa Cather, Emily Dickinson, and Vachel Lindsay.

And don't overlook your daily newspaper in your search for the lively idea and the graphic word. Sportswriters do some of the best (and some of the worst) writing of our time. And you'll find bright images and brisk prose in many a columnist's daily brooding on the passing scene—Inez Robb, James Reston, and Art Buchwald, to list only a few.

• *Study a how-to-do-it book on language and style.* True, such books are mostly about writers and the written word. But much that's true of the written word is true also of the spoken word. Four titles from a list that might be as long as an arm: *Watch Your Language,* by Theodore Bernstein, of the *New York Times; The Art of Plain Talk,* by Rudolph Flesch; *The Technique of Clear Writing,* by Robert Gunning; and Strunk's *Elements of Style,* edited by E. B. White, urbane stylist of the *New Yorker* magazine.

### What You Can Do about Weak Grammar

Flaws in your grammar won't guarantee success in talking to other people. But they won't stand in your way if you've got something worth saying, and if you say it earnestly and persuasively. So don't hold back in fear that weak grammar will defeat you. It won't.

When Julius Heil, late governor of Wisconsin, addressed a group of people the day after Pearl Harbor, he said, "Chentalmun! Ve iss attacked!" Yet thousands of Wisconsinites loved him—and voted his way on many an issue. Fiorello La Guardia, once mayor of New York City, butchered the king's English—but he was an articulate and successful political leader and a good mayor. In the campaign of 1948 presidential candidate Harry Truman tossed his carefully written speeches to the wind and talked in such mixed-up language that farmers and factory workers winced. But Mr. Truman ran through the campaign as a fighter—and came out a winner. Many a public statement of President Eisenhower, acknowledged leader of the Western world and object of the respect and affection of millions of Americans, runs blithely along, forgetful of syntax, yet is meaningful and often inspiring.

Granted, you'll sometimes find a sniper who will take pot shots at your split infinitives or your end-of-sentence prepositions. But the sniper is rarer than you think. And even he will lay his pistol down if what you say is worth saying.

The truth of the matter is that everyday talking in business and industry has little in common with classical speechmaking and painstakingly prepared oratory, such as marked the Golden Ages of Greece and Rome and the British House of Commons in the eighteenth and nineteenth centuries. Those orations were good for their purposes and well suited to their occasions. But people who live and talk in the rush and excitement of everyday events in our time have neither time nor need for such approaches to perfection. Indeed, painfully contrived grammatical precision can sometimes build a barrier between a businessman and certain kinds of listeners. It can give them the feeling they're beneath him rather than with him.

In the final analysis, most people really listen to the person more than they do to the words or the grammar. A twenty-year-old girl, foreign born, talks to a small group of Americans. She has lived in a Communist-run country. She has seen her family separated and her father shot. She's deeply moved by the threat of communism. As she talks you can hear a pin drop. Her hearers hang on every word and gesture. The fact that her talk is almost completely ungrammatical doesn't matter to her hearers. They listen because she talks from deep emotion and deep conviction. They hear her—not her ungrammatical blunders.

All this is not to say that sloppily built sentences are an asset when you talk to people. They aren't. In fact, the rules of grammar reflect man's need for uniform patterns in communication so that people who talk to each other will understand each other. Following these rules, the flow of thoughts becomes orderly and communication takes place. In the same way, traffic regulations provide a pattern by which you and other drivers avoid mix-ups and arrive at your destinations. Make no mistake—grammar is important. It's a barrier to communication only when it becomes a strait jacket—when it denies you the freedom to say, in your own best way, what you want to say.

So, if you're guilty of ignorant and offensive abuses of grammar, get yourself a grammar book and study it. You can find one in any public library—even a small library. Go after the rules the same way you go after the standards and practices stated in your business office manual, or the instructions for installing and operating a new machine in your plant, or the procedures for checking credit ratings in your office. First, master them. Then, having mastered them, you can command them to your own purposes.

## Why You Needn't Worry about Your Voice

A rich, resonant voice is a good thing to have. But you can get along very well with what you have, even if it's rasping or high-pitched or twangy. Arthur Godfrey's voice sounds like gravel being churned in a cement mixer. The late Fred Allen's voice was a mixture of rusty razor blades and sandpaper. Theodore Roosevelt's voice was high-pitched—almost soprano. The voice of Elmer Davis, one of the best of World War II radio commentators, had a heavy Indiana twang. And a courageous Middle Westerner, whose larynx has been removed and who must therefore talk through a tube in his throat, has become a successful salesman though he sounds like a man with a bad cold.

No, success doesn't hinge on your voice alone. It hinges far more on what you say and the clarity and conviction with which you say it. But if you are genuinely worried about the way you sound—and if this worry keeps you from speaking up when you have something to say—you can do any or all of three things:

• *Go to a professional who makes a business of training voices.* This is a long, hard pull. And unless you're prepared to go all the way with it, it can do you more harm than good. Why? Because you'll become even more self-conscious than you are. Cowed by this self-consciousness, you'll keep on shying away from opportunities to talk in the hope of reaching a perfection that you may never reach.

• *Get a good book on voice training.* Ten minutes a day with the right book and a set of exercises can work a lot of changes in the way you sound. But you must accept the fact that do-it-yourself voice training takes time. You won't reach perfection in a week—even in six months.

• *Use a playback recorder.* Record your voice, then listen to it. Maybe it sounds better than you thought. Whether better or worse, though, you'll see ways to improve if you listen objectively. Take the flaws you discover one at a time, correct each one in turn, then move on to the next. Don't stop with voice quality. Go on to diction —the way you enunciate your words. Lazy lips and a lazy tongue can make you sound indifferent, careless, even slovenly. Next time you have a chance to do so, check your diction with a tape recorder. You may get a rude shock—and some clear ideas about how you can improve.

Above all, keep your own personality in mind. The voice you want is the one that reflects the best qualities in your personality. If you're calm and deliberate, you don't want a booming voice. But if you're an outdoors man or a man of action, a booming voice may be just what you do want.

## What to Do with Your Hands

Best thing to do with your hands is to forget them. By and large, they'll take care of themselves. That is, they'll adapt themselves to the needs of the moment and the occasion.

People who worry about their hands and arms are afraid to do what comes naturally. A salesman talks to his sales manager about a new idea. It's exciting, and he's absorbed in it. He doesn't fret about what to do with his hands. Yet his hands move eloquently. They reflect his excitement. They become a part of his talk, adding color and movement to what he says, just as the inflections of his voice do. A stenographer gets upset about the air-conditioning unit that's blowing down her back. She lectures the office manager— with gestures. An insurance man argues with an adjuster—and his gestures back up his emphases.

The secret of the matter is that when your mind and your feelings act in concert with what you're saying, your body joins in with action. In a sense, your gestures are reflexes. They come naturally. When they come any other way, they look mechanical, contrived.

If you are like most people, there are three ways to make sure your gestures will come naturally:

• *Talk about familiar things.* If you talk about the things you know about—facts, figures, procedures, experience, people—your gestures will be free and natural. They'll reflect your confidence and assurance. Unfamiliar subjects will make you tense and fidgety, and make your gestures jerky and wooden.

• *Know where you're headed.* If your purpose in talking is clear in your own mind, your gestures will be firm and positive. If you're unsure of the reason for getting to your feet or if you're unprepared to talk, your gestures are likely to be aimless and fumbling.

• *Be eager to share your ideas with other people.* With this attitude your gestures will become free and outgoing.

But suppose you aren't like other people. Suppose you do talk about familiar things, know where you're headed, and want to share your ideas with other people—and still worry about your hands and arms. You can do several things: If this is a sitting-down talk, fold your hands in your lap. Or fold your arms. Or let your hands rest on the arms of your chair. Or fold them on the desk in front of you. Or hold your papers in them. Or light a cigarette (if smoking is in order). If it's a standing-up talk, step around behind the chair you've just got up from and rest your hands on the back of the chair. Or hold onto the sides of the lectern in front of you. Or lean slightly forward against your desk, bracing yourself with your hands palms down. Or push a book or some papers around. You may even put your hands in your coat pockets from time to time. Or grasp the lapels of your coat from time to time. Best of all, though—and toughest of all—is to discipline your hands simply to relax at your sides, moving them only when movement comes spontaneously from your thought and your imagery.

## What to Do about Your Mannerisms

Don't fret about your little peculiarities. They're part of your personality. Unless they're offensive, overdone, or in bad taste, they can add to the impact of your personality. Professor William T.

Laprade, long a popular professor of history at Duke University, used to blow his cheeks in and out several times after making a special point in his lecture. Edward R. Murrow, radio and television news analyst and commentator, is seldom without a cigarette in his fingers. Other people—even the best of speakers—hitch their belts, jingle the change in their pockets, wave their pencils, tug at their ears, or pull at their chins. These mannerisms don't hurt them. In fact, they may even become badges of recognition—and thus personal assets. For example, Charles Collingwood, who sometimes replaces Mr. Murrow, has been advised not to smoke while on camera lest his listeners think he's imitating Mr. Murrow.

On the question of mannerisms, the answer is the same as for what to do with your hands. Do what comes naturally. Just be sure your mannerisms are inoffensive. And be sure to keep them under control. That is, don't let them run so free that they distract your hearers from what you're saying, and don't let any one of them run on so long that it becomes tedious. In the final analysis, if you put all your thought and energy into communicating your ideas, your mannerisms probably will vanish altogether.

## Why Physical Handicaps Shouldn't Bother You

Think of the last time you saw a handicapped person—say, a blind man—face up to an important communication situation. The fact that he was blind really gave him an advantage, because his hearers admired his courage in speaking up in spite of his handicap. Indeed, physical attractiveness or unattractiveness shrinks into unimportance when you compare it with the heart and mind of the talker. Mahatma Gandhi, for example, weighed a scant 82 pounds. Franklin D. Roosevelt wore heavy steel braces on his legs. And Helen Keller is deaf, dumb, and blind. Yet each of these people touched millions of lives. Unmindful of their own physical handicaps, they grasped eagerly at every opportunity to communicate.

So, if you have some sort of physical handicap, don't let it keep you from taking part in conversations, discussions, and meetings. Your hearers will either (1) drown all consciousness of your handicap in their consciousness of what you're saying or (2) credit you with a bonus score because of your courage. Handicapped or not, you'll find the principles for commanding attention, stirring interest, and getting action are the same. These principles are fully developed elsewhere in this book. Here they are, very briefly:

• Speak with clear purpose. State it clearly for yourself—and for those who hear you. (Chapter 7)

• Know your listener or listeners. Word your purpose, state your thoughts, and seek to motivate those who hear you in terms of their own experience. (Chapters 1 and 7)

• Use concrete examples, familiar language. (Chapters 5 and 9)

• Use eye contact. (Chapters 1 and 2)

## Summary

Most of our fears about talking before groups and in business relationships are groundless. Groundless because our little shortcomings loom larger to us than to the people we talk to—or because, with so little effort, we could correct the faults that make us fearful of ourselves.

If your palms get clammy at the thought of talking in a group, if you quiver at the prospect of presenting a matter to your business associates or your boss, grasp your tension firmly and convert it into an asset. Most of us perform better under tension anyhow. Exploit the little opening tricks that will delay your start while you bring your thoughts to order. Nervousness is universal. All effective communicators have it—and do pretty well in spite of it (or because of it). So can you.

If you don't have a store of elegant words at your command, you may be better off than you think. Lots of the people who do have such elegant words in store fail to communicate because of those very words. In the hustle and bustle of everyday living, the clear, simple, purposeful word will serve you better.

And if you're reluctant to make a display of your lack of grammar, your voice, your mannerisms, or your physical handicap, take heart. Nobody pays as much attention to them as you do. What really counts in communication is what you are and what you say—not how you look or sound.

On the other hand, don't mistake the intent and substance of this chapter. If you think it means that you should accept mediocrity and self-satisfaction as good things, you're dead wrong. What this chapter says is this: You may be better than you think you are, and you shouldn't let your little shortcomings frighten you away from opportunities to talk. In fact, in some ways your shortcomings may be assets. But even if you do discover that you're better than you think you are, there's doubtless still room for improvement. How? By controlling your nervousness (not eliminating it). By studying your dictionary and your grammar book. By concentrating on what you say, not on how you look or sound. By smoothing down the rough edges of your voice and diction. And by wording your purpose clearly, understanding your listeners, keeping your words and examples concrete and familiar, and maintaining good eye contact with your hearers.

*Exercises*

1. There are three passages below. All of them are studded with heavy, multisyllabic words. Rewrite each passage without using more than two words of more than two syllables. Don't count "-ing's," "-ed's," etc.

*a.* Streamlining the circulation of engineering alterations brings economies of approximately $52,000 annually. The reduction in disbursements is a derivative of more efficient utilization of personnel, paperwork, and equipment. Reduction in personnel resulted exclusively from improvements in allocation of time rather than from dismissals.

*b.* The political novel has traditionally been a novel of indignation, animated by liberal ideology. Contrariwise, this new novel is a departure from this tradition. Essentially conservative in sentiment, it is dedicated to morality in politics rather than to ideology. The United States emerges as its collective hero.

*c.* The financial situation is undoubtedly lugubrious, particularly as envisioned by the financiers' mentality. But those who point admonitory fingers find it practically impossible to awaken interest. Some ascribe this to apathy or a profound confidence, as symbolized by the answer citizens occasionally give when discussing such complications: "All things will eventuate in an acceptable conclusion because fortuitous circumstances are on our side."

2. Invite a neighbor or friend to your home for the evening. Set up a recorder and make a record of your conversation. Play it back in his presence. Ask him to make notes about your voice and expression as you listen. Do the same yourself. Compare your notes with his, then set up a course of do-it-yourself drills and exercises that will improve your voice.

3. In the privacy of your home or office work out a simple, short talk about safety or health, using an example from your own experience. Rehearse it a few times. Then add all the unnecessary mannerisms you can think of—straightening your tie, mopping your brow, rattling your keys, and the like. Finally, go through the talk again, this time concentrating on your communication and leaving off the mannerisms. On this last time around, be sure you don't pick up some new mannerisms.

4. Repeat Exercise 3 above, but use gestures instead of mannerisms. Your aim at last: To feel comfortable even when your hands hang idle and relaxed at your sides, and to use your hands only when they respond to your own feelings.

*We have a lot of meetings at our plant. How can we stop wasting time?*

## 13

# How to Use Your Talking Skills
# to Improve the Meetings You Run

Take a sheet of paper and do a little arithmetic as you answer the following questions:

In the course of your regular work, how many meetings—group discussions, conferences, and the like—did you attend last month?

How many hours of your own time did these meetings take?

How many other people took part or attended?

What was the total number of man-hours given to these meetings by all of you?

How many of these total man-hours were wasted in aimless talk

about trifles, side issues, and personalities? How many were wasted
by habitual "aginners"? Chronic complainers? Long-winded talkers
who like to hear the sound of their own voices but really have nothing to say? Rambling talkers who never come to the point? Chairmen and discussion leaders who have no firm purpose in calling a
meeting?

Among the people who attended these meetings, what's the average value (in dollars) of an hour's time?

How much money did these wasted hours cost your organization
last month?

This last figure probably gives you a rude jolt. Think how well off
you'd be if you could add just this one month's figure to your
monthly income. Think how big your annual bonus would be if
your whole group could divide the year's total losses among yourselves.

Now think back and analyze what went on at these meetings. If
they were like all too many meetings, you can charge up most of
those wasted hours to chairmen, conference leaders, and supervisors who don't know how to keep a meeting moving toward its
objective—who don't know how to get through a meeting efficiently
and make it meaningful and gainful to everybody who attends. If
this is your weakness—if some part of these wasted dollars can be
charged up to your lack of know-how in running meetings—read
on. This chapter is for you.

## What the Leader of a Meeting Should Do

The conference or discussion leader is like the conductor of a
symphony orchestra. The conductor has a plan—the musical score
that lies on the music stand in front of him. With the score he brings
all the elements of the orchestra into play—violins, trumpets, cellos,
flutes, cymbals, trombones, clarinets, tubas, English horns, tympans,
and all the others. Under his baton each instrument adds its own
peculiar voice to the whole orchestration. He plays one off against
the other, keeps them all under control, blends their voices to
achieve his harmonies. He reconciles—brings into agreement—the

conflicting musical themes that run through the score, thus comes at last to the end of the composition with a feeling of achievement and completion.

Like the orchestra conductor, the leader of a meeting must manage all the various people who make up the group. His skill shows up in how well he can do the five following jobs:

1. *Stimulate ideas.* That is, life each person in the group up to a creative level, so that he gives his best to the discussion.

How can you do this? Well, you know in advance what the subject of the meeting will be. With the subject in mind, review the skills and experience of each person who will attend in the light of what he can contribute to the discussion. Then, as some one aspect of the subject comes to light in the meeting, invite the comment of the man whose skill and experience qualify him to talk most meaningfully about that aspect. If you show your need for him and your confidence in him this way, he'll give his best.

Another way to stimulate ideas: As leader, watch for ways to make provocative statements or ask provocative questions as the meeting moves along. You might even prepare some ahead of time. Suppose, for instance, you've got a meeting of foremen coming up. The subject for discussion: absenteeism. You might throw out this question at an appropriate place in the discussion: "They tell me the rayon plant across town has no absentee problem at all. How do you account for that?" Or "I've heard some complaints that our plant isn't as attractive as it ought to be. Any comments on that?" Or "This is a brand-new problem for us. We didn't have it six months ago. What's happened?"

2. *Inspire teamwork.* Sometimes this isn't easy. People like to argue—and argument, in a sense, is conflict. People get angry. Or they reveal their selfish, personal motives. Or they get defensive about their views. Or they bring personalities into the discussion.

Usually, though, you can create a teamwork approach in spite of situations like these.

First step is to set the stage properly—when you open the meeting. Take that meeting on absenteeism up above. You could start it off this way:

"This meeting is about absenteeism. Every week it's getting to be a bigger problem for us. As an offhand guess I'd say it's now cutting our production down by about 10 per cent. Our machine operators are giving us the most trouble. That's Shelton's department. But Shelton's trouble hits us all. Because if his department doesn't produce, the work slows down all along the line—plating, assembly, and packing. Absenteeism is a contagious thing, too. Just in the last couple of weeks it has picked up in other departments. What I mean is this: Even if the trouble is mostly in Shelton's department, it's a problem for all of us. It cuts down on our productivity, makes our weekly reports look bad, runs our costs up, and cuts our profits. I want us to try to find an answer for Shelton's problem. If we do that, we'll be solving some of our own problems, too."

What's achieved by this kind of stage setting? Just this: You show that the meeting has a constructive purpose. And you show that the subject has a bearing on every member of the group and that every member has a stake in what's said and done about it. With this approach, participants are less likely to attack Shelton for his shortcomings, more likely to help him (and the company) find an answer to the problem.

The second step in inspiring teamwork is to probe for the constructive element in every nonconstructive comment, however ill-tempered, ill-conceived, far afield, or poorly stated it may be. Often this will take some doing—even some stretching of your imagination. Once you find that constructive element, announce it to the group—but attribute it to the speaker.

Go back to Shelton's problem—absenteeism. Crawford, assembly-line foreman, is angry because absenteeism in Shelton's department last week caused three assembly-line workers to stand idle for two half days. Crawford takes out after Shelton: "I can't see any excuse for running a department as loosely as you run yours. I don't think you can stand up to your people. What you need is the guts to fire a couple of them."

Right there is where you come into the act. "Thanks, Crawford," you say. "I think you've added something to our discussion. We probably ought to take a new look at discipline throughout the plant. Maybe we're all too lax. Would you, Shelton, and Rodinski form yourselves into a task force, study the problem, and bring in some recommendations a week from now?"

This gambit will nudge Crawford off his selfish center—shift his attack from Shelton to the problem. You've probably seen skillful leaders do the same thing time after time in meetings. The more such a person as Crawford argues, the more the leader meets him with appreciation for his "contribution" to the discussion. At first the man is confused. But the strategy swings him around and he soon comes to realize that—in spite of himself—he's not really engaged in argument but is contributing to the answer for a problem. Gradually, as the leader reveals this contribution, the chip slips off his shoulder and he begins to see the others as companions rather than opponents. This way, he accepts his place on a team whose only adversary is the problem to be solved.

3. *Narrow the areas of conflict.* No use trying to fight a dozen battles at once. That way, you and the group will wind up in a brawl —or simply thrash around in the same spot and come to no conclusion.

There are four ways in which you can keep the area of conflict narrow, as follows:

• *Start with a clearly defined subject and a target time for closing.* Make these elements—subject and time—prime parts of your planning. Make the subject narrow enough to explore in the time allotted for the meeting. Announce the subject at the outset of the meeting, state how long the meeting will last, and tell what you hope to accomplish by the time the meeting is finished. This way, you'll give the group a sense of direction, purpose, and pace—a firm but invisible barrier to those who might want to go astray.

Here, for instance, is a typical opening that will get a group discussion off to a purposeful start:

"In our meeting today we're going to discuss discipline among our employees. That is, how we can get employees to observe our working rules, and what we should do when they violate the rules. It's now eleven o'clock. We'll stop at noon—in time for lunch. If we're going to cover the ground marked out for us, we can't wander off into other areas of discussion. When we break up I hope we will have framed some specific recommendations about which we can talk with top management and union officials. Now let's start in."

• *State the common ground.* If you can point out the common ground that the people in your group share, you may save them the time, trouble, and debate they would need to discover it for themselves.

For example, pick it up where you left off just above—same meeting, same subject, same people:

"Now let's start in. First I'd like to throw out a few remarks for background. Some of us have more discipline problems than others. Shelton, for example, suspended two men a week ago for smoking in a no-smoking area and another for 'borrowing' a power drill and trying to take it home. I believe Crawford has had only one case—an assembler who was suspended for being chronically late. But I believe we all agree that these kinds of violations are increasing. We also agree that they're a problem in every department. We agree that no one person among us is entirely to blame. And we agree that the problem won't hold still—either we do something to improve the situation, or the situation will get worse. Finally, we agree that whatever we're going to do, we must do fast. It's our task now to find out what we should do. With these points in our minds, would you like to tell us your views, Shelton?"

• *Keep the focus on the subject.* If your group is like most groups, it will stray from time to time, in spite of all you can do. Talkers will veer over into borderline subjects, reminisce, or drag personalities in. But in meetings of this kind there are always occasional pauses—swiftly passing moments when a man stops for breath, halts to gather his thoughts, or fumbles for a word. Also there's always that moment between the end of one man's comments and the beginning of another's. If you're a good leader you'll seize these moments to haul the discussion back to its base. And if the talk gets too far afield, you should feel no reluctance about breaking into the middle of a man's comments and bringing him back to base. After all, it's one of your obligations as discussion leader to conserve the time of the other people in the group.

Can you do this tactfully? Yes. In most situations a friendly reminder is enough: "I know you've had some breakdowns of your plating equipment recently, Rodinski. But I believe we could finish up this meeting on time if we got back to employee discipline." Or "Let me interrupt you a moment, Chaney, to say that the lubrication schedule will be the subject of a meeting next month. Right now we're talking about discipline. I feel sure you can help us by telling us how you see this problem." Or "We're not here, McGowan, to discuss the character of the industrial engineer. We're here to talk about discipline among employees. I'm sure you've got something helpful to say on this subject."

In other situations, it may take more than a friendly reminder to bring the discussion back to base. You may have to be downright firm. If you do have to cope with this situation, face it. Call the offender to order, politely but positively, and tell him bluntly that he's wasting the time of the group. You owe your group your best efforts to protect it against woolgathering, insolence, ignorance, name calling, and other kinds of time wasting.

• *Explore one area at a time.* Break the subject up into manageable pieces, feed them one by one to your group, clean up each one before you move on to the next.

To see how you can do this, go on with the meeting about discipline in a manufacturing plant. If you were leader of the group you might very well break up the general subject into several headings, each of which you would throw out for discussion in turn, as follows:

NUMBER OF DISCIPLINE CASES: How many in the past month? Is this more than in the month before? Is the increase big enough to warrant action?

KINDS OF VIOLATIONS INVOLVED: What kinds of rules were broken most often? Safety rules? Operating rules? Procedural rules? Rules of personal conduct?

CAUSES OF VIOLATIONS: Is union leadership (or lack of it) the root of the trouble? Poor housekeeping? Management indulgence? An ill-advised or poorly stated rule? Bad working conditions? Poor hiring practices? Inadequate training? Weak communications?

ACTION TO BE RECOMMENDED: What should management do? What should the union (or the employees) do? What rules need changing? Should enforcement be stepped up? Should penalties be lighter, or heavier?

4. *Keep the group under your control.* You're the leader. So act like a leader. Make your personality the dominant one. But do it without being domineering.

This is not a matter of personality and tact alone, though these are important. To keep a meeting under control you need confidence —the confidence that comes from purpose and direction. And you need a firm hand. There will be those who, wittingly or unwittingly, try to take the meeting away from you and run off with it themselves. If you give in to them, your meeting will be lost—and so will you. Later (Chapter 14) you'll find out how to handle these difficult people. For the present, suffice it to say that these people can be handled—by charm, by wit, by tact, by firmness, by brute strength of character, by rationalizing, or by understanding, depending on the situation and the person involved.

5. *Fix the purpose of the meeting,* shape the procedure that will best achieve that purpose, and then move relentlessly toward that purpose. The next part of this chapter will tell you briefly what a leader needs, what are the four most common types of meetings, and how you can plan and run these meetings.

## What a Leader Needs

Your job as leader is to plan the meeting, to stimulate the participants, to guide and integrate their thinking, and to bring the meeting to an effective close.

To do this complex job you'll need certain traits and attitudes. If you don't have these traits and attitudes now, don't despair. You can acquire and cultivate them. Here's what you will need to run a meeting successfully:

• *Faith in group achievement.* You must accept this fact: Though groups can turn into mobs—become unstable, highly suggestible, and even vicious—they can also be sound, wise, steady, and cooperative. If you show your faith in the group, its members will respond with trust in your leadership and with their best talents.

• *An understanding of people.* Individuals, that is. Before you damn a man for being unruly or stubborn or dense, try to find out why he acts the way he does. Understanding him is more than half of the job of getting him to give his best.

• *Ability to "take it."* Sometimes you may feel the people in your group are sabotaging you. Try to remember this: Some people just aren't used to making contributions to a group effort. They aren't used to deliberating, investigating, or evaluating. They tend to battle—and often make the leader the enemy. Give these people time. Be patient with them. They'll gain experience—see you finally as a skillful leader and pattern their conduct after yours.

• *Flexibility.* Don't cling to rigid rules of order just for the rules' sake. Use rules only to the extent that they help the group to function efficiently. But don't let them stifle discussion or imagination.

• *A gift for listening.* It's the best way of understanding the people in your group—and the only way of seeing how they look at their problems and their world.

• *Straight thinking.* You must be on guard against turns that lead the discussion away from the subject; adroit enough to bring the talk back to the issue or problem under discussion, and sensitive enough to see when an apparent drift away from the subject is really not a drifting at all but the revelation of a new facet of the subject.

• *Ability to articulate.* You must be able to put group ideas and group goals into brief, pointed language, throw in meaningful comments quickly and clearly, turn the group's groping phrases into crystal-clear phrases, sum up succinctly, and state results with strong impact.

• *Skill in evaluation.* You must be alert to conflicts of opinion, spot the main issues, lead the group on to the next point when the time is ripe, distinguish between what's pertinent and not pertinent, and sense the time when the group is ready to be led from discussion to conclusion.

• *Objectivity.* You don't have to be cold and impersonal. But you mustn't let your feelings and background stand in the way of logic.

If you must state a personal opinion, make it clear to the group that it is personal.

• *Personal warmth.* Use all your sensitivity to the feelings, the motivations, and the needs of the people in your group. Make each person in the group feel you're interested personally in him and that you place a high value on his ideas.

• *Know-how.* Know-how in the field of the problem under discussion, plus know-how about running a meeting. Both ways, you'll build the group's confidence in you as a leader.

• *A sense of humor.* Humor in the best sense, that is. You don't have to be a funny man. Indeed, you're better off not being one. The man with a sense of humor is the man who sees things in perspective—sees people's little failings against the background of their upbringing and their needs, handles their anger and indignation with a light but sympathetic touch, welcomes laughter as relief from tension, and resolutely seeks the cheerful and constructive side of everything that comes to light.

## Four Types of Meeting—and How to Run Them

By and large, meetings fall into one or another of four general types: problem solving, instruction giving, information giving, and idea generating. Each has its own purpose. Each calls on the leader to take a different approach.

Take them one by one:

### 1. The Problem-solving Meeting

Of all four types, this comes closest to pure discussion and asks the least active participation by the leader. In fact, if things go well —that is, if the people taking part are knowledgeable and creative and if they steer freely toward their purpose—the leader will have little indeed to do. He might even vanish from the scene.

*What subjects are suitable.* What are some typical problems that a problem-solving meeting can attack gainfully? Here are a few:

A bottleneck in the production (or accounting, maintenance, transcribing, filing, admitting, or personnel) department.

A sales dropoff in an upstate district—or in a product line.

An accident hazard that a new machine (or a new process, a new material, or a new building) will create.

The communications obstacles in putting across a new policy (or rule or procedure).

The antagonism of employees to a new procedure (or rule, policy, or personality).

Dissatisfaction with working schedules (or days off, shift switches, or working conditions).

Inability to interpret reports (or codes or instructions).

Failure to reach potential markets (or production goals or profit goals).

*How to get ready.* Start early, well in advance. Get your own creative processes going. Study all aspects of the problem—how it affects others now, and how the solutions your group may suggest might make life easier or harder for others. Study the members of your group, so you'll know what to expect of them and how to handle the situations they may create. Track down previous reports on the problem—or minutes of earlier meetings on the same problem. Define the purpose of the meeting to your own satisfaction, settle on an orderly approach to the various aspects of the problem, and make notes that will guide your own thinking. Tell your superiors about the coming meeting, thus alert them to the probability that recommendations may come out of it.

*What the pattern is.* Problems like those above, thrown out before a discussion group, call for a fairly uniform approach. It's your role as leader to plan this approach and to steer the group along the lines laid down. You should lead the discussion through these five steps:

• *State and clarify the problem.* You should take the first crack at this. Try to fit the problem into one clear sentence. Then invite the group to go to work on changing and clarifying it. Members of the group may want to bring their own experience and special knowledge to bear on the statement of the problem. Unless you get such clarification at the outset, you'll leave the door open for quibbling—maybe even quarreling—in later discussion. Why? Because some of your people will discover that they didn't know what others meant by certain words or phrases used at the beginning.

For instance, suppose you call a meeting of nurses to discuss their dissatisfaction with daily work schedules. If they discover later in the meeting that the problem as stated forbids them to discuss free weekends and vacations, they'll be a pretty unhappy lot. The discussion probably will end up in annoyance and frustration, and you'll have a still unsolved problem on your hands.

But if you, as leader, give these nurses freedom at the beginning to help define the problem—or freedom to revise the definition as the discussion develops—chances are you'll get a satisfying and constructive discussion.

Once you and your group have agreed on a statement of the problem, move on to the next step.

• *Marshal the facts.* The facts will show the dimensions of the problem—whether it's big, trifling, or not really a problem at all.

Go along with the nurses just above. How has this work-scheduling problem been showing up? What are the symptoms? If patients complain that Miss Caldwell is waspish, if Miss Ivey points out that she and Miss Hooper have worked three successive weekends, if Miss Petrov has had to go away for a rest cure, and if Miss McKinley collapsed in the operating room a few days ago, you'll probably get agreement that something is wrong, seriously wrong, with the work schedule and that the group had better get busy and find an answer to the problem. But if you find that Miss Ivey has worked three successive weekends as a private arrangement with Miss Volkel, so Miss Volkel could enjoy some weekend house parties, the group doesn't really have a work-scheduling problem. Miss Ivey, to be sure, does have a problem—her relationship with Miss Volkel. But that's not a problem for group discussion or group solution.

• *Get at the causes.* Let's say production is slowing down in your department. That's a real problem, whatever your department may be—accounting, assembly, stenography, maintenance, manuscript editing, or something else.

As discussion leader it's your role to spur the search for causes.

Urge the group to speak freely and openly—to say whatever comes off the top of the head. Seek answers from the people who are directly involved in the slowdown—they're likely to know many of the facts. Seek answers also from those who aren't directly involved —they may take a fresh, objective approach, see causes that are invisible to those who are close to the problem.

You'll probably come up with a long list of causes—some valid, others invalid. But as the exploration moves along the group will gradually boil them all down, fix on the standouts, and thus isolate the causes of real magnitude.

As leader, you can speed the process (being careful, though, not to cut off the flow of the discussion) by snatching favorable moments to review, synthesize, summarize, and otherwise point up and steer the discussion. You'll find some commonly accepted ways of doing this in the following typical lead-in sentences:

"Let me see if I've got your meaning clearly in mind, Winkler. If I understand you right, this is what I gather from your comment."

"I'm glad you brought that out, Thompson. It throws more light on what Sprague said a few minutes ago. You and Sprague may have put your finger on the root of all our trouble."

"Funny how things begin to take shape when you get them out in the open. I believe we now begin to see the pattern. To me, it looks this way..."

"I'd like to add a little something—go a bit beyond what you said, Baskovic. It may add scope to our view of the problem."

• *Move on to solutions.* With the causes agreed upon, the group now can suggest solutions. It's up to you to take the lead—to announce that the time has come to switch from cause-seeking to answer-seeking. This part of the discussion will develop in a more orderly way than the search for causes. Why? Because the causes you have settled on will naturally suggest solutions. Even so, you should encourage free discussion—free flow of ideas—lest you and the group miss something helpful or significant.

Your role in this part of the meeting is much the same as in the

hunt for causes—to review and summarize occasionally, to synthesize, to expedite, and to steer. And to do it tactfully, helpfully,
pleasantly, and constructively.

• *Verify the findings.* Glossy theories splinter pretty easily against
hard realities. That's why you must get your group to put its solutions to the test. Granted, the group can't very well carry out laboratory tests under controlled conditions. Nor can it be sure its answers
will work under all circumstances. But you can urge your group to
lay its solutions down alongside the everyday realities of the plant
or the office—the processes and procedures involved, the people
concerned, and the tangled interrelations of activity. Better to "de-
bug" the solutions at the conference table than in the shop or office.

Suppose your group has been wrestling with the problem of communication in the department. It has worked out an answer—reor-
ganize so the top man in the department has only three men report-
ing directly to him instead of eight.

Looks fine on paper—and sounds good in theory. But get your
group to put it up against the personalities involved—and you begin
to see trouble, real trouble. Smith is taciturn. Hodges is jealous of
McWhorter. Silverman is a lone wolf. Perez is an apple polisher.
Hamilton is inarticulate. Jamieson is a patsy for every rumor that
comes along. And Irving is trigger-tempered. The fact is, no man
in the group would willingly let another sit next to the top man.

In these circumstances the proposed reorganization just isn't the
right answer. Maybe another kind of reorganization would work.
Or maybe the workable answer isn't reorganization at all, but something entirely different. Good thing if your group can find this out,
too, before you try to make this untried answer work. It's your job
as leader to see that the group does find it out—to hold the answer
up before the group until it has been explored, probed, tested, and
weighed in terms of hard reality.

### 2. *The Instruction Meeting*

In this kind of meeting your role as leader is more open—more in
the center of the stage—than in the problem-solving meeting. This

time, you're in a selling role. Even so, it's a pretty subtle selling role, because you'll do your best instructing when you get the group to join you in moving toward an objective.

*What subjects are suitable.* Typical objectives for the instruction meeting would include the following, for example:

To explain a procedure in bookkeeping—or in paper work or material handling or interviewing or preparing written reports.

To train foremen in human relations skills.

To illustrate techniques in handling customers—or in running a machine or making a repair or answering the telephone.

To develop the skill of listening among insurance adjusters—or among department-store complaint handlers or social workers, or hotel desk managers.

*How to get ready.* For the instruction meeting you need good preparation. To begin with, you need a plan. A plan will help you work with seeming ease and spontaneity. It will help you stimulate your group to think and take part. What's more, it will help you guide the thinking of the group, keep discussion on the main line, move logically from one stage to the next, stress the key points, anticipate problem situations, and bring the meeting to an effective close. Your plan should include a statement of the purpose of the meeting, a logical organization and arrangement of the subject matter, examples that will explain or point up the key aspects of the subject, some provocative questions to throw at the group, and your conclusions.

Many a meeting, though, requires more than mental preparation. You may have to make physical preparations as well. If you do, make a check list of mechanical aids you'll need—charts, films, paper, pencils, chalk, blackboard, signs, notebooks, ash trays, and the like. Also make a check list—just to be sure your meeting won't fall flat on its face—that will assure you of an assigned meeting room, ventilation, heat, light, seats, projector, screen, and sound amplification.

*What the pattern is.* As leader, you'll want to follow the best pattern for the instruction meeting. It goes like this:

• *Set the stage.* Open by saying that you have an objective to reach, not a problem to solve. State what this objective is—to focus attention on the method, the policy, the technique, the skill, the theory, or the principle to be taught.

Why present it as an objective rather than a problem? If you let your people think you're giving them a problem to solve, they'll expect a major voice in shaping conclusions (which have already been shaped, else there'd be no reason for instruction) and they may resent your dominant part in the meeting. But if they hear the word *objective,* they'll gather that the conclusions have already been pretty well settled. They'll know that you're seeking their ideas and that you'll welcome some say in the matter from them. But they'll also know that your main purpose is to instruct—not to solve a problem.

For instance, you might open a supervisors' meeting this way:

"I've called this meeting today with one specific objective in mind. That objective is to lift the level of our skills in interviewing. I've talked with a good many thoughtful people about this subject recently, and I've done some boning up on it at home, too. I believe there are some helpful things I can suggest to you. Meanwhile, I hope you'll speak up from time to time if you have any questions, or if you have something you'd like to add from your own experience."

• *Get the group involved.* But get it involved on a contributing and participating basis—not on a conclusion-making basis.

How can you do this? Any one or more of several ways. By asking questions of the group. By staging demonstrations, using whatever props you may need—sample parts from the assembly line, typical ledger sheets, commonplace articles (like a dozen lemons) with which you can illustrate complex mechanisms and reactions (like atomic fission). By getting some member of the group to manage your props for you. By role playing. By using the blackboard. By citing case histories from the plant or the office. By making provocative statements ("Some people pretty close to our business say the company pays all of us too much money"). By asking for a show of hands on common experience or opinion. By setting up discussion panels within the group. By inviting challenge of your position or somebody else's. In fact, there's hardly an end to the devices you can command to spur your people's participation in the learning process.

• *Sum up.* Having made your points, half by stating them yourself and half by inducing group members to state them for you, you've got things fairly well crystallized. It's now your chore to bring the meeting to an end. You do this by summing up. If you've prepared properly for this meeting, you knew before the meeting began just about what you would say in your summary. Indeed, you probably brought some summarizing notes along. Also, if you've been smart about running the meeting, you've taken notes on what group members have said in the course of the meeting. Put your pre-meeting notes together with those you've taken at the meeting, and you'll come up with an effective summary in which your group members will feel—with good reason, probably—that they've contributed as much as you have to what they've learned.

Imagine, for instance, that you've reached the end of an instruction session with the three secretaries who do most of the phone answering in your office. The objective of the meeting: To make the phone a sales help in addition to its merits as a communications device. You might summarize this way:

"For my part, this has been an interesting and helpful meeting. We have all learned something from each other. Let's see if we can pull a few things together before we break up.

"We use the phones here in our office for talking to outsiders. But these outsiders can't see our faces when we talk, or our hands. And that's why nearly every one of us has made the point, in one way or another, that our voices alone—not our hands or faces—represent us when we're talking on the phone. They can make us seem pleasant, hurried, angry, bored, impatient, inviting, happy, or helpful. In one or another of those ways, we impress the people who call in here. I think that's an important thing to remember, and I'm glad you're aware of it.

"I'm especially glad to have your ideas on getting the bonus values from our telephones. Miss Turner, you remember, told us how she took the opportunity of answering a simple question a few days ago to suggest that the caller see a display of our product in a downtown store window. Miss Milstein not only made a complaining customer happy by reviewing the printed instructions with him and thus solving his problem. She also suggested that one of our attachments would make the product even more useful in this particular customer's home. And Mrs. Sloan, talking to a jobber whose shipment hadn't arrived on time, worked out a new shipping route for him, then and there. He'll get good service from now on.

"I believe we've also skirted the fringes of some other ways of making the phone work harder for us. Let me see if I can pull you over these fringes and into the heart of the matter—and at the same time make still more practical suggestions for everyday use."

From here on, you're on your own. This is the time when you state your own suggestions—when you fall back to the notes you made as you planned the objective of the meeting and wrote down, for your own guidance, what you expected your people to learn about bonus values in the telephone. With that, you bring the meeting to a close—instruction mission accomplished.

### 3. *The Information Meeting*

Here's where the leader usually plays an even stronger role—stronger than in the instruction meeting. Why stronger? Because he has the information (or most of the information) that's to be imparted to the group. Or because he has command of the people who do have the information and will impart it.

*What subjects are suitable.* What kinds of things do you talk about in an information meeting? The information you want to pass out, of course. Take a few typical situations:

The president of a company tells a meeting of employees (or department heads or directors) about the company's standing, or about its profits, or about its new profit-sharing plan.

The chief engineer of one division of a large plant tells people in another division about the operations (or problems) of his own division.

A manufacturer's installation engineer tells supervisors how a new material-handling system works.

A supervisor tells mail clerks about a new way of distributing mail.

A specialist or consultant (in safety, or quality control, or insurance, or client relationships) tells department heads how his system fits into their needs and operations.

*How to get ready.* If you're to be leader as well as the information giver, you prepare for this kind of meeting just as you do for the instruction meeting (above). That is, you must think the meeting through in advance—plan it from start to finish. But if you're to be only the leader—that is, conduct and coordinate the meeting while others impart the information—your task demands not only that kind of planning, but another kind as well. You must set up the order in which your information givers will talk, arranging the sequence logically and for best effect. And you must carve out the areas that each information giver is to talk about, plan your transition remarks as you bridge the gap from one speaker to the next, set up a time schedule with clear limits on each speaker, plan for orderly and efficient handling of questions and answers, make up your mind that no part of the meeting will overrun its allotted time, and outline in advance much of what you will say to bring the meeting to an effective end. Notes and a watch are indispensable.

*What the pattern is.* The usual pattern for the information meeting is the one-man lecture (or informal talk), followed by questions and answers. But whatever the pattern may be (and there are some variants), you're the leader. You're in control of the meeting. You control the hearers and the information (or those who impart it). And when time runs out, or when you think the ground has been thoroughly covered, it's your job to summarize and synthesize the information briefly and thus bring the meeting to a close.

Here are the most common variants from the usual pattern, any one of which (or almost any combination of which) you may set up to pass out information:

THE PANEL: You call in experts—usually outsiders. They talk as a group for a while. Then you open the meeting for questions and suggestions from the group. But you steer the panel by throwing in your own remarks or questions from time to time, by bringing in

new views and aspects for the panel to discuss, by passing opportunities to talk from one panel member to another, and by keeping any one member of the panel from running away with the show.
You control the group's questions by making yourself interlocutor
between panel and audience.

THE DIALOGUE: You get two knowledgeable persons (maybe you're
one of them) to pass questions and answers back and forth between
themselves. Usually one of the persons will ask most of the questions
and the other will answer them. Later, these two will answer
questions from the group.

THE SYMPOSIUM: You set up a group of two or more people, each
a specialist in his own field, and arrange for each to talk for a given
time on his particular field. When they've finished talking, you invite listeners to direct their questions at one member or another of
the symposium. Again, if you want to keep firm control of the meeting, you'll receive the questions from the group and relay them to
the experts as your best judgment directs.

## 4. The Idea-generating Meeting

Some people now call it brainstorming. Whatever it's called, its
purpose is the same as that of the problem-solving meeting. But
the climate and the technique of conducting it are so different from
the usual problem solving that it requires a special approach by
leader and participants alike.

Roots of brainstorming lie in Alex Osborn's book, *Applied Imagination*. One chapter in that book tells how groups in Osborn's
advertising agency sat around a table in an informal setting and laid
siege to a problem until it yielded answers. The ground rules:
Quantity of ideas the goal, rather than quality. Every person speaking up with his ideas. Hitchhiking on another's idea encouraged.
Every stated idea recorded (by a nonparticipating secretary), no
matter how wild or crazy or remote. No evaluation of ideas permitted. No criticism permitted. (Evaluation and criticism came
later, in another setting and by a different group.)

What does this every-idea-welcome, no-idea-barred approach
do? It opens the gates wide. Nobody fears criticism or mockery or

a brushoff. Everybody speaks up. Everybody is on an equal foot-
ing. There's no time lost in argument or debate. Nobody gets mad.
Everybody works together. The climate quickly becomes constructive—and electric. Once the session gets under way, the leader
practically vanishes into the group and becomes part of it, contributing his share of ideas along with the others.

*What are suitable problems?* Almost any tough, urgent problem
that requires the play of several minds is fair game for a brainstorming session. For example, here are a few typical problems:

Cost reduction on a punch press (or in monthly report making,
mailing, or interviewing).

Design of a handling device on an assembly line (or a check-
processing procedure in a bank or a paper-work form or a magazine
article).

Words and drawings or pictures for an advertisement.

Handling an unruly or profane customer.

Developing more referrals from related businesses.

Managing the Easter crowds at a church service.

Stretching the research budget to cover a new project.

*How to get ready.* Brainstorming seems like a random attack on
a problem. You deal with vagrant, spur-of-the-moment, half-formed
ideas. Yet back of every successful brainstorming session lies a well-
shaped plan. It's your job, as leader, to make that plan. Here's how:

• *Word the problem.* Keep it concrete and specific—even narrow
in scope. For instance, you'll get a better response from your group
if you limit the problem to ways of dealing with one well-known
quarrelsome customer rather than ask the group to brainstorm your
entire public relations problem.

• *Do some solo brainstorming of your own.* Do it before the meeting. Store up some ideas. They'll be useful in getting the meeting
started off. And they'll be fillers-in if the pace of the meeting slows
down.

• *Think up some provocative questions to throw into the meeting.*
Be prepared to bait a few well-chosen people, prod them, or kid
them into activity.

• *Plan the make-up of the group if you can.* Best size: six to ten people. Mix them up—men and women, standpatters and progressives, pros and cons, people from different departments, old and young—so you'll get enough conflict to stimulate ideas.

• *Be sure you know what you're doing.* Conduct of a brainstorming session requires a pretty high order of skill. So sit in on a few sessions that somebody else runs before you try one of your own. Read up on brainstorming, too. If the leader flubs the meeting, the thing can backfire. One company, for instance, turned its leaders loose without adequate training to conduct brainstorming sessions on cost reduction. Before long, the training department began to get angry phone calls. Seems costs were rising instead of falling on some products that had been brainstormed for cost reduction.

*What the pattern is.* Though brainstorming sounds utterly disorganized and catch-as-catch-can, you can be sure of a successful session if you follow a pretty regular pattern. It goes like this:

• *Set the stage.* Make the surroundings comfortable and informal. Seat the group around a table. Try to keep the top brass out. A boss might hinder free flow of ideas, might draw attention to himself rather than the problem, might not be able to keep himself from passing judgment as ideas flow.

• *State the problem.* This is up to you, as leader. For best results, select concrete problems—the kind that call for action rather than reflection and discussion. Make the problem specific, like those above. For instance, the problem of getting more referrals from other businesses is much more specific than the problem of improving public relations. In the same way, the problem of improving a training program is much more specific than that of ways to meet a manpower shortage. Above all, state the problem clearly—unmistakably.

• *Prepare the group.* Give the participants some background a few days before the session. It needn't be more than a paragraph or two, stating the problem and offering two or three sample solutions. If it's your first session as leader, be sure you give each member of the group a set of the ground rules well in advance. That way, everybody will know how to act and what to expect.

• *Explain the procedures.* The group will need explanation if brainstorming is a new experience. Charts, flipovers, flannel boards, cards and the like will help. You can get them from such organizations as Creative Thinking, Inc.

• *Warm up the group.* It sometimes takes three to five minutes to get the group in the right frame of mind. During this period you, as leader, must provide most of the ideas. Once the ideas begin to tumble out of the group, though, brace yourself for the avalanche.

• *Keep things moving.* But keep order, too. Nod your head as a sign of recognition when somebody raises his hand. Don't let any brainstormer contribute more than one idea at a time. Don't tolerate any speeches—cut them off quickly and move on to another person. If more hands fly up than you can handle, take them one at a time around the table. Don't let anybody bring a list of prepared ideas to the table—he'll inhibit the others. Encourage hitchhiking (that is, adding one idea onto another) by prearranging a fixed signal (a snapped finger, two hands raised, or something similar) and recognizing such a signal immediately.

• *Record every idea.* Have a secretary present, not to take part in the session but to put every idea on paper—every idea without exception. This will reassure the group. Nobody will be afraid his idea will be lost.

• *Stop when the time is ripe.* Usually an hour is long enough. After that, zeal begins to wane. Par for the course is about 60 ideas per hour—an idea per minute.

• *Follow up.* Some of the best ideas may come to mind after the session has closed down. Ask your group to send you memos about their delayed-action brainwaves. Put these late arrivals together with the secretary's list of ideas from the meeting. List and classify the whole lot. Then pass the finished list on to the next higher level of management for analysis, criticism, discussion, and evaluation. Fact is, the brass probably will go way beyond screening and evaluation. Why? Because such a review will offer the upper-management group opportunities for further development, elaboration, and application.

## Summary

Business meetings take time. They cost money. So, if it falls to your lot to conduct a meeting, you're duty bound to make it as gainful as possible—and thus to get the most for the time and money that you, your company, and the group invest in it.

If the ability to conduct meetings were a gift, you might have some reason to despair. But it's not a gift. It's a skill—a skill you can learn and perfect if you go at it with hard work, common sense, and a resolve to understand people and bring out their best. The chapter above will bring this skill within your grasp.

To justify the time and money it costs, your meeting must have a purpose—to solve a problem, to instruct, to pass out information. As leader you must shape that purpose and state it clearly to the group. You must settle on the meeting pattern that best suits that purpose. And you must steer the group singlemindedly toward accomplishing the purpose, all the while drawing out the best resources of your group and bringing them to bear on the problem under attack or the subject under study.

## Exercises

Take any one of the following general subjects:

Nervous tension in the plant (or office)

Cost reduction

Public (or customer) relations

Discipline

Wider markets for a product or service

Now, with your chosen subject, do the following things:

1. Frame four sets of opening remarks (including statement of purpose)—one each for a problem-solving meeting, an instruction meeting, an information meeting, and an idea-generating session.

2. Draw up an outline guide to steer the leader through each of these four meetings.

3. Prepare a set of summarizing remarks for each of these four meetings.

*I have trouble with people who want to take over a meeting and run it themselves.*

# How to Overcome Common Obstacles to Running a Meeting

Sometimes, hard as you try, you just can't get on with a meeting. It bogs down, or veers off on another track, or wanders aimlessly, or breaks up in frustration or anger, or just trails off inconclusively. First thing you know, your time is gone, everybody is weary of the whole business, and you haven't advanced an inch from where you started. The obstacles have been too much for you and your group.

It's bad enough when, in spite of all you can do, meetings founder on obstacles you foresaw and prepared for. At least you have the satisfaction of knowing you thought ahead and tried hard. But it's even worse when a meeting splinters on obstacles you didn't even expect. That's when you can feel pretty dumb—ready to chuck the whole business of running meetings, whatever the cost to your career. "Anybody should have foreseen that," you say to yourself after it's all over.

This chapter will tell you about some obstacles you might not expect unless you've had a lot of experience in conducting meetings. And it will suggest ways in which you can leap over these obstacles, thrust them aside, or skirt them. The obstacles include hard-to-handle personalities, stratagems and attitudes that can throw a meeting off its course, and that old bugaboo of group meetings—the bog-down.

## Handling Hard-to-handle People

You'll meet strange and difficult people when you lead meetings. It's your chore, as leader, to keep them in line, bring out the best in them, and protect the other members of the group from their failings.

Here are some of the types you'll surely have to deal with—and a few hints for handling them:

*Sage Sam.* He sits quietly in his chair, taking an Olympian, sometimes disdainful view of others in the meeting. He leaves to others the workaday job of wrestling with problems. It's beneath his dignity and his learning. He scorns the sometimes bumbling, impromptu words of his fellows. He contributes nothing. Instead, he holds back until the tumult and the shouting die, then rises ponderously from his chair and talks with a this-is-the-way-to-do-it-I-knew-it-all-the-time air.

How to handle him? Treat his offering as just one more contribution that will stand or fall on its own merits. Don't overlook the weak points he made. In fact, make it clear that the whole meeting might have gone better if he had contributed something rather than set himself up as judge of what others contributed. But do this helpfully, not hurtfully. Try to show him that there's more satisfaction in talking with people than in talking above them. Probe for the cause of his aloofness. Try to help him understand himself.

*Affected Al.* You can't get through to him. And he's not interested in getting through to others unless they rise to his own lofty plateau. He cloaks himself in his assumed intellectual superiority, thus hides his natural self. To talk with him, you have to speak his language, his special little codes, his special jargon. He looks down his nose at others, a little pained because they don't know this or that authority, don't have this or that business or professional background, don't hold this or that title or degree. He doesn't dislike other people. He just feels sorry for them.

When this kind gets in the way of your meeting, pin him down to cases—specific examples and facts. That will break down his pose. Ask him what action he would take to follow up his learned discourse, why he would take it, and how his experience would justify such action. Later, if you have a chance, see if you can fathom the reason for his affectation. Maybe you can bring him back to his natural self.

*Glowering Glenn.* He sees nothing ahead but depression, inflation, a world gone to the dogs. That's because of all these new ideas. They're ruining everything, he believes. He backs away from (or snarls at) every experimental approach, every symptom of an open mind, every creative move, every enthusiasm. "If it hasn't been done before, it's no good," he says.

Here's one way to handle Glowering Glenn: Just keep trying to fish something optimistic out of him. The law of averages may be against you, but you've got a sporting chance. So latch onto any clue he may drop inadvertently, any slip of his tongue, or any ambiguity he utters—anything that will give you a chance to give a constructive interpretation to his remarks. Move him just an inch, and he may give a yard.

*Timid Tim.* The world has kicked him around—and he hasn't kicked back. He's shy. He's unaggressive, neutral—eager to please but afraid to speak up or state an opinion. He'd rather die than oppose you—or anybody else. If there's one thing he dislikes, it's difference of opinion. For that reason he's not much help in a meeting.

As leader, you must bring him out. How? Search for any little sign of interest—leaning forward in his chair, a slight nod or shake of his head, a sudden glance at somebody who's talking, a smile or a frown. When you detect one of these almost furtive impulses to get involved in discussion, draw him out gently: "Tim, you look as if you had something to add to our discussion." Or "Tim, I seem to remember you got involved in a situation like this a few days ago. Would you tell us about it? It might help us solve this problem."

Above all, don't let others in the group take out after Tim. It's easy to embarrass him and drive him back into his shell. Move quickly to get in ahead of anybody who's likely to be blunt or rude to him. Make it your job to thank him for his contribution and thus build up his confidence.

*Victrola Vic.* As a child, Vic was scratched with a talking-machine needle. He's never got over it. He takes an hour to say what anybody else could say in minutes. He likes to "begin at the beginning," "fill you in on the background," "get at the underlying philosophy of this situation," "review the history of this question," "look at some remote but nevertheless related aspects of the problem." He repeats. He generalizes. He drifts. Sometimes, in fact, he gets almost incoherent, as if mesmerized by the sound of his own words. Usually, if Vic has a point at all, the group knows what it is within the first two or three minutes. Everything he says after that only clouds his meaning—and tortures his listeners.

You have to be firm with Vic—firm, but polite and pleasant. You can't let him destroy the morale of the group, as he surely will if you let him run free. Don't hesitate to interrupt him and ask him, in a friendly way, to come to the point. Or break in with some such questions as these: "Do I gather this is what you're getting at, Vic?" Or "Isn't this the same point that George made a few minutes ago? Our time is limited and we've got to move on to the next point." In short, hurry him along, crowd him, bring him to a halt. In the long run he'll be grateful to you, for this is one way you can help him improve his speaking skill.

*Blunt Ben.* This fellow thinks everybody has the same tough hide he has. Nothing stops him. He boasts of his so-called realism, insists on calling things spades even if they're not spades at all, believes truth isn't truth unless it's shocking. His favorite opening goes like this: "I'm plain spoken and honest. I believe in saying exactly what I think." His greatest joy is to view with alarm. This way, no matter how bad things become, he can always say, "It doesn't feaze me. I told you it would turn out just this way."

Some Blunt Bens are simply ignorant and noisy. Others are secretly fearful or sensitive and cloak their true feelings in bluntness.

How can you handle this sort? First you pin him down to the facts. Don't let him get by with generalizations or unfounded conclusions. Ask for his evidence. If he can't satisfy you and his other listeners this way, at least you will have revealed him for what he is—an ignorant and noisy talker. Once you establish that fact, you can let him know you're onto him and you can afford to deal with him uncompromisingly.

If he responds to your probing for facts, however, you can be pretty sure Blunt Ben's bluntness is a cover for his fear and sensitivity. It's your job to bring out his better side. You can do this by putting his facts into perspective, reinterpreting his conclusions, and thus softening the blow of his bluntness. With you to guide him, he can develop into a valuable member of your group.

*Prejudice Pete.* Pete has fixed ideas. He's immovable. Twenty years ago, for example, a certain kind of typewriter gave him a little trouble. Today it's a fine machine, but Pete won't even talk to a salesman from the company that makes it. His mind is shut tight.

Pete is a tough one. In fact, he may be so tough that you can do only one thing: Tell him that the majority will rule and that he'll have to make the best of it. But if you see even a faint clue that he'll move from his fixed position, grasp it and work at it. Ask the other members of the group to restate the thinking and the facts that led them to their conclusion. And ask Pete, in the spirit of fair play, to take another look at the ideals by which you conduct discussion—one ideal being that the members accept group conclusions when they are based on valid evidence and sound reasoning.

## How to Foil Stratagems

As you conduct more and more meetings, you'll begin to recognize the little tricks and turns that people use, deliberately or innocently, to turn a meeting aside from its purpose, to disrupt it, to win a point, or to distort somebody else's point. Doesn't matter much how these stratagems creep into your meeting, it's your job, as leader, to spot them, thwart them, and thus keep your meeting moving in the direction you've set for it.

Here are some of the most common stratagems you'll have to contend with:

*Overstatement.* Watch out for the man who's bent on coming to one conclusion—his and his alone. He overstates what the facts warrant. He generalizes without facts to support his views, offers dogmatic rather than reasoned conclusions. He brushes past proof and states questionable assertions as if he had proved them or as if they were universally accepted.

Example? Take this typical comment: "Our badly needed expansion in these good times demands a new south wing to house our research division. Our competitors have outdistanced us here. With respect to markets, we're in the Dark Ages."

Sound good? Sound valid? At first hearing, yes. But listen again. Who knows whether expansion is badly needed? Has anybody proved it? Maybe these *are* good times. But how good are they? Good enough to justify a big capital investment in a new research wing? So competitors are out front. How far out front? Are they on the right road? Do their new-product sales reflect their forward position?

It's your job as leader to protect your group against this sly assumption that things that are really debatable aren't debatable at all. And to keep your group from being carried, in one long, hazardous leap, from few facts (or no facts at all) to a sweeping conclusion. So be on guard against overstatement and the half-hidden assumption. Challenge each one. Insist on the facts. When the occasion calls for it, don't hesitate to say, "Just a minute, East-man. You moved a little too fast for me there. I don't follow you. Can we back up and look at the facts?"

*Double talk.* Maybe it's not double talk to the talker. But it is double talk to listeners. Because they don't understand what the talker is saying. He's using words they don't know—and using them so fluently, so confidently that they dare not reveal their ignorance by asking what he means. So the meaning goes right past them. Or a fruitless argument develops because they don't know what he means—or thought he meant one thing when he really did mean another.

For example: "There's bad exposure in our insurance coverage. The coinsurance clause obligates us to coverage of 90 per cent value. We would be in bad shape if a fire occurred, from the stand-point of sound value and reproductive value. We need a professional appraisal of our plant at once."

That's the controller of a company talking. He's bought the com-pany's insurance for ten years. He knows what he's talking about. But do his listeners, who probably never got deeper in insurance than to buy a general all-risk policy for their homes? "Bad exposure" could mean a poor photostat of the policy. Or it could mean that gas tanks are too close to the main building. Or it could mean simply an embarrassing tear in somebody's pants. But what does it mean in this context? And what is coinsurance? What is sound value? Reproductive value? How many people in the group know?

It's your duty to keep things clear for your group. So there's nothing at all wrong with your reminding the controller from time to time that not everybody in the group speaks his language. It's a chore you can do pleasantly and courteously. But you may have to resort to firmer tactics if some speaker persists in double talk, in spite of your warnings, with the clear purpose of misleading the group or keeping the group in the dark. That's when you have to be strong, and insist on the right of the group to know what's going on.

*Sidetracking.* You must not tolerate diversion, whether it's planned or done in innocency. The time of your people is too valuable for exploring side streets and back alleys. You've set the purpose for your meeting. Stick to it.

It's perfectly natural for the mind to stray from one subject to another. But the productive mind is the disciplined mind. Same with meetings. They need discipline to produce their best—the discipline of concentration on an issue, a problem, or subject until it yields the reward you seek. It's your job to impose that discipline without impairing the free play of minds—and without letting wandering minds lead the group afield.

Suppose you've called a meeting to review pay policies for secretaries in your office. Sam Liveson breaks into the discussion with this: "Your seniority makes me think of that girl Doris down the hall. I wish I knew what work I can and can't ask her to do. She's always negative and antagonistic. If she's overworked (and I doubt it), she sure lets everybody know about it."

Your job is cut out for you here. Get the discussion back on the track. "That seems to me to be unrelated to the question of pay policies, which is what we are here to discuss," you reply. "You're talking personalities, and we're talking policy. Let's stay on the track. We can discuss the problem of discipline, if we need to discuss it, at a later meeting."

*Stubbornness.* This can be a serious roadblock if you let it. What makes people stubborn? Why do they hold to their stated views in spite of the evidence of fact and the persuasions of the group? It's not always easy to know. But you can make some smart guesses. Stubbornness may come from prejudice, which is another way of describing a blind spot. Or it may come from fear of losing face by surrender of a position previously taken. Or it may come from a man's selfish wish to satisfy his own needs regardless of the welfare of others.

If you think stubbornness comes from prejudice, handle it in the way outlined for Prejudice Pete earlier in this chapter. If you can't bring him around on the basis of fair play and evidence, simply tell him that the majority will rule.

If you think it comes from selfish aims, try to persuade him to submerge his own need for satisfaction into the good of the whole. If that doesn't work, question him ruthlessly until he risks exposing his own selfishness and backs down in fear of embarrassment before the group.

If you think it comes from fear of losing face, provide some kind of escape hatch for him. "I'm afraid we may have misunderstood your position in the first place, Bennett," you might say. "Would you be good enough to state it for us again in different words?" Or "We all started out with agreement in principle. In fact, Hendrickson, I think you fought hardest for this principle and stated it for us more clearly than anybody else. Now if we still agree in principle, I don't believe we can be very far apart on this one detail. Would you state once more the principle for which you fought so hard, Hendrickson? Then let's come back and take another look at the detail."

*The dogmatic air.* Arrogance, aloofness, and disdain have no place in a group discussion. They not only inhibit free exchange of ideas. They also provoke anger, and very quickly switch the orientation of the meeting from problem to personality.

You must deal with this attitude promptly, calmly, and firmly. Bring out the fact that fruitful discussion can flourish only in a climate of courtesy, tact, and regard for the views and feelings of others. Let it be known that you expect a constructive approach, not a destructive one.

*Going blank.* Don't let it throw you if some member of your group clams up. He may be preoccupied temporarily with some aspect of the problem you're discussing. If so, he'll get back into the stream in a few moments. Even if he's sulking, or deliberately sabotaging the meeting, you may be able to swing him around. Whatever the cause of his silence, throw an occasional question at him. Invite him to get whatever it is off his chest: "You're sitting there in a brown study, Hamilton. I wonder if you'd tell us what's on your mind." Appeal to him on the basis of a fair hearing for all and an equal opportunity for everybody to contribute his best to the meeting.

*Cross-examination.* Some people, like some football coaches, believe that the best defense is a strong offense. To cover the weakness of their position they become aggressive—fire questions right and left in a campaign to throw their opponents into confusion.

Best way to handle this situation: Match question with question, shaping your questions to reveal the weak spots that the aggressive member wants to conceal.

*Flippancy.* A few people are pretty successful at dodging questions and issues by ridiculing them or minimizing them.

YOUR BEST PROCEDURE: Stick with the question or the issue. Come back to it again and again. Rebuild it every time it's knocked over.

*Reverence for tradition.* This is an old tearjerker. Granted, traditions and great reputations do—and should—play a strong role in conduct, and sometimes even in decisions. But they're often dragged in by the hair to support views and positions they're altogether unrelated to. And many of them have long outlived their usefulness. Many a manufacturing plant, for example, is now hemmed in by growing city slums, penalized by lack of water supplies, and burdened with heavy taxes simply because somebody invoked the ghost of old Throgmorton, who founded the company 100 years ago, saying that he would turn over in his grave if the company ever moved from its original site.

YOUR ACTION: If tradition is beside the point, say so, clearly and firmly. As for old Throgmorton, he founded the company to make a profit. It did just that. And if any tradition is to guide the company, the tradition of fair profit on investment ought to be it. The old man was fond of the site before slums surrounded it. He certainly wouldn't be fond of it today.

*Bandwagon thinking.* This is emotional, not rational. It doesn't weigh the facts. It simply follows the crowd. It's contagious—and dangerous. "Everybody else is doing it" is a weak reed to lean on when you're shaping the conclusion of a group discussion. Don't let your group members give in to that kind of argument.

Insist on objectivity. Keep your group's attention focused on the framework within which the results of the discussion must go to work. Bandwagon thinking has led some small, growing companies into mergers that never should have happened. It has lured other companies into labor relations situations that they should have avoided at all costs. And it has drawn still other companies into new product lines that would have been much better left alone.

*Tricky logic.* Proverbs are the big culprits here. Most of them make good sense some of the time. But some don't. And none of them are valid in all circumstances.

EXAMPLE: "This is the exception that proves the rule." Fact is, there are exceptions to many rules. But how can an exception make a rule true? The proverb really means, "This is the exception that puts the rule to the test." In other words, you measure the strength of the rule by the way it stands up against exceptions.

So keep your ears cocked for such tricky logic as this proverb and other old saws seem to support. Make sure they don't lead your group astray. And call the hand of anybody who tries to use them to prove a point.

## How to Keep a Meeting from Bogging Down

A meeting won't get very far without a head of steam and a track. It needs somebody—you, that is—to bring the boiler up to working pressure and keep it there, and to steer the talk down the track. Without that, a meeting is sure to bog down.

Here are several tips on keeping a meeting in motion:

*Get things off to a good start.* This is part of your business as leader. A good start is the secret of a meeting that covers all the ground laid out and moves without interruption to its end. The start creates the setting, stakes out the territory, sets the pace, and identifies the goal. The way you start will tell your group, right away, whether this is to be a gainful, thought-provoking session or a dreary, aimless waste of time.

How can you get off to a good start? Several ways. For example:

• *By tying subject and people together.* This will show your group members how the problem (or the subject) is related to their interests. Suppose you're a hospital administrator. You call a meeting of ward nurses to talk about job enlargement for nonprofessional hospital employees—nurse's aides, orderlies, porters, and the like. You hope that by the time you reach the end of the meeting you'll have a long list of suggestions for better use of these nonprofessional employees. Here's how you might open that meeting:

"I've asked you to meet with me today to talk about the kind of help you have—and need—on the wards.

"If I know nurses (and I've worked with them for nearly fourteen years now), they would be far happier and would do better work if they could get back to nursing. Today, I know, you have to sort and deliver mail, do a lot of housekeeping, keep records, take care of visitors, run down to the pharmacy—even sometimes launder a convalescent's nightgown. Those are not the skills you learned in nursing school. I want us to find a way of training our nonprofessional helpers that will let nurses be nurses again."

• *By stating the over-all issues involved.* This will put the subject of discussion in perspective—relate it, that is, to matters of larger scope and thus give it importance. Suppose, for instance, you're the head of an industrial research organization. You call a meeting of your accounting department to reexamine your procedures. Your opening might go like this:

"We're going to take a new look at our accounting procedures today. What we wind up with will become an important part of the thinking of our board of directors. The board is weighing the advantages and disadvantages (taxes, mailing privileges, and the like) of putting our organization on a nonprofit basis. It's exploring our need for this kind of change, the various plans that are available, and the ways in which our operations would be changed if we did go nonprofit. We can be a big help to the board when the time comes for decision."

• *By defining the problem or the subject.* You can do this yourself. Or you can ask the group to help you. This latter method has the merit of getting the group into the act right at the outset. Whichever way you go about it, key words and phrases must be clarified so that everybody understands them in the same sense.

Maybe you're a teacher. You have to conduct a discussion with a subcommittee of the parent-teacher association. Purpose of this meeting is to discuss the way teachers report on their pupils. You know that as the meeting moves on you'll be using words that are perfectly clear to you but may not be clear at all to the parents in your group. You might start like this:

"By the time this meeting is over I hope that we teachers will understand some of the things that puzzle our parent group, and that our parents will understand why—and how—we do some of the things we do. That, in substance, is the purpose of our meeting this afternoon. Stated another way, our problem is to clear away some of the obstacles to communication between parent and teacher. But before we get deeply involved in discussion I want to be sure we're all talking the same language—that we all understand the words we're using. Take these five key words to begin with: average, median, mean, percentage, and percentile. You're a banker, Mr. McLeod. What do they mean to you?"

• *By using a case history.* This will nail the problem (or the subject) down to reality right away, give your group members the feeling that they're wrestling with everyday, meaningful matters. For example:

"I have here in my hands—and will pass out copies to you—a ledger sheet that's a real case in point. It shows how bookkeeping procedures at our home office are impairing our efficiency here in our branch office. Let's go through the facts and use this case as a jumping-off place for our discussion."

• *By stating briefly the history of the problem.* This, like stating the over-all issues involved (above), puts the problem in perspective, gives it significance in relation to other facts or events. But keep it brief. That way, it can speed your meeting. If you string out the history, you'll be the major cause of the very bog-down you hope to avoid. Imagine, for example, that you've called a meeting of your managing group to talk about a new proposal for profit sharing. You could get into it this way:

"To set the stage for this discussion of profit sharing, let's take a fast look at our company's past interest in the subject."

*Keep things on the track.* This takes a quick mind, a firm hand, and sound planning. As leader, you must be prepared—must have an outline that covers the ground logically and systematically. You must watch for those personal traits (like those of Victrola Vic, for instance) that can sidetrack a meeting; for the attitudes (like stubbornness) that can derail a meeting; and for the mechanical failures (poor planning or lack of structuring) that can bring a meeting to an inglorious end, nothing accomplished. You've already seen ways to handle these situations in this chapter and in the preceding chapter.

*Swing smoothly from one matter to the next.* In other words, when you spot the turning points in a discussion, lead your group to new ground. Try to sense these turning points before the group begins to back and fill.

Helpful transition sentences? Here are three samples:

"It seems to me we've come thus far in our discussion. (Here you summarize very briefly.) This seems to lead us naturally to ..."

"Since we're agreed on that point, it's logical that we should explore this next area of discussion."

"I think we've about exhausted that aspect of our subject. Are we now ready to move on to the next phase of the problem? It's ..."

*Keep the talk logical.* It's your duty to protect your group against flummery and fallacy, gaps and tricks in reasoning, and the pitfalls its own faulty logic may dig. So if some member of the group is reasoning from example—that is, drawing broad conclusions from specific cases—be sure he cites enough cases to justify his conclusion. If he's reasoning from analogy—that is, drawing a comparison between two cases that seem similar—be sure his cases are really similar, not just superficially or partly similar. If he's reasoning from cause to effect or from effect to cause, be sure the gap is fully bridged; that is, that the cause cited (and not some other cause) really produced the effect, or that the cause can be deduced from the effect cited and not from some other effect.

*Spur ideas with questions.* This is a sure way to stir up ideas and points that may be lying dormant in the minds of your group—and to make sure people don't forget the ideas they intended to bring up. There are several kinds of questions you'll find useful from time to time. Here they are:

• What, why, *and* how *questions*. These lead people to take thought—to think aloud, take a stand, commit themselves, move toward action. Use them often. You'll get good results. Examples? "Why do we do it this way?" "What should we do about this?" "How can we solve this problem?"

• Who, when, *and* where *questions and questions that call for* yes *or* no. These are somewhat more pointed. They put people on the spot—sometimes make them uncomfortable. So use them sparingly—only when you have to force the facts into the open and only when you feel the time has come to be blunt and direct. Examples? "Who's responsible for this?" "When did this happen?" "Where did you leave it?" "Did this happen in your department?"

• *Catch-everybody questions*. You'll throw these at the group as a whole and invite thoughtful answers from everybody. If you're leading a meeting of tellers at your bank, for instance, you might ask, "Do our customer's comments give us any clues for improving our services?" If it's a sales meeting, you might ask, "Have any of you picked up clues from our customers about how we might broaden our product line?"

• *Nailing-down questions*. These are the kind that you throw at hard-to-handle persons. They force such people into the open, make it hard for them to hold back facts, make it even harder for them to ignore the views of others. For instance: "You tell us, Jones, that our product is tops in quality. That's why you oppose this appropriation for a new electronic inspection device. How, then, do you account for the complaints we got from our Chicago sales office last week?" Or "What you urge on us as company goals sounds good, Smitherman. Do you have any concrete suggestions as to the money involved, the manpower needed, and the probable time schedule involved?"

• *Leading questions*. These throw fresh material at the group, set out a new line of thought, bring out unexplored points of view. Examples? "Should we try to see how this change in the lubrication

schedule will affect our assembly-line operations?" Or "What would
happen if we employed a research chemist instead of a mechanical
engineer?" Or "Have we overlooked this line of thinking?"

• *Pass-along questions.* When you get a question from a member
of the group, you can easily pass it along to some other participant
—usually somebody you think can handle it. Sometimes it takes no
more than a flick of your eye to make the relay, because the person
who can best answer the question is usually sitting on the edge of
his chair anyhow, eager to get into the act. At other times you may
want to pass the question to somebody who needs urging to get into
the discussion. This is when you might say, "McGregor, I wish you'd
take a crack at that question."

*Cite examples to create attention.* Keep a few stories and real-
life cases up your sleeve, haul them out when they seem to be in
point. They should be rich in interests the group can share. Imagine,
for example, you're conducting a session with foremen on wage
incentive rates. Comes a time in the discussion when somebody
raises the question of when the rates should be revised. "Soon as we
can," you might reply. "I'm thinking about our punch presses right
now. Last week we added some new transfer devices that make
the work faster and easier. It's time we took another look at the
rates—before they get out of hand. Three years ago, some of you
remember, we redesigned our assembly line. We let things rock
along for nearly two years without revising the rate. Then we saw
how far out of line our costs had run. But by that time our as-
semblers and the shop steward had come to look on the old rate
as right and proper. So we had a real battle before we could get
a new rate accepted. I don't want that to happen to us again. I
think we'd better move in on these punch presses right away."

Or maybe you're running a sales meeting. The problem: To increase sales of your line of vacuum cleaners. One of your men tells
about a tough distributor he can't sell. The distributor, he reports,
says his sales have moved slowly this last month and he's just not
in a position to take on more cleaners right now. "That reminds
me," you say, "of what I heard at lunch yesterday from an insurance
salesman. He said his prospects often tell him they don't have the

money right now to buy more insurance. When they tell him that, he says, he knows there's a fatal flaw somewhere in his sales story. It's not that the prospect doesn't have the money. It's just that the salesman has failed to create the strong desire that would compel a prospect to give up something else so he could buy more insurance. So whenever this insurance salesman gets a turndown, he takes another look at his sales story. Does this give us a clue about our own sales approaches?"

*Use conflict as a help.* Naturally, you'll cut off senseless arguments. They only waste your time and the group's. But constructive conflict is useful. It adds life and movement to a meeting. So don't hesitate to encourage it—and exploit it. From time to time you may find occasion to say, "Two of us seem to be on opposite sides of this question. Suppose you thrash it out for a while. Why don't you begin, Appleby? Then we can hear from Wilkins." A bit later you can come back in with this: "Have we explored these views thoroughly now? Are we ready to push on to our main objective?"

Good discussion leaders, in fact, sometimes take on the role of the devil's advocate and thus purposely create conflict—and rouse interest into the bargain. There are many places where you can interrupt a meeting, taking an improbable or even impossible position simply for the sake of provoking discussion. "The truth is," you might throw out, "I think nearly every man in this room is overpaid." If that doesn't bring forth some lively rejoinder, nothing will. And the group may uncover some fresh ideas into the bargain.

*Summarize periodically.* Every discussion ought to be stitched together from time to time. Why? Because words dissolve into thin air. And ideas vanish unless they're captured. So it's a good thing to pause briefly—to add up progress in these little summaries along the way. You'll review the facts that stand out thus far, state the areas where there's agreement, point out the places where there's still honest difference of opinion, and restate the action the group thinks should be taken.

These quick summaries will do three things for your meeting. They'll highlight the high spots of the meeting and make them memorable. They'll give group members a series of progress reports and thus create a sense of accomplishment. And they'll provide a springboard from which you and the group can move ahead into the next aspect of the discussion.

Above all, don't overlook your over-all summary at the end of the meeting. It should tie together all your little summaries into a meaningful package that your group members can take along when the meeting breaks up. They'll leave with a sense of real achievement.

## Summary

Steering a meeting all the way through to a successful end may not be a triumph. But it is personally satisfying—and another forward step in your career. You can be justifiably proud of it. Why? Because obstacles lurk at every turn of a meeting, and brambles and briers crowd in from every side. Any leader who comes through unscarred is skillful—or just plain lucky.

In this sometimes scrambled world of human relations you can't tell what will happen next to slow your meeting down, turn it aside from its objective, or make it sputter, like a burned-out candle, to an inconclusive end. About the only thing you can be sure of is that it will somehow fulfill Murphy's Law: "If anything can go wrong, it will."

How, then, do you rescue this meeting of yours from disaster? You do it by looking ahead—by anticipating as many as you can of the things that make meetings go wrong. Maybe you can't foresee all of them. But the more of them you can foresee—and prepare yourself for—the better your chance of bringing off your meeting in good style.

The fact is, there are certain typical people, certain typical twists of argument and debate, certain typical situations that crop up in most meetings. They threaten trouble. They jeopardize success. But they needn't ruin your meeting. Indeed, if you're prepared to handle them (and that's what this chapter is about), you can meet them head on and defeat them or, better still, turn them to your own advantage and thus bring your meeting to a meaningful end.

Three things you should always keep in the forefront of your mind as you conduct a meeting:

1. *Your meeting has an objective.* Everything you do—and everything you let happen—must move toward that objective.

2. *Time is worth dollars.* You must make every minute count for the people who attend. That means you can't permit the quibbling, the selfishness, the meanderings, or the eccentricity of anybody (including yourself) to take over.

3. *It's a rare person who can't contribute something to a meeting.* Maybe you'll nearly despair of getting anything helpful from the malcontents, the snobs, and the other troublemakers. But keep trying anyhow. You can nearly always find some way to bring out a man's best, however deep he has buried it.

## Exercise

Pick a willing partner—a classmate, a friend, a brother or sister, your wife or husband. Ask your partner to join you in a little drama, with you cast as the leader of a meeting and your partner cast as a participant.

Tell your partner to put aside his true character for five minutes and, instead, take on the character of Prejudice Pete or Sage Sam or any other of the hard-to-handle people described in this chapter. Tell him you want him to play his role hard and earnestly. You play yours the same way.

Pick a meeting objective from the list below:

Find ways to broaden employment policies.

Develop a plan for cutting costs (in some activity you're both familiar with).

Plan a sales campaign for a new product.

Frame a policy for better relations with customers.

Now get started with your drama. Remember, you two are acting out a meeting in which your partner tries to disrupt everything while you try to keep control—and bring out the best in him. Keep it up for five minutes.

When it's all over, enlist your partner's help in finding out how well (or poorly) you performed as the leader of a meeting.

*How can I read a report without putting people to sleep?*

# How to Read
# Reports and Papers Aloud
# Without Putting People to Sleep

Do you ever doze off while somebody is reading aloud to you? Sounds cozy if you imagine it before an open fire on a winter night. Sounds nostalgic when you remember yourself as a child, tucked snugly in bed while a favorite aunt read to you.

But there's nothing cozy or nostalgic about it when you're reading something aloud in a business meeting or conference and suddenly realize that your listeners have become sleepers—or squirmers, whisperers, doodlers, daydreamers, or maybe even walker outers.

When this happens you feel the rude jolt of failure. The report or paper you thought was going to be interesting—or informative, provocative, or convincing—turns out to be none of these things. You've lost your chance to put your point across to your hearers. Or you've disappointed the people who trusted you to speak for them. Or you've failed to block a move that will injure your company. Or you've lost a cause that could have put your company far out in front of its competitors.

A common experience? Yes. Too common. Because it falls to the lot of many men in industry, in business, and in professional and civic life to read papers and reports. Trouble is, few of these men ever bother to acquire the knack of reading aloud.

Don't be mistaken. This book doesn't advocate reading your talks aloud to your listeners. But it does accept the fact that you sometimes have to make reports that are intricate or heavily loaded with facts. Or you have to quote something difficult or complex within a talk. When these occasions arise, reading is the only way to be sure you're right. But this reading doesn't have to be dull. If you handle it right, it can be the high point—rather than the low point— of your talk. To find out how to make it so, read on.

## Five Pitfalls in Reading Aloud

What's wrong with the way so many people read aloud? Why do so many people who talk interestingly turn dreary and dull when they read from a manuscript?

The villain in the act is the manuscript—the written report or prepared paper. There it is, in your hand or on the lectern in front of you. You can't just throw it away. You've got to live with it. You've got to read it. It's the reason why you're talking.

But that doesn't mean you have to stumble into the traps the manuscript sets in your path. What traps? These five:

1. *The wooden recital.* There's the manuscript, all written out for you. It's inflexible—nothing you can do about it. It fixes your

HOW TO READ REPORTS AND PAPERS ALOUD

HOW TO READ REPORTS AND PAPERS ALOUD

course. You can't branch out on your own. It's cold and formal. Whatever spark of spontaneity it once had seems now to have vanished—lost somehow in the translation from spoken to written words.

It's easy to make a wooden recital of reading a manuscript. And that's the trap you'll fall into if you take the attitude that your reading job is a cut-and-dried chore—that all you have to do is stand up, rattle off the report, and sit down. It's your job to make the words and figures live and meaningful.

2. *The downcast eye.* The paper in front of you is a magnet. It draws you because you're afraid of faltering or leaving out something important. The result: Your eye clings to the manuscript, and eye contact—that living link with your hearers—dissolves. First thing you know, your listeners are woolgathering. You've lost them.

3. *The faraway mind.* There in front of you, word for word, is all you have to say. You don't have to think at all. The thinking has already been done. So, before you know it, your mind wanders to other matters. You begin to read by reflex. There's no connecting thread between what you're saying and what you're thinking—if you're thinking at all. A little of this faraway mind on your part, and your listeners, too, will drift far away.

4. *The hypnotic drone.* No thought about what you're doing, no spark of interest in your own words, no occasional upward glance to link you with your hearers—and before you know it you're droning along in dreary monotony. Your voice goes flat and listless —no peaks, no valleys. Or it slips into singsong. Either way, your listeners will drift off into hypnotized slumber. But don't blame them. In fact, be glad for them, because their slumber will be merciful rescue from the pain you're inflicting on them.

5. *The race against time.* "This has been thought out already. It's here in black and white. It's plain as a pikestaff. No need for anybody to reflect on it, analyze it, take a second thought about it. No need, therefore, for me to pause. Thing to do is go straight through. Waste no time. Make it quick."

If that's your approach, you're not being fair to the substance of your manuscript. And you're not being fair to your listeners. You'll sprint far ahead of your hearers, arrive breathless at your goal, and looking back, see not a listener in sight.

## How to Improve Your Reading-aloud Skill

It's not hard to avoid the five traps above. What you need is contrast, variety, and spirit in your reading. The secret, as pointed out earlier, lies in reading the same way you talk.

Reading the same way you talk is fairly easy if you have time to prepare—that is, if you can study the manuscript before you read it. It's a little harder—takes a little more skill—if you pick up the manuscript "cold"—that is, if you don't have time to study it before you read it. But you can still do a creditable job even without preparation.

Take it both ways—preparation and no preparation:

*When you've got time to get ready.* This is really no problem. It just takes a little time for study and practice. Here are nine simple steps to follow before the time comes for you to read a report or paper:

1. Make sure you understand the material. Go through it thoroughly. Look up the words you don't know. Get the meaning of every phrase, every sentence. Read it through several times, until you grasp the over-all meaning—the purpose and significance of the material—and its submeanings. If you've written the material yourself, be dead sure it has a single, clear-cut purpose.

2. Underline every key word and phrase. If it's a statistical report, underline the key figures.

3. Read the material aloud. Do it several times. Stress the words and phrases you've underlined.

4. Seek out the natural pause spots. These are the places where you think your listeners might want to reflect on what you've just said—or the places where you think a point needs time to sink in. Put a slash mark (/) at the pause spots. If you think a prolonged pause is called for, put in two or three slash marks. Don't rely too much on punctuation (commas, semicolons, periods) when you

mark the pause spots. If you do, you'll wind up with too many pauses and thus weaken your impact. Let your good judgment (and your sense of drama) tell you where to pause.

5. Read your material aloud. This time, pause at the places you've marked, and stress the words and phrases you've underlined.

6. Read aloud again. This time, add the word "Bob" at some of the pause spots. Pretend Bob is a friend you're talking to. Visualize him. Make your tone conversational. Try to create the illusion that you're simply talking to him, not reading to him.

7. Read aloud again. This time, drop the word "Bob" but keep your tone and manner conversational. Also this time, see how often you can lift your eyes from your material—and how long you can keep going without dropping them again. Practice the "sweep" action. It goes like this: Drop your eyes to the sentence and then, while you're speaking the words you see, let your eyes sweep ahead to the last part of the sentence. While you're speaking the words in the last part of the sentence, lift your eyes and scan your make-believe audience. Don't get rattled if you have to go back to the page. And don't push the panic button if you can't find your place the first instant. You'll find it in good time if you stay calm—just the right time for an effective pause.

8. Pick a friend (or a willing listener) and read the material to him. Or read it into a tape recorder. Stress your key words and phrases, pause at the places you've marked, keep your tone and manner conversational, and look at your page as seldom as possible.

9. Whether you've read your paper or report to a friend or a tape recorder, analyze your performance. Here are some questions to guide your self-analysis:

Did I sound eager to communicate?

Did I sound friendly?

Did I sound confident?

Did I stress my key words and phrases?

Did I pause at the right places? Too long? Not long enough? Just right?

Did I sound and look conversational?

Did my delivery and my approach bring out the over-all purpose?

If you have to answer "No" to any question, better go back and brush up.

*When you go at it "cold."* Suppose your supervisor is called out of town unexpectedly. As he leaves, he thrusts his departmental report at you and says, "Here, take this. I'm supposed to be meeting right now with the production committee, but I've got to leave. Read this report for me at the meeting, will you? I'll be back day after tomorrow."

What do you do then? You fall back on the experience you've gained by reading reports that you did have time to study. Even if you don't have time to study this new manuscript, you can come through all right—if you don't get rattled, and if you take your time.

Here are five helpful tips:

1. Don't worry. Sure, you'll make a few flubs. Who wouldn't? But take this attitude: "What I gain from contacting this group—looking into their eyes and talking right to them—is a lot more important than a few flubs." That's the attitude of calm confidence you need.

2. Go slowly. No need to hurry. The slower you go, the fewer flubs you're likely to make.

3. Think as you read. Try to grasp meanings fully as you go along. Keep saying to yourself: "This fellow is trying to put across an idea (or a fact or a cause). What's his purpose? Have I got his meaning right?" Chances are, if you don't understand what the report means, nobody else will. So take time to think as you read.

4. Pause where you think pauses will help you. If you take this approach, you'll probably pause where your listeners, too, feel the need of reflection, or where they'll recognize some key point in the report. Punctuation and paragraphing, of course, will help you. A clear, unflustered mind will help you even more.

5. Use the "sweep" action. You can't lift your eyes as often as you could if you were familiar with the material. But you can—and should—lift them from time to time, thus keeping the bond strong between yourself and your hearers. Your pauses will give you some opportunities to look up. And sometimes you can find places to throw in transitional or explanatory remarks of your own—being

careful, of course, not to distort the meaning of the material you're reading. Such remarks as these, for instance, will give you a chance to maintain eye contact with your listeners: "At this point the reports moves on to another aspect of the problem," you might say. Or "There are some statistics here that I think bear repeating." Or "This is the same view Applewhite explained to me a few days ago." Or "That's the end of his comment on this problem. He has marked what follows as his conclusion."

## Summary

If you think this chapter means that you should always read your talk, you couldn't be more wrong. It means nothing of the sort. It simply means that when you do have to read something to a group, you should try to give it some style, some impact, some personality and meaning.

The occasions when it is better to read than to talk informally are rare. Examples: When you have technical or otherwise intricate material to present—something you can't entrust to your memory. When you have a report that's full of statistics. When you're talking about some sensitive issue and want to be especially careful about the way you state your thoughts. When you have material created by (or belonging to) somebody else, and you get stuck with the job of presenting it.

When you turn to reading rather than talking to put your message across, it's all too easy to forget your primary function—to communicate dramatically, clearly, and persuasively. That's why so many men slip into monotony and lose contact with their hearers when they read a report or a paper. You don't have to face that failure, now that you've studied this chapter.

Reading needn't be dull and dreary. In fact, if you go at it the right way, it can be exciting and stimulating. What's the right way? Just this: Create the illusion that you're not reading at all but are talking warmly, freely, and imaginatively to a group of listeners whom you must interest and carry along with you. To do this, you must prepare carefully—if you have time to prepare. If you don't have time to prepare—if you have to read material that you've never seen before—read it as if you yourself were a listener, eager to get the message. Sure, it takes skill to read "cold" copy effectively. But it's a skill that you, too, can have—because it comes with practice.

## Exercises

Pick out a couple of paragraphs (200 to 250 words) from some reading material that will interest or help the people you work closest with. Maybe the passage is about selling insurance or merchandise, or winning new customers for a bank or a service corporation, or getting more production from people or machines, or brightening the day of a hospital patient, or designing a curriculum for especially bright children, or setting up a sense-making municipal tax program.

Whatever subject you choose, go after the material this way:

1. Read the paragraphs through two or three times. Circle the words you don't know. Look them up in your dictionary. Write on a separate sheet of paper the main idea—the purpose—of your two chosen paragraphs.

2. Underline the words and phrases that need special emphasis.

3. Read the material aloud, emphasizing the underlined words and phrases.

4. Mark the pause spots with slash bars.

5. Read the paragraphs aloud again, pausing where the marks tell you to pause and stressing the words and phrases you've underlined.

6. Read the material aloud once more, introducing the word "Bob" from time to time, as if you were talking to a friend.

7. Omitting the word "Bob" but keeping a listening friend in mind, read your two paragraphs aloud again. Practice the "sweep" motion as you read.

8. Read your material to a friend or into a recorder.

9. Play back your recording and look for the things you did well and those you did poorly. Or talk over your performance critically with your associate.

10. Try again, this time correcting the mistakes you made the first time.

**16**

*People say I gab all the time. I need to develop the skill of listening.*

# How Good Listening Can Make You a Better Communicator

If you can talk skillfully and persuasively, you've got a priceless asset. Talking is what this book is all about. But it would fall short of its mark if it didn't help you become a better listener, too. Because listening at the right time is just as important as talking at the right time. And listening, like talking, is an art. Without it, you'll find it hard to succeed in business, in industry, or in community and social relations. Skillful listening makes other people talk well—makes them believe that their own monologue has been a discussion or a conversation. They're right—if you've listened actively and helpfully. In fact, if you're a good listener you can win a reputation as an effective communicator without opening your mouth more than half a dozen times in the course of a discussion. What's more, you can be as persuasive and helpful as a skilled talker.

People often pay a high price for talking when they should be listening. And an equally high price when their listening is flabby or half attentive. What price? A company president, only half informed because he didn't listen, can make a ruinous decision that will put him—and his company—on the skids. A salesman, failing to listen attentively, can lose an order—and even a long-time customer. A superintendent or foreman, impatiently brushing aside a half-heard warning, can issue an order that will wreck his plant and kill or maim his employees. A personnel director, ignoring a worker's veiled plea for attention and understanding, can cause a skilled but sensitive man to quit his job in anger or frustration. A head nurse in a hospital, listening with only half an ear, can miss the key point in a nurse's report and thus unwittingly cause the death of a patient. A clergyman, preoccupied with preparation of his Sunday sermon, can fail to sense a parishioner's desperate need for spiritual help and thus fail in the highest aspect of his noble calling. A woman at a civic luncheon, letting her mind wander from her neighbor's conversation, can miss what her neighbor says and thus lose support for a worthy cause—and jeopardize a cherished friendship into the bargain. All these people—head nurse, clergyman, salesman, and the others (maybe you, too, sometimes)—pretend to be listening. But they're really slipping off into their own thoughts (perhaps what they'll say in reply). This way, they're missing a vital link in communication—genuine listening.

These are just a few of the many disasters that befall people when they don't listen as well as they talk. They bear out the truth of the old saying: "Silence (at the right time) is golden." They explain why it's sometimes said that listening wins more friends and influences more people than talking.

In a sense, active listening is conversation. The eyes of talker and listener meet. The listener's face and hands signal acceptance or denial, warning or enthusiasm. He shows amusement, grief, anger, annoyance, agreement, disgust, joy. He gives the impression that an attentive ear sticks out all over him. His manner invites confidence. It welcomes a bond between talker and hearer. It tells the talker, silently, that what he has to say is worth saying—and worth listening to.

## Why People Talk

People talk, of course, for many different reasons. And whatever their reason may be, more often than not there's good cause for you to listen—some gain in store for yourself, or some help you can give them.

Look at a few of the reasons why people talk:

• *To make friendly contact.* There's Mr. Harvey, mowing his lawn. The neighbor's boy from across the street ambles over, stands there watching for a while, and then says, "Whatcha doin', Mr. Harvey? Cuttin' the lawn?" The boy just wants to be friendly. For him, talking is fun. And if Mr. Harvey responds, it will be fun for him, too.

• *To pass ideas and information along—to explain or instruct.* Hank Morley leaves his punch press and strides quickly to the foreman's office. He starts talking as soon as he opens the door. He's got an idea for a new mechanical feed that will boost production 25 per cent. Or he has just spotted a hazard in the plant—wants to describe it and explain how to eliminate it.

• *To persuade.* Vito Ferrari, crack space salesman, talks ten minutes to tell why his magazine leads the field. He wants to persuade his client to double his advertising appropriation.

• *To entertain.* Henry Harrison is host to some plant visitors in the company lunchroom. He keeps the conversational ball going with one story after another. For example: "Reminds me of one of the plate passers at my church. One of his fellow collectors asked him why he always fished in the plate for a large bill—a $5 or a

$10—then put it on top of the plate if he found one. 'Because the preacher always looks at the plate when I hand it to him down front. If he sees a $5 bill, we get a better sermon.'"

• *To give shape to half-formed ideas.* Miss Lopez, buyer for ladies' coats in a large department store, has the germ of an idea for better display. She talks it over with the merchandise manager, and as she speaks, the hazy hunch she started with becomes an eye-catching window display that's keyed to the headline news of the week.

• *To solve problems.* Alan McElroy, training director, is puzzled about how to organize his annual report to top management. He invites the industrial relations director to have lunch with him. As McElroy begins to outline his problem, his answers begin to fall into place. By the time he has talked through lunch, with scarcely a word from the industrial relations director, he knows exactly how his report will move from one point to the next.

• *To relieve pent-up emotions.* Phil Samson has a deep worry. Hasn't slept well for a couple of nights. Looks haggard. Can't keep his mind on his job. Can't hold in any longer. He stops the first friend he sees and spills out his story. He doesn't say so, but everything about him pleads, "Just let me sound off—get this off my chest. Please don't interrupt me or disagree with me. That can come later, when I'm more reasonable. Right now all I want is to talk freely, until I feel better."

These cases are typical. You could probably call to mind hundreds of others, much like these, from your own experience. Every one offers good opportunity for active, creative listening—listening that will help the talker, and listening that will help you, too. To find out how to listen actively and creatively, read on.

## Six Rules for Listening to Help Others

To a man who has problems, troubles, puzzles, or worries, the good listener is a rich resource. The helpful, sympathetic ear is what people often look for in their bosses and their associates, sometimes in their subordinates, and always in their friends. If you want to be the kind of man to whom people turn when they need help, these six rules will guide you:

1. *Take time to listen.* Somebody asked an expert not long ago, "What's the secret of labor's advantage over management these days?" The expert replied, "Listening. Management is just too busy to listen. It can't be bothered. Labor leaders take time to listen."

So don't ever say, "I'm too busy to listen." Don't pass your listening responsibilities (and opportunities) along to the clergy, the psychologists, the professional counselors. Do your own listening, even if it does take time. Consider it a compliment—that the person came to you. The higher up the ladder a man climbs in business or industry, in politics or professional life, the more listening he has to do. He learns quickly that much of his success hinges on his attentive ear, because that ear of his often guides an associate or subordinate to the root of a tough problem—and thus makes life simpler and easier for everybody, including the boss.

2. *Let angry, impassioned people talk themselves out.* Chances are, they'll reason themselves into a sound position if you give them time.

Take it this way: An angry nurse storms into the personnel manager's office at the hospital. She attacks the hospital's housekeeping in general and a few housekeepers in particular. "Why do we nurses on Ward B have to throw laundry down the chute? Nurses on Ward D don't have to." That's only the beginning of her tirade. She goes on and on. The personnel manager sits quietly and hears her out. At last she calms down. But the personnel manager keeps right on listening as she becomes more rational. At last she reveals her real problem: She feels nobody is willing to listen to her problems. She apologizes for letting off steam, thanks the personnel manager for listening, says she now feels better.

What has the personnel manager gained by listening? He has won the high regard of the nurse, and he has spotted a cause of low morale—a weak link in staff communications. That needs some fast repair, and he knows how to go about it.

3. *Signal your attention to the talker.* This is easy. You can repeat snatches of his spiel from time to time—words and phrases that

you feel are important to him. You can come in now and then with
a "Yes, I understand," or "I'm glad you told me that," or a plain
"Uh huh." You can nod your head in agreement, or wag it in amaze-
ment or doubt. You can gesture with your hands. You can even let
certain pauses pass without interruption, thus making them expectant and inviting your talker to go on.

4. *Let a worried man talk himself out.* Two men traveled together
overnight to a bankers' convention in a distant city. They had barely
boarded the train and settled down in the club car when Brown began to talk: "Smith, you think everything is fine and dandy back at
my home. It isn't. And the fault is mine . . ."

Smith knew Brown hadn't been quite himself at the bank recently.
He began to see this trip as an opportunity for some helpful listening. It turned out just that way. Smith listened half the night.
Next day, after the convention, he started listening again—and listened all the way back home. As they got off the train and headed
out of the station, Brown took Smith's hand and shook it firmly.
"Thanks a lot," he said. "Everything's going to be all right now. It
will take a while. But I think I've now got a way to make things better at home."

Smith had spoken hardly a word. But he had listened helpfully
—no advice, no judgment, no interruption. Just attention.

A good listener is indispensable to a man who has heavy responsibility—the head of a corporation, a military commander, even the
President. With a good listener close by, such men can air their
deepest thoughts in private and move toward solution of the problems that press in on them from all sides. For instance, Carl
Sandburg tells the following story about Lincoln:

> In the labyrinth of viewpoints [about emancipating the slaves] in
> which Lincoln found himself, encircled by groups trying to infiltrate him
> with their special ideas, he sent a telegram to Leonard Swett at Bloom-
> ington, Ill., asking him to come to Washington at once. Swett got on a
> train, traveled two days, arrived in Washington, and went at once, with-
> out breakfast, to the White House. The two met, old partners in trying
> law cases, sleeping in the same bed in zero weather at taverns on the old
> Eighth Circuit. . . .

Lincoln turned to Swett and began a discussion of emancipation in all its phases. He turned it inside out and outside in. He reasoned as though he needed to think out loud in the presence of an old timer he knew and could trust. Swett watched the mental operations of his friend until, after an hour, they came to an end. The President asked for no comment, hoped that Swett would get home safely, sent his best wishes to acquaintances, and the interview, as such, was closed.

5. *Steer the talk in helpful directions.* Suppose, for example, an acquaintance of yours—maybe a subordinate—has failed in some project or is disappointed at the way something has turned out. He comes to you to unload. He blames himself and, in talking to you, reveals things that would be harmful or even ruinous if made public.

When this happens two undesirable things are happening. First, your friend is tottering on the brink of maudlin self-blame, if he hasn't already plunged over. This is unhelpful, unconstructive. Second, you may be coming into possession of dangerous information —information that could make your friend fear and distrust you later.

What can you do? Steer the talk into constructive channels. And do it quickly. Don't hesitate to break in. How? With comments or questions like these:

"I begin to see the fix you're in, Walt. Let's see now if we can find a direction that will lead you out of it."

"Things do look pretty grim, don't they? But they can't be as bad as they seem. Isn't there another side of the coin we can look at?"

"I'd rather not know those details. They're not really important now. The important thing is to find out where you go from here."

6. *Leave decision making alone.* As listener, you're playing the role of guide and helper—not decider. It's your task to bring the problem into the open and to throw light on it so your man can see it. But he must find the answer himself—make the decision, come to the conclusion.

Suppose your man asks, "What should I do?" Don't tell him what you think. Instead, ask this question: "Well, what could some of the answers be?" Or "Why don't you review the facts for me once more

—very quickly?" This way, you'll lead him up to his answer but
not into it. In the end, he'll find the answer by himself. Having
found it himself, he'll live with it. And he'll remember you warmly
as a helpful listener.

## Four Rules for Listening to Help Yourself

You've got two ears and one mouth. That's just what you need for
doing half as much talking and twice as much listening. Why so
much listening? Because nobody ever learned much while talking.
Listening, on the other hand, pays big dividends in information, understanding, and performance. To make your listening dividends
bigger and better, try these four rules:

1. *Erase your prejudices.* Even in this enlightened age there are
too many people who let color, race, ancestry, appearance, mannerisms, and job levels come between themselves and opportunities to
listen—and learn or enjoy. A foreman in a New York garment factory turns a deaf ear to a machine operator who wants to suggest
a simpler way of doing a job. The operator is a Puerto Rican. The
foreman thinks, "I know all about these Puerto Ricans. They're always causing trouble—street gangs, can't speak good English, and
all that." So he lets his prejudice block an opportunity to save his
company $5,000 a year in production costs.

A wholesale paper salesman makes one call on a potential customer, and never stops in again. Why? He didn't like the man—
thought he was cold, aloof, conceited. "Wouldn't call on him
again for $1,000," the salesman told an old acquaintance. Fact is,
the prospective customer was painfully shy and self-conscious, sensitive about not even having finished high school. But his close
friends knew him to be warm, intelligent, and remarkably self-
educated. If the salesman had been willing to submerge the prejudice formed on first acquaintance, if he had probed a bit for the
finer qualities of the man, he would have won rich rewards of
friendship—and many times $1,000 in repeated sales.

2. *Concentrate.* Pay attention. Don't let other things distract you
—rank, or action on the side—of your own concerns. Your failure to
concentrate could keep somebody from getting through to you on

a critical point or at a crucial time. For example, a vice president asks a foreman in a drop-forging shop a question. Simple yes-or-no answer. But the foreman gets flustered—this is top brass he's listening to. He hears the question wrong, says "Yes" when he should say "No." The vice president takes the wrong answer to the president. Result: a $7,000 loss because top management acts on misinformation.

Take it another way—this time, in a bank. Two tellers are out sick. The assistant cashier has to backstop them. He runs back and forth between his desk and the teller's cage, answering the phone here and accepting deposits there. Mrs. Plumston phones in, wants certain securities delivered to her broker before three o'clock. The bank officer, harassed and distraught, pays little attention to Mrs. Plumston. He does have some securities delivered—but they're the wrong ones. Result: Mrs. Plumston's bonds are sold at a loss. And the bank loses a good customer.

Take it still another way. Sam Parkins, office manager of an insurance agency, is worried about his fourteen-year-old. She's not doing well in high school. He plans to spend a while with the principal late this afternoon. He's planning what he'll say. That's when Doris Mitchell comes into Sam's office. Doris says the girls are unhappy about vacation schedules—talks on about Joanne, Millie, and Eleanor, even makes some suggestions about schedule changes. But Sam is a thousand miles away. He's not really listening. Result: Millie and Joanne quit, find new jobs in another agency down the street, leaving Sam with the task of hiring and training two new girls. Doris and Eleanor stay on, but they're not the happy workers they used to be.

3. *Take it easy.* Don't interrupt. Don't cut the talker off. If you're too worried about getting in your own two cents' worth, too eager to rebut, or so smart you think you don't have to listen, you're in for trouble. When you're thinking about what you're going to say next, you aren't listening at your best listening level. Instead, you're "thinking off." When you think off, communication stops. That's when frustration, fatigue, and failure take over a conference or a meeting.

Look at Jack Prince. He's boss of the machine shop. He's wrestling with some puzzling cost problems in the plant manager's office. His assistant, Tom Hawkins, breaks into the office:

"About that Stillman order, Jack..." Tom begins.

"Don't tell me anything about it. Just get it out," Jack shouts. "The boys know it's got to go this afternoon. The truck will be backed up the ramp at four o'clock."

"But Jack, I thought you'd like to know ..."

"Don't bother me now. I'm too busy. Just get back on the floor and see that nothing happens to that Stillman order."

Tom backs out, shrugging his shoulders.

If Jack had just listened to Tom, here's what he would have learned: The vice president for manufacturing had come into the plant while Jack was in the plant manager's office. He had brought an urgent government order. Not finding Jack on the floor, he had told Tom to stop all work on the Stillman order and get going on the government order. Meanwhile, he had scheduled completion of the Stillman order for the second shift and had ordered the truck not to come for it until next morning.

Like Jack, we all have talents, knowledge, abilities. But how can we use them to help others (as well as ourselves) unless we listen to find out where the problems are? How many times have you talked on and on to somebody with a problem, only to have him say as you turned to leave, "What I really need help on is ..."? That's when you realize you've done all the talking and none of the listening. "So that's your problem," you say: "Well, now ..." And you can focus on the area of real need.

4. *Adopt the talker's orientation.* Don't get so wrapped up in your own purposes and your own frames of reference that you don't hear what the other fellow is saying. To understand him and to get the real value of what he's saying to you, probe for his purposes and put what he says into his own frame of reference. Ask questions that he can answer in his frame of reference.

Not long ago two brothers spent an evening together. One was an engineer, the other a psychologist. They talked shop—each to his own.

"I've got a real problem out at the plant," said the engineer.

"We're making small electronic parts. Specifications are tight, especially on coatings. Every part—and we make 7,000 of them a day —has to be completely coated. Can't have a chink anywhere. We've spent $50,000 for a fancy electronic inspection device. When it works, it's fine. But it's down more than half the time. Something's nearly always wrong with it."

"What you need," the psychologist said, "is something with sharp, tireless vision and a simple nervous system. Why not pigeons? I've worked with pigeons a long time in the lab. They've got just what you need."

"You're crazy," the engineer said. But he kept on listening.

"Takes about three months to train a pigeon for the simple job you need. A pigeon will live twenty years—and work for you as long as he lives. Your capital investment will be $1.25. He'll cost you about $1 a month for food. He'll work sixteen hours a day for you, and never get tired. His error will be less than 1 per cent. That's better than your electronic gadget can do."

The point of this story is not that it's amazingly true. (It *is* a true story. It was reported in *Factory* magazine, a McGraw-Hill publication, in December, 1959. Only reason why the trained pigeons never went to work in the engineer's plant is that management feared the labor-displacement problem.) The point here is that the psychologist brother was tuned to the engineer's frame of reference. Their orientations, though worlds apart, were no barrier to profitable listening.

## How to Get People to Talk—So You Can Be a Good Listener

There are some people you have to draw out—lure into talking. If you don't, they won't say anything at all. And you can't be a good listener—or any kind of listener, for that matter—unless somebody says something.

Suppose you've got a shy, silent employee in your department. He never speaks up. In fact, he clams up every time you come around. Yet you feel there's more to him than he's willing to show.

If you can bring him out, he'll be better off—and so will you. Or suppose you've got a sullen worker. He glowers and glooms around, seems to be nursing a grudge, seldom if ever utters a word. His sullen spirit is catching on in the shop. You want to find out what's troubling him and help him find the answer. It's important to morale.

What can you do? These things:

• *Put him at ease.* To do this, you have to know something about him. Your own sharp eyes and the comments of his friends and associates will give you some clues. You can find out about his likes and dislikes, his religion and his friends, his schooling and his job, his children and his hobbies. Where does he live? How did he get into his kind of work? What does he like to do most of all? What about baseball? Woodworking? Bird watching? Fishing? Bridge? Travel? Vacations?

Once you know the kind of man you're dealing with, snatch every chance to break through his barrier. Somehow, somewhere, if you keep trying, you'll hit on something he's likely to talk easily and openly about. His first moves may be tentative and even reluctant, but with a little encouragement from you he'll open up. Once he does open up, you may have trouble stopping him. You may find yourself in the midst of a lot of small talk. Don't worry. The gates are down, and you can move pretty easily now from small talk to meaningful talk.

• *Move from small talk to meaningful talk.* Sometimes this just happens. Suddenly, without quite knowing how you and your troubled friend got there, you're in the midst of the problem. That's fine. It's been easy, and you're lucky. Most often, though, you'll have to lead him by the hand, ever so gently and subtly. You'll have to snatch some clue or hint in the small talk and contrive a transition from that to the area where the problem lies. If the small talk is about contract bridge, maybe some mention of a finesse or a renege will lead the talk over to trickery or less-than-straightforward conduct in the shop. If the small talk is about school days, it may lead to serious talk about on-the-job training. And that may lead in turn to more serious talk about your man's feeling that he was passed over for a promotion he thought he deserved. Chances are, he'll unbottle his thoughts and feelings once he reveals what his real trouble is.

• *Probe with questions.* But do it gently and tactfully. Watch your man closely. If you do, you can sense the difference between the "red" areas, where the whole situation will explode if you blunder in blindly, and the "yellow" areas, where you can advance if you do it more slowly and cautiously. The key to success is to ask questions that skirt the trouble area—or the area that you believe is troublesome. Watch for the go ahead—some favorable response from your man, like a look of interest in his eyes, a drawing in of breath as if to speak, a smile or nod of assent. When you spot these signs, you can move in closer with your next questions. Whenever you can, though, let your man himself make the final revelation of his trouble. It's your job to lead him right up to the point of revelation.

Take the case of the real estate man and the reticent farmer. It shows how ruinous a single blundering question can be. The real estate man wanted to buy a certain 20-acre tract bordering on a lake. The farmer owned this tract and didn't want to sell it. The real estate man wanted to find out why. "Aren't the other people worried about what's going to happen to the land?" he asked the farmer.

The neighbors were the farmer's "red" area. "Those folks have already got their noses too deep in other people's business," he snorted, and walked away.

The real estate man was licked before he had got well started. He had plunged ahead where he should have felt his way. He hadn't put his feelers out. He hadn't probed at all. He had just stabbed blindly.

• *Follow up after you've listened.* First, though, be sure your talker has talked himself out—has reached a plateau where he can talk calmly and rationally. If you're sure he's talked out, then go ahead with your follow-up. The purpose of follow-up? To help him find his way from problem to solution.

Now's the time to ask questions that will help your man explore his problem on a broader basis, or on a higher level, or from a new

angle. "What does your boss think about this?" you might ask.
Or "Have you thought how adoption of your views in sales might
affect production scheduling in the plant?" Or "Put yourself in the
customer's position. Would your way be the best way to handle this
situation?" Or "Think of Moseley in terms of his job. Would you
have acted differently if you'd been in his place?"

You can pick up clues and hints you've spotted here and there
as your man talked. He may have said, for instance, "Charlie's
brother has given me trouble before." Now's the time to come back
to that passing remark. "You mentioned Charlie's brother a few
minutes ago. What about him?" you might ask.

One word of caution: Don't snatch the first facts that come to
light as the answer to your man's problem. They may lead you nowhere at all—or even in the wrong direction. So be sure you fish out
all the facts with your follow-up questions. As he remembers them
and brings them to light, your man will begin to weigh them himself.
That way, he'll find his answer or come to his conclusion all on his
own.

How can you follow up? There are three ways, as follows:

DIRECT ADVICE: But unless you're a psychiatrist or a professional
counselor, better shy away from this. Sound direct advice can come
only after careful probing and exploration—and not many of us have
the time or the skill for that. Better to give no advice at all than
misguided advice based on shallow understanding.

INDIRECT GUIDANCE: You can ask leading questions that will show
your man another side of the problem that's worrying him. This
way, you might bring a union man to see management's side of an
issue, or a management man to see the union's side.

NONDIRECTIVE QUESTIONING: You can ask questions for which you
know neither the direction they will lead your man in, nor the
answers they will provoke. You'll ask such questions for one purpose: to help the other person see himself more objectively and thus
help him solve his problem. This way, you'll establish a feeling of
helpful "we-ness," as if to say, "Together we can get at the root of
this thing and solve it."

## Summary

Do you know somebody who has a reputation as a good talker, a good conversationalist? In the course of a business discussion or a social evening he probably says no more than a dozen sentences. Yet he's a pleasing, constructive communicator. He's a successful listener. He listens so well, he's so attentive, and he's so skillful at drawing other people out that when they leave him they feel his conversation has been refreshing and stimulating.

Good listening is an art. But it's an art you have to keep working at, because the temptation to abandon it—that is, to talk when you should listen—is sometimes hard to resist. Listening is a tough discipline. You get impatient with the problems and shortcomings of other people, or you're pressed for time, or you want to put in your own two cents' worth, or you simply don't understand what drives others to talk and how their own talking helps them.

Good listening is also an asset. The man who listens well earns dividends in information, in understanding, and in esteem. Listening at the right time has won many an argument, cemented many a sale, helped many a man to a solution for a desperate problem, calmed many a ruffled employee, cleared the way for many a man to the next step up the ladder of success.

So it *is* important to listen—to listen attentively and constructively. Most people spend a big share of every day listening—or seeming to listen. If they don't do it well—if they don't really listen—they're simply wasting time. And time is not their only loss. When listening is flabby, communication breaks down, misunderstanding builds up, information goes by unnoticed, truth and fiction get all mixed up, fact and prejudice become blurred, hasty generalizations pass unchallenged, meaningful clues and hints slip by ungrasped, and decisions go the wrong way.

How good a listener are you? Now that you've studied this chapter, you should be better than you were before. Next time you have a listening job to do, check yourself against the following questions:

1. Do I take in only the words and ideas I want to take in? Or do I reach out for new things to hear?

2. Do my prejudices block out facts and ideas? Or do I keep my mind open to facts and ideas stated by somebody I don't like or related to subjects I don't like?

3. Do I let distractions keep me from listening—such distractions as the high rank of the talker, the hustle and bustle of my own office, or the problems that press in on me? Or do I thrust such distractions aside and listen attentively?

4. Do I go blank on a talker because I'm thinking about how I'll add to what he says, or what I'll say to rebut him? Or do I really listen to him?

5. Do I listen in terms of the talker's experience and frame of reference? Do I take on his orientation?

## Exercises

1. Pick a teammate from among your classmates or friends. The two of you will play out a three-minute drama. Your friend will be talker—the one who sounds off. He'll talk about one of the eight subjects below. It's something he feels strongly about. It's been bothering him a long time. He's angry. In fact, he's downright unreasonable. He opens up on you. He goes on for three minutes. (In a real-life situation, such a talker probably would go on for much longer.) At last, he asks what you think he should do about his problem.

Meanwhile, you're the listener. Act the role as this chapter tells you it should be played. Mostly, you'll be listening—but you'll show that you're an interested and helpful listener. At the end, see if you can steer the talker to a rational calm and a sound answer to his problem.

Now, if you're both ready, let your teammate pick a subject. Then go ahead with your drama. Here are the subjects:

He never does what I say.
He gripes all the time.
He's jealous of me and my job.
My boss has one failing.

They always want to quit early.

The man's not fit for the job.

Here's what my department really needs.

This problem has been bothering me a long time.

Take down this listening session on tape if you can. But whether you can tape it or not, sit down with your teammate and analyze what took place after it's all over.

2. Your teammate pretends he has a serious problem at work (or at home or elsewhere). He doesn't show much emotion when he talks to you about it. Yet you feel he's talking to unburden himself of a great worry. So you listen to him.

You listen for four minutes. Then you begin to ask him indirect and nondirective questions that will lead him to find his own solution in his own way.

Tape your conversation if you can. As you play it back or recollect it, analyze your listening technique, note the ways in which you might have been more helpful.

*Can I use some little formulas to help in certain situations, such as giving orders, reprimanding, spiking rumors, and talking on safety?*

# 17

# *How to Handle*
# *29 Common Talking Situations*

You never know what kind of talking situation you may be thrust into next. But you can be sure of this: In business, in industry, in civic affairs, and in social relations, wherever you are and whatever you do, you'll have to face up to situations that require you to talk.

Some of these situations come on you unexpectedly. Others you can foresee and prepare for. Some of them develop just as you expect them to. Others take surprising turns and twists. But all of them challenge your skill and ingenuity. All of them call for the best that's in you. And, more often than not, the way you handle them will tip the scales toward success or failure in your career, business, or social relationships.

If you've gone after the 16 preceding chapters of this book with strong purpose, if you've done all the end-of-chapter exercises faithfully, if you've been self-critical and self-analytical all the way along, and if from now on you keep practicing what you've learned, you can face almost any talking situation and be confident of success. You'll be one of those select few who see every talking occasion as an opportunity to help yourself and others, not as something to shy away from as a threat.

In a sense, this final chapter is a review of all the earlier chapters in this book. But it differs from the others in this way: It assumes that by this time you've mastered the theory and principles that spell success in talking and that you can now apply them in a wide range of situations. That's why you won't find discussion and examples in this chapter. Instead, you'll find 29 accepted ways—time-tested helps—for meeting and handling 29 commonplace talking situations—situations that are likely to confront you time after time in the everyday course of events. So, for a roundup of tips on what to do when you're thrust into such situations, read on.

## What to Do When You've Got to ...

### 1. Give an Order

Be crystal clear about what you want done. Start with the over-all assignment—for example, "I want you to repair a leaking value in the steam line." That way, your man won't have to interrupt you with "Wait a minute. What's this all about?" When he understands the over-all job, then go into the details. Details for ordering any job should cover the following questions:

• Who? Who is to carry out the order? Who will help? Who's in charge?

• What? What's needed to do the job? What tools? What materials? What instruction books?

• When? When is the job to begin? When is it to be finished?

• Where? Where is the job located? Where is it to be performed? Where are the equipment, tools, materials, helpers? Where is the completed job to be placed or shipped?

• How? How is the job to be done? How is it to be moved or installed or prepared for? How is completion to be reported?

• Why? Why does the job need doing? Why must it be done this way, and not some other way? Why have you picked this man (or these men) to do it?

## 2. *Issue a Reprimand*

Lead your man aside—away from others and out of their hearing, even out of their sight. If you don't, you'll humiliate him —hurt his self-respect and make him lose face among his friends. He'll resent you, and so will his friends.

But before you launch into your reprimand, think a moment or two. Try to figure out why your man acted the way he did, how his background directed his conduct, how his conduct and your reprimand will affect him in the long run. Above all, get the facts—even if it means delaying the reprimand a while. This way, you'll have time to cool off, muster your patience, and analyze the situation.

Use plain words to tell your man what's wrong. Don't beat about the bush. Be direct and firm. But keep your self-control. And end on a constructive basis. That is, show your man how he can avoid similar mistakes in the future.

## 3. *Spike a Rumor*

Get the facts as fast as you can. Then recite them, in plain words, to the people who've been spreading the rumor and to those who've been listening. If you can spot the one person who started the rumor, be sure that he above all others hears the facts.

Are the facts unpleasant? Bring them into the open anyhow. Rumors, good or bad, breed unhealthy excitement and speculation. Your people will be far better off knowing unpleasant facts than cherishing false visions.

Suppose safety or security forbids your telling all the facts. What then? Just tell what you can. Meanwhile, seek out those who started the rumor and question them about their sources. Keep after them. This way, without revealing forbidden information, you may bring them to doubt the truth of the rumor they've been passing around.

When you state the facts, state the rumor as well. This approach will bring fact and rumor face to face, so there'll be no doubt about what's true and what's false.

### 4. *Put a Stop to Malicious Gossip*

Go after this much the same way you go after rumor. That is, get the facts—as many as you can and as fast as you can. Meanwhile, move quickly to nail down the source of the gossip. Why move fast? Because malicious gossip aims at what your best people prize highest of all—an untarnished reputation. Gossip is ruinous. It hurts people, undermines morale, breeds prejudice.

The trouble with spiking gossip is that you can seldom make a public announcement of the truth without some risk of revealing the gossip to people who haven't heard it. This could compound the harm. But you can do three things:

• Find the source, and let him know, in no uncertain terms, that the gossip must stop. How find the source? Just keep probing. Every time you pick up a shred of gossip, ask where it came from. Eventually you'll get your clue. Then you can move in fast—and hard—on the source.

• Take every opportunity, in private conversation or in public talking, to bolster the reputation of the injured person among his fellows and to show your own confidence in him.

• Turn the gossip to a constructive purpose. Where gossip is concerned, it doesn't take much to tip the scales one way or the other—toward prejudice or sympathy. You can put your weight on the side of sympathy, thus thwart the purposes of the gossip starter and win support for his intended victim.

### 5. *Refuse a Request*

Tell your man the reason why you can't grant his request—for a day off, a new company car, a special expense-account item, a job for his nephew, some secretarial help, or whatever. Whatever the reason, it must make sense. If you give excuses instead of reasons, try to stall, or try to evade the issue, he'll see what you're doing and judge you accordingly.

If you're personally sorry you can't grant his request, it's all right to say so. But take the responsibility yourself. Don't tell him that you'd like to go along with him but that your own boss blocks the way. That puts you in conspiracy with your man, leads him to believe that you have no influence with your superior, and undermines his own respect for management.

### 6. *Apologize*

Look your man squarely in the eye. Tell him you did the wrong thing. Tell him you're sorry. Tell him it won't happen again. And be sure you mean what you say, because most people have a shrewd way of sensing insincerity. Above all, don't alibi, don't dredge up excuses, don't weasel out, don't blame somebody else.

Don't be ashamed to apologize when you've been wrong. The ability to face up to a mistake and acknowledge it is one good measure of a man.

### 7. *Straighten Up a Troublesome Youngster*

First of all, remember that he's young—inexperienced, not yet settled down, unsure of himself, a little impatient with tradition, chafing under restraints. Try to understand him in this light.

There's no pat, one-shot way of handling such a young person. For the most part it takes talking at repeated intervals—mostly spontaneous occasions. That is, you snatch talking opportunities when they turn up. On these occasions you talk specifically to the point at issue —the immediate offense or violation. But you talk understandingly and calmly. You reason with your young man, point out the infraction, and put it in perspective against his over-all job opportunities. After all, your purpose is to help him develop his ambitions and move toward their fulfillment, and to bring out his latent qualities of leadership.

Don't overlook your persuasive listening skills when you're dealing with a young person. Give him a chance to talk—and he'll tell you what's bothering him and why he acts the way he does.

And don't limit your talking to the occasions when your young man is in error. Look for times when he's right—and commend him. This way, you'll win his confidence.

### 8. *Tell a Man He's Being Promoted*

This is an occasion for congratulation. It's also an occasion for clear analysis and helpful comment.

First, tell your man why he's being moved up—good work in his present job, a special project of his that revealed his hitherto hidden talents, the need for new blood in the upper echelon, the retirement of an oldster, or any combination of these and other reasons.

Next, tell him what the new job requires and what he can hope for by way of future promotion. Let him know what help he can expect in getting started in his new job.

Then tell him frankly about any personal traits or professional shortcomings that may stand in the way of his success in the new job. Fact is, you may not have to tell him. If you talk provocatively about the scope of the new job, he may tell you what his failings are. Help him find ways to offset these weaknesses.

Finally, give him all the encouragement you can reasonably give him. Make him no promises. But let him know that you rely on him and expect the best he can give.

### 9. *Tell a Man He's Being Demoted*

This is a toughie. You just have to pull yourself together and go after it.

Tell your man why he's having to step down a peg—company policy, reorganization, his own inadequacies, a serious mistake he made, or whatever. Be honest. Give him the facts. But cushion the shock when you can. With his pride already wounded, there's no point in hurting his other feelings as well. Often the man who isn't quite good enough for a high-level job can give a good account of himself in a job one notch lower. But if you wound him beyond repair, he won't do well even in that lower-level job you assign him to.

Let your man talk as much as he will. Draw him out, in fact, and encourage him to state his case fully. Meanwhile, listen closely. He may reveal some way you can help him—or even some way you've failed him. The truth is, if you give him a chance to talk he'll often confess his inadequacies and failings and thus spare you the pain and embarrassment of stating them yourself. If you let him bring them to light, you'll stand a better chance of maintaining a fruitful working relationship with him.

Finally, challenge him to make good in the future. But make clear that his future depends on him—and that he'll get as much help as he deserves.

## 10. Move a Man Laterally

That is, transfer a man from one job to another without changing his salary, status, or degree of responsibility.

There's really nothing troublesome or hard about this. Not if you get into it the right way. What's the right way? Begin with the advantages of the new job—different things to do, a change of pace, an opportunity to broaden experience, new people to work with.

From there on, it's easy. Tell him in detail what the new job is, what his responsibilities will be, whom he'll report to, whom he'll work with, what the problems and opportunities are, and when he'll begin.

## 11. Retire an Old Timer

Before you start talking to him, spend some time and thought on what you're going to say—and on how you're going to give him opportunities to talk by asking him provocative questions and throwing out leading statements. As much as you can, plan your approach so he'll tell you why he should retire, rather than have you tell him. There's no guarantee your strategy will work out as you plan it. But the rewards in good feeling that grow from this strategy will be worth all the effort you make.

Open your remarks by complimenting your oldster on his long and fruitful years of work. Reminisce with him for a while. Let him talk —and listen to him. Don't hurry him.

When the time is ripe—and you'll probably sense it—tell him gently that the time has come for him to retire—that he's earned a long rest—that it's now time for him to enjoy some of the things he's worked for all these years.

Be sure he understands company policy—those aspects of it that bring him to retirement, and those that will ease his life after retirement—pensions, retirement clubs, and the like.

Appraise him (and if he looks promising and interested, sound him out) for a continuing productive relationship—as consultant, adviser, occasional trouble shooter, part-time helper, or whatever.

Finally, wish him good luck and Godspeed.

### 12. Turn Down an Unqualified Job Applicant

This gets you into the area of public relations. How can you do it without risking some offense to some fraction of public opinion? Well, you can't eliminate the risk altogether, but you can minimize it. Here's how:

Be courteous all the way. But keep the burden of talking on the applicant. If you reveal the details of the job in question before he has a chance to talk, he'll probably try to describe himself in terms of the job's needs. But if you keep him talking, he'll reveal his skills —if he has any—and his inadequacies as well. This way, you'll be in a better position to tell him, kindly but clearly, that his skills aren't suitable for the job.

Two important things: First, compliment the applicant on the skills he does have, even if they aren't suitable for the job. Second, don't delay—tell him as soon as possible that you must turn down his application.

### 13. Interview an Employee

There are lots of reasons for talking to an employee. For example: to gather information, to give out information, to adjust complaints, to establish a better relationship, to study his personality (try to find out what makes him tick). For these and similar situations, the following approach is a tried-and-tested one:

• Greet your man with a smile. If you can't greet him that way right now, wait until you are in a frame of mind to do so.

• Give him your undivided attention when he's talking. Don't interrupt him.

• Gather facts—not opinions or judgments.

• Keep the talk friendly on your side. Don't argue.

• Stick to the subject. If the talk veers off to one side, bring it back with questions and comments.

• Put yourself in your man's place. Try to see things from his point of view. That way, you'll understand him even if you don't accept his views.

• Help your man narrow down his views and define them. Help him analyze his problem—if he has one. Give him the facts that will lead him to sound decision or constructive action. Don't try to state his views or his solutions for him.

• Stay inside the limits of your own knowledge, experience, and authority.

• Be courteous all the way. Don't criticize.

• Ask good questions—not those that can be answered "Yes" or "No" but those that lead to exposition, discussion, and explanation. What leads off a good question? The words "Why?" "What?" "Where?" "When?" and "How?"

• Treat touchy subjects gingerly if you must bring them into the conversation. If you expect to talk about such subjects, hold the interview in private.

*14. Hold an "Exit" Interview*

A man is leaving your employ to take a job elsewhere. This is a twofold opportunity for you. First, if you make his departure friendly, he can become a public relations asset for your company. Second, if you go at it right you can uncover the real reasons for his leaving. His real reasons may be quite different from those he has announced and thus may reveal weaknesses you had never suspected in your company—even in yourself.

Departures of this sort usually are announced two weeks to thirty days in advance. So make your interview appointment well in advance of your man's last day. Meanwhile, study his record, watch him at work, even quiz his associates about him. Get all the facts you can.

When he comes into your office, welcome him. Try to win his confidence—show your sincere interest in what he's been doing for your company and in what he expects to do in his new position. Tell him the favorable things you've seen and heard about him.

But give him plenty of opportunity to talk. Probe him with questions—about his job, the people he's been working with, his expectations and hopes when he first joined your organization, about his recollection of standout events and milestones, about his transfers and promotions, about his family and other interests. Chances are pretty good that as he talks he'll disclose his real reasons for leaving. Those reasons may suggest what you can do to hold on to the next good man who joins your organization.

### 15. *Tell a Man to Do His Job a New Way*

This takes some motivation. Start by saying that the job method is going to be changed. Then tell why: You're about to bring in a new machine—or to add a new device to an old machine. Or you've got to boost production to meet competition. Or you've got to cut costs. Or your methods department has discovered a better, easier, faster way to do the job. Try to win his acceptance by your manner and by the strength of your reasons.

Next, tell your man just what the new way is. Explain it to him in detail, pointing out, as you explain it, why the new way is better than the old way: It's faster or easier. It turns out more units per hour. It means fewer errors, less spoiled work, higher quality. It's a challenge to his skill and ingenuity. It means more stature for him.

Finally, get your man to go through the new procedure step by step while you watch. Correct him where he needs correction, encourage him when he's right, and leave him with the thought that if he needs you he can call on you for more help.

### 16. *Handle a Complaint*

The way you do this is important. Handle it right, and you probably can keep it from festering. Handle it clumsily, and you can get into deep trouble.

First step: Listen. Listen hard and listen long. Be patient. Give your complainer every chance to get things off his chest. When he has settled down (as he will if given time), probe for the facts as he sees them—but do it calmly, tactfully, and pleasantly. By your own attitude, show your man that you take his complaint as seriously as he does. Don't lose sight of the fact that he's in dead earnest. This is no time for you to be flip, or make jokes, or patronize your man.

Don't try to come to a decision then and there. Tell your man you want to think the matter through, look into it further, and thus make sure he gets the fairest possible treatment.

Next, check the facts. Check your man's entire story. Not that he would tell you a tissue of lies—few people would. But personal interests do sometimes color facts. You want the uncolored facts. So go after them. Make your investigation thorough. Get all the facts—and all the details.

Now check your findings against the union agreement and your company's policies, find out whether the complaint is really a legitimate complaint. While you're at it, find out, in terms of the union agreement and your company's policies, what you can and can't do.

Thus armed, you're ready to see your man again. Prepare carefully what you're going to tell him, then call him in. Be straightforward with him. If the company is wrong, admit it. If your man is wrong, tell him so—but give him a complete explanation. Be clear and firm—and polite. Bring the interview to an end as pleasantly as you can.

One more thing: Follow through. Drop in on your man shortly afterward to see whether he's satisfied or still nursing a grudge. His future attitude is important—to you and to him. A show of interest on your part may swing him around even if he was dissatisfied when he left you.

### 17. *Talk above Distractions*

Traffic noises outside, chronic coughers in the room with you, clacking typewriters close by—even a pretty girl passing by—these distractions and others like them can play havoc with your talking, whether you're talking to one person or a group. They often rattle the talker, and nearly always draw off the attention of his hearers.

Bad as they are, you needn't be altogether helpless against these distractions. Here's what you can do:

- Concentrate harder on what you're saying—and shoot harder at the interests of those who should be listening.

- Make some passing remark about the distraction, thus showing that you, too, are aware that it's a threat to communication but that you'll simply ignore it as a thing of no consequence. In short, share the distraction momentarily with your hearers, then bring them back with you to the subject. If you brush it off once and for all, chances are they will, too.

- Hit your key words and phrases more forcefully than you ordinarily would.

- Broaden your gestures. The eye is a great attention guider. If you can hold the eyes of your hearers, you've got a good chance of holding their attention as well.

### 18. *Cope with a Hostile Listener*

A hostile, uncooperative, or negative listener in a group is fairly easy to spot. He's restless. Or he doesn't look you in the eye. Or he glares at you. Or he mutters to himself or his neighbor. Or he shakes his head. Or he deliberately shows his inattention or lack of respect for you by busying himself with a book or a paper or a fingernail file.

What can you do about this unsympathetic character?

Most important of all, don't antagonize him further. Don't scold him, or invite attention to his conduct, or make light of his attitude.

Look pleasant. If you catch his eye, try to hold it.

Make it clear, as a principle, that you lay no claim to full knowledge of all subjects and that you welcome expression of all views, even if they do differ from yours.

Drop some comments on subjects that you know will interest your problem listener. Make some reference to his special skill or knowledge or experience. If this is a discussion meeting, ask him for comment, especially when you come to some subject in which he shines.

If he shows anger or insolence, brush it aside. Don't fight fire with fire.

Finally, if he insists on making a jackass of himself, let him go ahead. He'll hurt himself—not you.

### 19. *Introduce a Guest Speaker*

If there's opportunity beforehand, ask the speaker if there's anything he'd especially like you to tell the audience—something he'd rather not say himself.

Bear in mind that the wider the fame or the greater the stature of the speaker, the less you need to say about him. The accepted form for presenting the President, for instance, is simply this: "Ladies and gentlemen, the President of the United States."

Your job, as introducer, is to set the tone for the speech to follow and to make it easy for the speaker to take over. This really isn't hard to do. But it does take preparation—gathering the information you need about the speaker and his subject, organizing it, and going over it aloud in a kind of private rehearsal. If you're afraid of muffing the vital facts, write them down—but try to read them as if you were talking, not reading.

Avoid clichés. Audiences long ago got tired of hearing "Without further ado" and "...a person who needs no introduction." If you can't do better than that, get somebody else to introduce the speaker.

Be sure to do the following in your introduction:

• State the speaker's name. Make it loud and clear. Be sure you pronounce it the same way he pronounces it.

• State his rank or title, if he has any.

• Tell why he's an authority—why the audience should listen to him.

• Humanize him. Is he a good golfer? Does he have a family? What connections does he have with local people?

• Briefly, very briefly, interest the audience in his subject. But go no further. Some misguided introducers try to make a speaker's speech for him.

• State the title of the speech the audience is about to hear.

• Present the speaker.

### 20. *Present an Award*

For the man who receives an award, the presentation should be a red-letter occasion—happy and memorable. It's up to you to make it so. Here are tips:

• Fill in the background of the award. Who created it? Why? On what occasion? What's the history of the award?

• Tell what the award stands for. Is it for achievement in science? In battle? In industry? In charitable causes? Is it for long service? Or accumulated merit? Or some special accomplishment?

• Say how the winner is picked. By judges? By popular vote? Or how?

• Tell why the person who is to receive the award deserves it.

• Make the presentation. Talk directly to the winner, but stand at an angle to the audience. If it's a plaque or scroll or certificate, read it aloud, so the audience can hear. Hold it at an angle, so the audience as well as the award winner can see it. Shake the winner's hand and, if it's part of the program, give him a chance to say his words of acceptance.

### 21. Receive an Award

People expect you to be a little flustered when you're presented with an award or a gift. But that doesn't entitle you to abuse their indulgence or to slight the occasion or the people involved. Unless you're taken completely by surprise, prepare your acceptance. You owe it to the people who are witnessing your honor.

Your acceptance remarks should include the following:

• Thanks to the people who made the award possible

• Credit to the people who developed your talent or contributed to your know-how or shared in your achievement

• Your promise to keep on striving

• Your thanks once more

Address your remarks to the one who presents the award or gift, but turn yourself partly toward the audience so they can see your face and hear you. If there's some visible token—a plaque or scroll or cup—hold it up for the audience to see.

### 22. Say Goodbye to a Job

Whether you're moving from one department to another within an organization, or leaving an organization you've been with for some time, or retiring to enjoy your golden years, chances are somebody will arrange a goodbye occasion for you. Naturally, you'll be expected to say something appropriate.

Above all, keep it lighthearted. An affair of this sort becomes maudlin all too easily. Don't try to be flip or funny. But don't dissolve into tears, either.

Here's what you might do with your farewell remarks:

• Reminisce a little. Recollect your first arrival, and touch on the high spots that followed.

• In telling your narratives, bring your associates in by name.

• Tell what you aspired to do and become.

• Tell what you feel you've accomplished—but be modest about it.

• Express your appreciation for those who've worked with you and supported you.

• Tell what you think the future holds for you.

• Tell what you think the future holds for those you're leaving behind.

• Say kind words about your successor.

• Say goodbye.

### 23. *Run a Formal Meeting*

This is not the usual round-table discussion, but a meeting in which you have to control debate, hold people in check, and bring the group to a vote on an issue.

There are generally accepted rules for this kind of meeting— rules that have grown up because long-time experience has showed them to be the best way of getting through a meeting fairly, efficiently, and decisively. To find these rules, go to your public library (or your company library) and ask the librarian for a simple handbook on parliamentary rules of order. There are dozens of good ones. If there's no library handy, go to your local bookstore and ask for help.

With book in hand, sit down and study the important rules—how to call a meeting to order, how to determine who talks and who keeps quiet (and when), how to bring a motion to a vote, how to handle an amendment to a motion, and the like. Take the book with you to your meeting, keep it close at hand for reference. It will guide you through many a tough situation—when argument threatens to get out of control, when chaos threatens, when a dominant person (or group) seems bent on snatching the meeting away from you and running off with it.

## 24. *Explain Something Complex*

Here are the time-tested steps:

• Start with the simple and familiar, then go on, by careful stages, to the complex.

• Take one thing at a time.

• Go slowly, carefully, deliberately.

• Repeat the important things often.

• Take nothing for granted. Assume that the listener doesn't understand.

• Be sure your hearer hears every word.

• Use examples, comparisons, and analogies.

• If you have time, prepare visual aids.

• Speak in plain language that your listener will be sure to understand.

• Keep your eye on your hearer. If he seems to wander, or if he seems puzzled, backtrack.

## 25. *Instruct on the Job*

First, get ready. You can't instruct successfully if you go at it cold. Here's how to get ready:

• Break down the job that's to be learned. List the important steps. Pick out the key points. Don't overlook safety.

• Set up a timetable. Looking at the breakdown of the job, decide how long it should take to learn it.

• Set the stage. Get everything ready—equipment, materials, and supplies.

• Have the workplace (stenographer's desk, machine, sales counter, teller's cage, receptionist's room, hospital bed, or whatever) properly arranged, just as you expect the learner to keep it.

Now that everything is ready, start in with your man. In general, follow this pattern:

• Prepare the learner. Put him at ease—maybe with some friendly personal comments. Tell him what the job is, and find out what he may already know about it. Get him interested in learning the job, pointing out opportunities, challenges, intriguing aspects of the work.

• Present the operation. Tell, demonstrate, and illustrate one important step at a time. Stress the key points. Be clear and patient. Give your learner no more than he can master in one session. Invite his questions.

• Let him run through the job himself. Correct his errors as he moves along. Get him to explain each key point to you as he moves from step to step. Make sure he understands—and keep on teaching until you know he understands.

• Follow up. Put your man on his own. Tell him whom he can go to for help. Check up on him often at first, then gradually taper off.

## 26. *Make an Announcement*

Tell why you're making the announcement and how it will affect your hearers. State the facts of the announcement—who, what, where, when, and how. Explain the whys behind the facts. Give your hearers opportunity to ask questions—even to object. But be conciliatory about objections. Finally, summarize the announcement —and tell where your listeners can see the announcement in print (bulletin boards, company magazine, local newspaper, and the like).

## 27. *Tell an Amusing Story*

Some people (maybe you're among them) have a hard time making a funny story sound funny. Comes the punch line, and there's a deafening silence—or at best a long-suffering smile. If this is your unhappy experience, take heart. Here are a few tips that can sharpen up even the dullest of storytellers:

• Take it easy. Good humor should look easy and natural. Relax. Enjoy the story yourself—and show that you enjoy it.

• Make it clear that you're joking—even if you use the dead-pan approach. Humor is tricky—and people are sensitive. If they don't know you're joking, they'll take you seriously—may even walk away in anger.

- Build your story on surprise—sudden and unexpected contrast.
- Move quickly to the pay-off, the punch line. A long, repetitive story soon becomes dull—dismally dull.
- Tell your story in a framework that's familiar to your hearers. Don't stray from the people and places your listeners know about.
- Dodge dialect unless you're exceptionally skilled at it. It can offend sensitive people among your hearers.
- Time the elements of your story—especially the pay-off lines.
- Keep it clean.

### 28. *Ask for Money for a Cause*

Many of us get tapped for service on drives to raise money—for the community chest, the Red Cross, our church, research foundations, health organizations, colleges and schools. And most of us dread getting involved in such enterprises. We feel embarrassed to ask for money, we fear a turndown, we feel apologetic for taking up the time of those who listen.

Is there a way to make these tasks less burdensome for ourselves, less tiresome to those we call on, and more rewarding to the causes we represent? The answer is "Yes." The answer comes from John D. Rockefeller Jr. In a nutshell, here's what he prescribes for those who seek gifts for a good cause:

- Base your approach on your own answer to the question, "How would I like to be approached for a gift?"
- Inform yourself. Look at the gift the same way you look at an investment. That is, get the facts and estimate the gains. How sound is the organization behind the appeal? How great is the need? How does help get to the need?
- Know the person you're going to call on. Plan your approach in terms of his interests, his friends, his participation in former years.
- Tell your prospect the facts—about the cause, the organization, the need, the results of filling that need.
- Have in mind a dollar range to suggest—in some instances, in fact, if you know your man well, a firm figure. Why? Because lots of people are unsure of what's expected of them, and a tactful suggestion from you can be helpful. But bear in mind that nobody

likes to be told what he should give. In a tactful approach you might say, for instance, "The gifts of others in your group (or line or classification) are ranging from $5 to $50 (or from $5,000 to $50,-000)." You might even say: "We need $10,000, and we're hoping you will want to give $1,000. That would help and encourage us. Of course, we'll be glad if you have it in mind to give more. And if you feel that's more than you can give, we'll understand. What we do ask is that you think this matter over carefully."

• Keep your approach friendly and pleasant.

• Don't apologize for asking for money if your cause is a good one and if you're sold on it yourself.

• Keep your urging gentle and tactful. Never press. After all, a man's decision to give is—and must be—his own.

## 29. *Talk on Television*

The first few times are always hard. Even so, here are some tips that will make even your first TV appearance easier—and more effective:

• Be yourself. Don't try to imitate Ed Murrow—or any other TV personality, for that matter.

• Relax. Don't take yourself too seriously.

• Imagine you're talking informally to a small group of people at your office or in your home.

• Treat the camera as you would a person sitting just a few feet away. Pitch your voice for conversation, vary it from time to time. Don't freeze your eyes to the camera. Let your gaze wander from time to time, as you would if talking with a friend.

• If you read your remarks, don't try to hide the fact.

• Use gestures sparingly. TV has a way of magnifying them. And don't let a gesture pass between your face and the camera.

• If you're a member of a panel, address your remarks to a particular panel member, not to the TV audience generally.

• Speak in plain, simple language. Lots of people listening just won't understand your professional jargon.

• Don't scorn the gadgets—prompting devices and the like. Remember, the TV people are professionals. They know what amateurs need—and know how to make amateurs show up to best advantage.